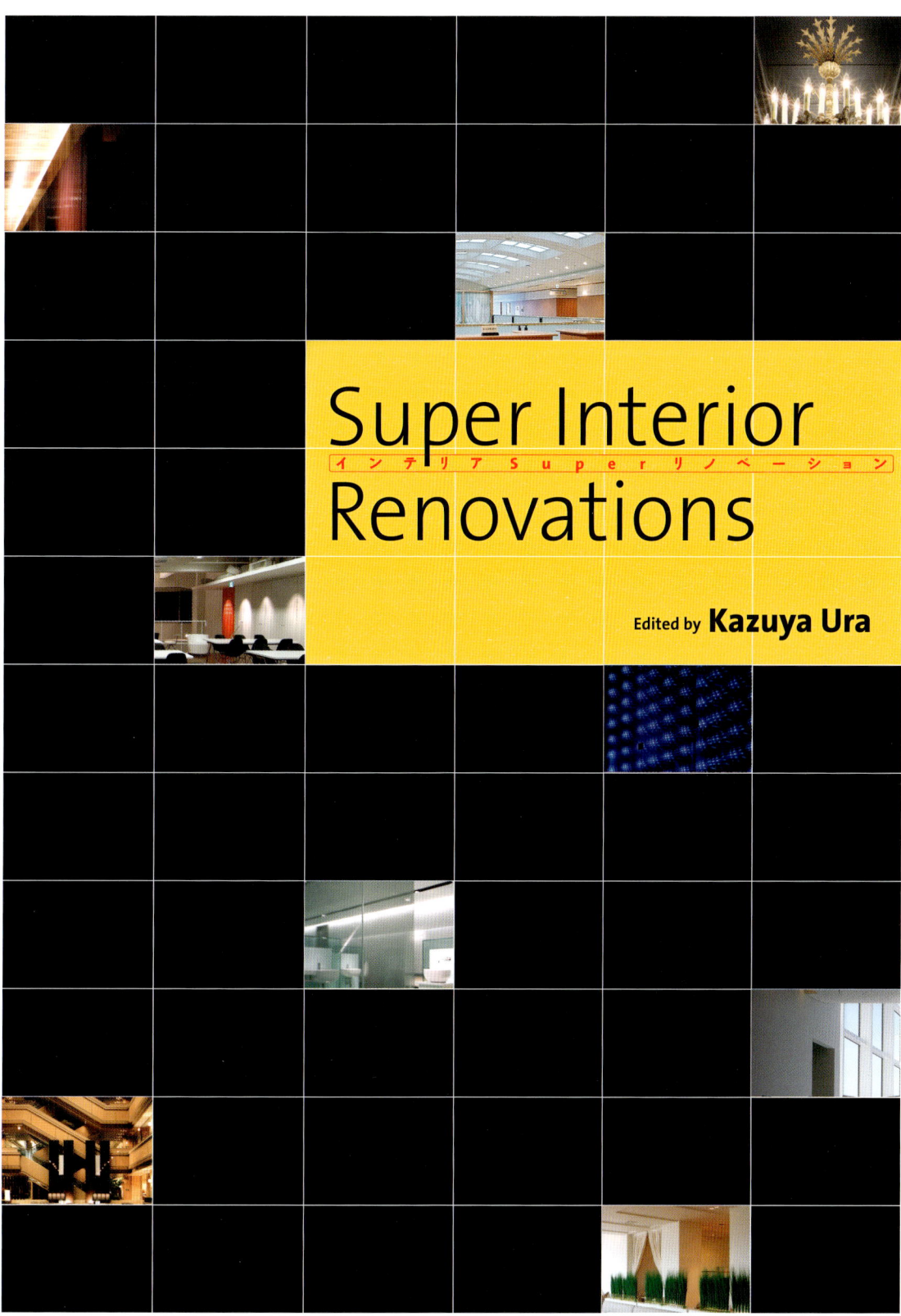

[まえがき]

スペースヴァリューを さらに高めるRenovation

浦 一也

英語のRenovationには「革新、改善、回復」というような意味がある。Renewalは「更新」であり、Reformは「改正、矯正、改良」。Repairが「修理、回復」、「改築、改装」はRemodelというほうが近い。Conversionには「転換、転向」といったニュアンスがある。

いずれも建築関連の世界で行われている、原型や躯体、スケルトンにあまり手をつけずにインフィルとしてのインテリアなどを改修・改装するという内容にぴったりすることばではないのだが、本書ではこのような「空間をよみがえらせるような改修」を規模の大小を問わずRenovationととらえることにしたい。また、建物用途にいたるまでの大幅な転換を図るようなものをConversionとして捉えたい。

昔から当たり前に行われてきたはずのこのような手法が、なぜ現在取りざたされているかといえば、よくいわれるようにスクラップ＆ビルドの時代から限られたエネルギーを持続可能な手法で使いまわす、エコロジカルでサステイナブルな時代への移行の過程にあり、保全や永続性という概念にモノの価値が移ってきたということなのかもしれない。あるいはスケルトンに値する社会資本としての建築の質が向上したのかもしれない。あるいは建物の新築を容易に赦していたハコモノへの投資はIT関連などにまわってしまったからなのかもしれない。あるいは……。

日本には20年サイクルの伊勢神宮の式年遷宮に象徴される、技術の保全と永続性に関する極めて秀逸な手法がある。木材の成長やヒトの寿命と技術の伝承という観点からも20年とはうまいサイクルであり、旧建物の解体で発生する材が各地に降下されていくこともよくできたシステムである。しかし、これを単なるスクラップ＆ビルドの代表例と「かんちがい」する向きも少なくなかったところに日本のRenovationが出遅れた一因もあるのではないかと思われる。たしかに地震や台風の多い高温多湿の風土では、木材による建て替え、建て直しこそサステイナブルな手法であったといわざるを得ないが、それを十分にゆるす自然と、社会構造があったのである。中国では限られた自然材料を使って数千年を耐える石造りの構築物をつくりあげる技術を確立し、砂と土だけの世界では日乾煉瓦を使った大構築物も造られていた。森の樹を使い果たした欧州では石と煉瓦を手にして風雨よりも隣人や部族間争いの襲撃に耐えるシェルターや城壁を造ることに邁進していた。

したがって日本の建物には壁がなく、柱と梁で構成した架構に粗末な屋根を葺き、外界とは建具だけの仕切りであったから西欧風の閉鎖的なインテリアの概念が生まれる素地はまったくなかった。建具や間仕切りは畳と同様、サイクルの短い流通品であったし、茅葺屋根の更新は集落総出で葺いてまわるというような仕組みすら社会に存在していたのである。そのような時間軸を伴ったモノつくりの絶妙な連環が断ち切られたのはやはり無暴な近代化にほかならない。破壊と無秩序な開発が世界に蔓延したからこそ、CO_2問題も起きた。京都議定書を引き合いに出すまでもなく、先進国と開発途上の国の立場も問題も逆転した「今」、どこの地域でも再生や再利用という手法による永続性のありかたが改めて共通の課題となり、Renovationの本義とその役割が大いに問われているのである。

インフィルのひとつとしてのインテリアのありかたは室内を飾りたてるようなものではなく、ヒトの生活空間を生活の変化とともに使いやすく、住みやすいものに常に変化させていく「しつらい」のありようである。ヒトという「自然」がいつまでも自然であるというアイデンティティを保っていけるための大切な人工物を肌に近いところでしつらえることである。そのインテリアをプランニングし、長寿命を目指すシェルターとの良好な関係を保って変化に対応する手法こそが今問われているRenovationと一致すると考える。

求められるべきはRenovationによって得られるSpace Varueのさらなる高まりである。そのための手法はデザインとマネジメントが両輪となったプランニングにある。建築空間のもっている価値は不変ではなく社会のニーズでどんどん変わるものだ。その社会が求める価値を手に入れるためにインフィルが差し替えられる。それも原型から較べてもさらに高い価値を求められる。逆に新築では得られないほどの空間の価値を発揮できるもの……。それこそがRenovationの真骨頂である。「時」を味方につけた空間は美しい。新築したばかりのホテルより、反省を込めてよく考えられ、Renovateされたホテルのほうがずっと心地よいのもそんな理由からだ。

本書では2005年という断面における住宅以外のRenovationの膨大な事例のなかから、インテリアの手法として有効で「ためになりそうな」例を収集した。住居施設については定住的な空間だけに視点を変えるべきであるし、それだけで編集が成り立つほどであるため、あえてセレクトから外し、非住宅に限った。また日々最適な例が生まれている状況であり、好例が他にある場合、それもご容赦願いたい。

2005年8月

[Preface]

Renovation to further enhance values of space

Kazuya URA

There are many architectural terms with similar meanings but different nuances. The term "renovation" suggests a renewing by cleansing, repairing, or rebuilding. It may also suggest innovation, improvement or recovery. "Renewal" implies a restoration of what had become disintegrated so that it seems like new. "Reform" suggests an improving by making corrective changes while "repair" means to restore by replacing parts or putting together what is disassembled or broken. "Remodel" is an act of altering the structure. To "convert" means to change from one function or form to another.

Each of them cannot perfectly describe an act of renovating or refurbishing the interior without major changes to the original construction, framework, or skeleton. In this book, however, we will consider any such act of restoring spaces as a renovation, regardless of its scale, and an act of drastically altering the form or function of the building as a conversion.

Why are these methods that have become common and even customary now drawing attention? There are many possible causes. Perhaps we are in the process of transition from an age of "scrap-and build" to an age of ecology and sustainability, where limited energy is used and reused in a sustainable manner, and our values are thus shifting toward conservation and maintenance; or, the value of structural skeletons as social capital has improved enough to justify renovative approaches; or, investments in buildings that previously enabled new building construction are now simply applied to IT-related projects.

Japan has an excellent approach toward conservation and maintenance of technology, symbolized by the act of rededicating a shrine every 20 years at the Ise Shrine. The cycle of 20 years is very effective in terms of wood growth, men's longevity, and succession of technology. This is an excellent system because wood materials that become available by disintegrating old buildings can be recycled for other uses. There has been, however, widespread misunderstanding that this represents a simple scrap-and-build method, and this way of thinking probably resulted in Japan's late start in renovations. We must admit that rebuilding or reconstruction was once a sustainable method in the hot, moist climate and environment with many earthquakes and typhoons. However, it must also be noted that, at the time, nature was rich enough to sustain this method, and the Japanese social structure could afford it. In China, they established technologies to build stone constructions that could last for thousands of years by using limited natural resources and materials, while in the world of sand and soil, even huge structures were built using adobe. In Europe, where wood resources were almost used up during the Middle Ages, they chose stone and brick to build shelters and castle walls that could withstand attacks by neighbors or other tribes rather than weather.

Japanese buildings traditionally had skeleton constructions composed of columns and beams without walls. They were thatched with straw, and separated from the outside by fittings. Thus, unlike the West, there was no background for the concept of the enclosed interior to be produced in Japan. Fittings and partitions were, like tatami mats, dispensable components with short lifecycles, and there was even a customary system to re-thatch roofs by all the members of rural villages. This well-balanced and continuous cycle of construction was broken by the sudden onset of modernization. As destruction and disordered development have prevailed globally, the CO_2 issue has occurred. Now that related environmental issues cannot be resolved through a simple classification of developed and underdeveloped countries, not to mention the Kyoto Protocol, a common challenge is how to approach sustainability through recycling and reuse, and the true purpose of renovations are now strongly questioned.

How the interior should be, as part of infills doesn't mean the lavish decoration of the interior. Instead, it should be a set of ever-changing furnishings that turn space into something easy to live in and use, in accordance with the changes of the occupant's lifestyle. In other words, it means the creation of artificial things that can naturally fit our daily lives, and are appropriate for enabling us to maintain our identity as part of nature. I believe that the renovation in question means a method to plan the above-described type of interior, and to respond to continuous changes while maintaining compatibility with designs of shelters or frameworks that require longer lives.

This requirement further enhances the value of space through renovation, and the approach for this goal lies in planning based on an ideal combination of design and management. The values of architectural spaces are not permanent, but are ever-changing depending on social needs. Infills are replaced in order to realize values required by the society. In addition, values after replacements should be much better than those of the originals. The true worth of the renovation is a creation of spatial values that cannot be obtained from newly built constructions. Spaces with history are beautiful. This is why a hotel renovated on the basis of reflection and consideration is more comfortable than a newly constructed hotel.

This book features a collection of completed renovations that serve as examples of effective and useful approaches to interior design for non-residential buildings in the year 2005. Please note that the book covers only a few examples, and that excellent and optimal designs are currently being created every day.

August 2005

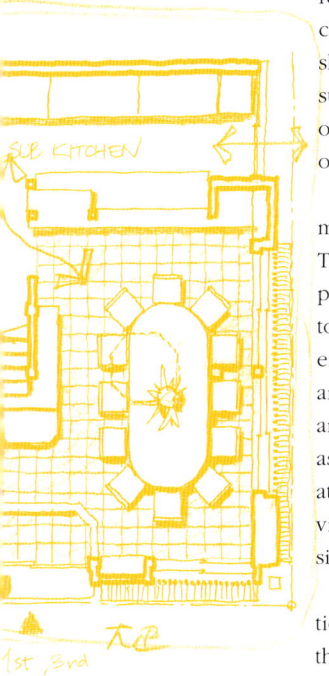

目次　Index

002　まえがき：浦 一也　Preface: Kazuya URA

008　スタッフ紹介　Staff

第1章　Chapter 1
ホ テ ル　Hotels

010　名古屋東急ホテル　NAGOYA TOKYU HOTEL
クラシカルな既存部分に重ねた新しいデザイン
Basing the new design upon the existing classical structure

016　ホテルエルム札幌　HOTEL ELM SAPPORO
構造躯体以外は全て一新したプチホテル
Everything except the structural skeleton was renewed with this petit hotel

020　ホテルニューグランド「スカイ・チャペル」　Hotel New Grand "Sky Chapel"
プールの水の重さでチャペルをつくる
Making a chapel utilizing the weight of the water

024　ホテル日航東京 ブライダルサロン「ブルー・ブリーズ」＆地中海料理レストラン「オーシャンダイニング」
hotel nikko tokyo Bridal Salon, Blue Breeze and Mediterranean cuisine, Ocean Dining
「海・空・風・光」をテーマにした料飲施設リノベーション
Restaurant renovation on the theme of the sea, sky, wind and light

028　ホテル ニューオータニ高岡　Hotel New Otani Takaoka
スタイリッシュに変身した高岡市民のコミュニケーションホテル
Takaoka citizen's communication hotel has transformed itself into a stylish place.

032　ホテルグランヴィア大阪　HOTEL GRANVIA OSAKA
新しい出会いを求めたホテルロビーの全面改修
Full renovation of the hotel lobby for new meetings

034　六甲山ホテル　ROKKOSAN HOTEL
昭和初期のクラシカルなホテルを再現
A classical hotel of the early Showa style recreated

036　エクセルホテル東急　EXCEL HOTEL TOKYU
「伝統・革新」をコンセプトにしたホテルブランド再構築
Rebranding the hotel based on the concept of the tradition and renewal

040　クラブハウス ウエディング リビエラ　Club House Wedding Riviera
さまざまな顧客のニーズに応え、進化しつづけるウエディングハウス
Ever-evolving wedding house meeting various customers' needs

044　成田全日空ホテル　ANA HOTEL NARITA
エアポートホテルを全面リニューアル
A fully renovated airport hotel

048　京都ロイヤルホテル　Kyoto Royal Hotel
古都のホテルを全面リノベーション
Renovating a hotel in an old capital

052 クレイトン ベイ ホテル『クリスタルチャーチ』 Crystal Church, Clayton Bay Hotel
既存の屋上に張り出した空に浮かぶチャペル
A chapel that floats in the sky, placed on top of an existing roof

054 サンルートプラザ東京B棟改修計画 Renovation Plan of the Building B, Sunroute Plaza Tokyo
狭い客室を長所に変えた客室デザイン
Creating a small guest room into a charming space

058 伊豆エグゼクティブ・センター IZU EXECUTIVE CENTER
耐震改修で美しく生まれ変わった研修所
Training center beautifully reborn after antiseismic renovation

062 ホテル日航茨木 大阪 hotel nikko ibaraki osaka
リブランディングによって生まれ変わるホテル
Regeneration of a hotel through rebranding

066 渋谷東急イン SHIBUYA TOKYU INN
「利用者の声」を尊重したゲストルームのリノベーション
Guestroom renovation respecting users comments

068 客船"飛鳥"リド・カフェ改修計画 Renovation plan of the Lido Cafe on the passenger ship, Asuka
機能優先だったカフェテリアを船旅が楽しめる空間にリニューアル
Renewal cafeteria from functional to cruise-ship atmosphere

072 千里阪急ホテル「パオーレ」 Paole, Senrihankyu Hotel
プールサイドの休憩所がウエディングヴィラに大変身
A resting place by the pool is dramatically transformed into a wedding villa

074 千里阪急ホテル「サンシャインテラス」 Sunshine Terrace, Senrihankyu Hotel
老朽化が進んだ喫茶室をバンケットホールに再生
A dilapidated coffee shop revitalized as a banquet hall

第2章 Chapter 2
オフィス Offices

078 日本財団ビル The Nippon Foundation Building
設計者・吉村順三氏の設計コンセプトを継承したオフィス
Office building , Designed by the late Junzo Yoshimura's concept was described as follows

082 菱化システム Ryoka Systems Inc.
オフィスの生産性をより高めるためのリノベーション
Renovation to elevate the spirit and thereby increase office productivity

084 丸紅東京本社 Marubeni Corporation Tokyo Headquarters
自然光を取り入れて威圧感をなくしたオフィスエントランス
Non-intimidating office entrance taking advantage of natural light

086 陶山國男記念室 Dr. Kunio SUYAMA Memorial
スケルトンを残す理由、インフィルをつくりこむ理由
Reasons for leaving the skeleton, reasons for building in the infill

088 日建スペースデザイン 大阪設計室 Nikken Space Design Osaka Office
スケルトンを顕わしたオフィス空間
Office space with exposed skeleton

第3章　Chapter 3
病　院　Hospitals

092　ふれあいホスピタル・シニアホテル横浜　Fureai Yokohama Hospital/Senior Hotel Yokohama
ホテルの居心地をそのまま病院にコンバージョン
Comfort of a hotel converted to that of a hospital

100　福井県済生会病院 外来診察部門　Out-patient Department, Fukui-ken Saiseikai Hospital
スタッフの顔が見える外来診察部門に改修
Renovation of outpatient department to
promote face-to-face communications between staff and patients

104　楠樹記念クリニック　Nanjyu Memorial Clinic
装飾性の強いサロンから、リラックスできるラウンジへ
From a highly ornate salon to a lounge where you can relax

106　IVFなんばクリニック　IVF Namba
やわらかな光で包むクリニックにコンバージョン
Conversion into a clinic surrounded by soft radiance

108　大阪府済生会中津病院　Saiseikai Nakatsu Hospital
記憶に残るデザインの継承
Inheriting design to remember

第4章　Chapter 4
商　業　施　設　Commercial Facilities

112　資生堂パーラー 銀座4丁目店　Shiseido Parlour, Ginza 4-chome Branch
記憶に残る「心の高まり」をつなぐフォルムと光
Form and light to produce "the rising of emotion" to remember

116　ポーラミュージアムアネックス　POLA Museum Annex
1、2階を開放した銀座の古いビル
An old building in Ginza renovated with a sense of openness

118　三木サービスエリア　Miki Service Area
お土産コーナーから脱皮したベーカリーショップ
A bakery that was originally just a small souvenir shop

120　セラトレーディング乃木坂ショールーム　CERA TRADING Nogizaka Showroom
ショーウインドウに入る感覚のショールームつくり
A show room designed so that you feel as if you are entering a show window

122　はん亭　HANTEI
100年を生き抜く商家
Shop house surviving a century

124　上野精養軒　Ueno Seiyoken
鹿鳴館の香りを残した次世代レストラン
Next-generation restaurant with the ambience of the Rokumeikan

128 日本料理「JAKARTA basara」　Japanese Restaurant JAKARTA basara
現地の建材で造るインドネシアの日本料理店
Japanese restaurant built with local construction materials in Indonesia

130 宝塚ホテルケーキショップ　Takarazuka Hotel Cake Shop
新しさと伝統が組み合わされたケーキショップ
Cake shop combining modernity and tradition

132 ヴァンドーム青山 銀座並木通り店　VENDOME AOYAMA Ginza Namiki-Dori
ショーケースにもアイデンティティを求めた路面店
Street-level shop with even showcases having

134 MOVIX本牧　MOVIX HONMOKU
家族で楽しめる非日常空間
Non-ordinary space for families

138 世界貿易センタービル スカイホール　SKY HALL, WORLD TRADE CENTER BUILDING
超高層トップのウエディング・バンケット改修
Renovating a wedding banquet hall at the top of the skyscraper

142 浜松町東京會舘／宴会場「チェリールーム」、離宮飯店内宴会場「天山」　Hamamatsucho Tokyokaikan
夜景もリノベーションのエレメント
Night view is another element of renovation

144 MOKUZAI.com　MOKUZAI.com
インフィルは全て商品
All the infills are products

148 スカイビルレストエリア改修計画　Renovation project of the restroom, Yokohama Sky Building
リラックス＆リフレッシュスペースにリニューアル
Renewal to create a relaxing and refreshing space

第5章 Chapter 5
クラブ施設　Private Club Facilities

152 日本工業倶楽部会館　The Industry Club of Japan
都心に建つ歴史的建築物の保存再生
Preservation and renovation of a historic building in the city center

160 交詢社倶楽部　The Kojunsha Club
光の密度が綾なす知の空間デザイン
Space design of intelligence compiled by density of light

第6章 Chapter 6
公共施設　Public Facilities

168 秋田市立新屋図書館　Akita City Araya Library
新しい建物(モノ)と古き良き倉庫(モノ)の共生する地域図書館
Community library where a new building and a good, old warehouse coexist

172 産業技術総合研究所　National Institute of Advanced Industrial Science and Technology
　　自然光を生かした楽しく心和む空間にリニューアル
　　Renovated into an entertaining and relaxing space ulitizing natural light

174 CLUB ANA　CLUB ANA
　　空港ラウンジの部分改修
　　Partial renovation of an airport lounge

176 旧第四銀行住吉町支店　Former Daishi Bank Sumiyoshi-cho Branch
　　文化遺産と共存するレストラン
　　Restaurant in a cultural heritage

178 女子美術大学　Joshibi University Of Art And Design
　　自然の色彩にビビッドなカラーがマッチする、ファサードの再生
　　Facade renewal where natural colors are in perfect harmony with vivid colors

182 展示係留保存船「羊蹄丸」　FLOATING PAVILION「YOTEI MARU」
　　海上文化交流施設として生まれ変わった連絡船
　　A ferryboat renovated as a floating cultural exchange facility

186 バイオグラフィ　Biographies

190 あとがき　Afterword

スタッフ　Staff

企画	大田 悟（グラフィック社）	Planner	Satoru OTA (Graphic-sha)
装丁	工藤強勝（デザイン実験室）	Book Designer	Tsuyokatsu KUDO (Design Laboratory)
本文組版	伊藤滋章（デザイン実験室）	DTP	Shigeaki ITO (Design Laboratory)
整理作業	流王 天	Data Arrangement	Takashi RYUO
翻訳	宮坂聖一	Translation	Seiichi MIYASAKA
	R.I.C.出版株式会社		R.I.C Publications Asia Co., Inc.
制作協力	井筒英理子　井上敬三	Execute Cooperator	Eriko IZUTSU　Keizou INOUE
	小倉謙二　黄川田大介		Kenji OGURA　Daisuke KIKAWADA
	柴崎香恵　鈴木雅子		Kae SHIBAZAKI　Masako SUZUKI
	富田美香　長澤智子		Mika TOMITA　Tomoko NAGASAWA
	名波千尋　野田理絵		Chihiro NAWA　Rie NODA
	冨士由起子　古澤美登里		Yukiko FUJI　Midori FURUSAWA
	吉原浩司		Kouji YOSHIHARA

第1章 ホテル

Chapter 1
Hotels

名古屋東急ホテル
クラシカルな既存部分に重ねた新しいデザイン

NAGOYA TOKYU HOTEL
Basing the new design upon the existing classical structure

改修前のアトリウムラウンジ。
The atrium lounge before renovation.

ロビーとラウンジを一体で計画。（写真：ナカサ＆パートナーズ）
Seamlessly planned lobby and lounge. (Photo: Nacása & Partners Inc.)

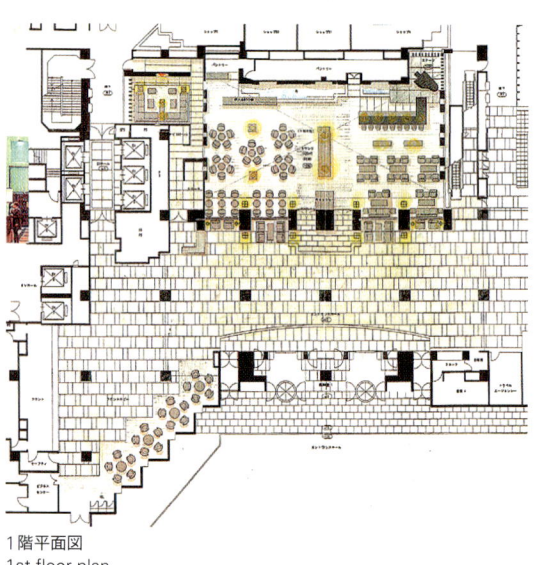
1階平面図
1st floor plan

名古屋では確固たる地位を占めているこのホテルの一連の改修計画である。新チャペルの増築のコンペに始まり、それに続いて客室・コーヒーハウス・アトリウムラウンジと改修を順次行うこととなった。
最大の課題は新築時のコンセプトであった、ヨーロッパの伝統に基づいた様式的な設えを、どのようにフレッシュに現代に蘇らせるかであった。
現代のヨーロッパの街並みの中には、古いものの中に現代的な感覚を共存させた、すぐれた例がある。このことが改修計画のヒントとなった。

The project was part of a series of renovations of a well-established hotel in Nagoya and started with the competition of the extension of the chapel, followed by a series of renovations of the guestrooms, coffee house, and atrium lounge.
The biggest challenge was how to succeed the concept passed down unbroken since the completion of the building and giving a new look to the facilities whose style was based on the European tradition.
In the present European urban landscapes, we could find excellent examples of old structures added with a sense of modernity, and they served as cue for our renovation planning.

Client:	NAGOYA TOKYU HOTEL CO., LTD.
Construction:	Obayashi Corporation Nagoya Branch (Coffee House), Matsuzakaya Co., Ltd Nagoya Business Division (Guestrooms & lounge), Obayashi Corporation (Chapel)
Designer:	Shoyo Izu / Shinya Suzuki / Sadao Nakayama: Nikken Space Design
Location:	Nagoya-shi, Aichi
Renovated area:	Guestrooms (3,069.7 sq m); Coffee House (430 sq m); Lounge (500 sq m); and Chapel (320 sq m)
Completion:	Guestrooms / Coffee House / Chapel = March, 2003, Lounge = September, 2003
Materials:	Guestroom = Floor: Long carpet, Wall: vinyl cloth Coffee House = Floor: Flooring, Wall: Natural wood, Spraying paint Lounge = Floor: Tufted carpet, Wall: Natural wood, Tile

アトリウムラウンジ

ホテルの1階メインロビーの4層吹き抜けに位置するダイナミックな空間で、利用する人々に寛ぎのひと時を与える、ティーラウンジである。
ホテルの顔となるような、ステイタスを持つグレードとした。
デザインのコンセプトは、ヨーロッパの伝統様式の中に、現代のデザイン感覚を採り入れ、古いものと新しいものが共存し、その重厚な時代の積み重ねが空間の新しい価値を表出させることとした。
またエントランスとラウンジに一体感を持たせ、疎外感なく、親しみやすい空間とした。
吹き抜けのトップライトの天空よりふりそそぐ光を、朝・昼・夜の自然光と人工照明を駆使し、一日の光の変化を演出した。
またウエディングにも利用されるため、シンメトリーの空間の中に、祭壇を設置できるスペースを設け、セレモニーなどを行えるよう考慮している。

Atrium Lounge

This tea lounge is located on the first floor in the four-story air-well-void in the main lobby of the hotel, providing guests with relaxing time.
The lounge is given an upscale image representing the hotel.
The design concept is to integrate the European traditional style with modern design approaches so that things new and old should coexist in harmony and present a new spatial value based on accumulated layers of tradition and renovation.
The entrance and the lounge give a sense of seamless continuity, which make them familiar and relaxing.
In the well, the light coming overhead from the top light is combined with artificial illuminations to emphasize natural light changes over the course of day.
As the lounge is also used for wedding ceremonies, a space is provided to create alter setting.

アトリウムの様式的シンボルを残し現代のデザイン感覚と調和をとる。（写真：ナカサ＆パートナーズ）
Modern design approach integrating the atrium's symbol of style. (Photo: Nacása & Partners Inc.)

屋上に増築されたチャペル『フェアリア』。（写真：ナカサ＆パートナーズ）
Fairyair, chapel added on the roof. (Photo: Nacása & Partners Inc.)

コーヒーハウス。(写真:ナカサ&パートナーズ)
Coffee House. (Photo: Nacása & Partners Inc.)

ケーキ・ベーカリーのテイクアウトコーナー。(写真:ナカサ&パートナーズ)
Take-out corner (cake and bakery). (Photo: Nacása & Partners Inc.)

改修前のコーヒーラウンジ。
Coffee lounge before renovation.

コーヒーハウス

設計条件として、新築当時からの店名である「モンマルトル」を改修後も使用するということであったため、これを何かの形で表現することを考慮した。

そこで意匠上の一つの手法として、パリのモンマルトルの地図をグラフィックアート化し、壁面に設置することとした。

内装・家具は濃い系と薄い系の二色の天然木やフローリングの床などにより、正当なカフェの設えとし、シックであるが明るいイメージを持った、インテリア空間としている。

家具レイアウトでは、改修前は固定的であったが、それをフレキシブルにして、一人客・カップル・家族・団体などの、あらゆるニーズに合わせ、対応できるようにしている。

またホテルの朝食をコーディネートするための、ビュッフェ形式の大カウンターを設けたり、ディスプレー等の演出なども考慮している。

Coffee House

As one of the design requirements was to use the original name of the coffee shop, "Montmartre", due considerations were given to associate the design with this famous spot in Paris.

As a means of implementing this, a map of Montmartre is turned into a graphic art and mounted on the wall.

The interior and furniture give an authentic impression of cafe terrace by employing two types of natural wood, dark and light, and wood flooring, which results in the interior space with a chic yet cheerful atmosphere.

Before the renovation, the basic layout of furniture was fixed type; in the new design, however, the furniture can freely be moved to meet different needs from single travelers, couples, families and groups.

In addition, provided is a large buffet counter for hotel accommodations with breakfast, and design considerations are given to displays, etc.

朝食時はブッフェカウンターに早変わり。（写真：ナカサ＆パートナーズ）
Also serving as a buffet counter during the breakfast time. (Photo: Nacása & Partners Inc.)

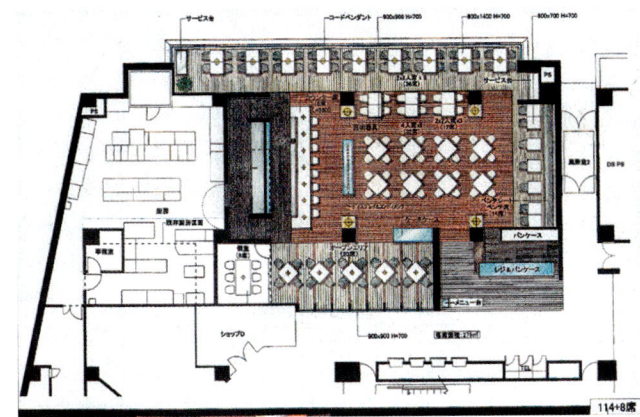

明快で機能的なレイアウトプラン。
Clear-cut and functional layout plan.

団体・パーティーに利用できるコーナー。
（写真：ナカサ＆パートナーズ）
The corner suitable for groups or parties.
(Photo: Nacása & Partners Inc.)

シングルルーム。(写真：スタジオワーク)
Single room. (Photo: STUDIO WORK)

客室改修工事

2フロアー、94室・シングル・ダブル・ツイン・スイートを約2ヶ月で改修を行った。現代感覚に合った都会的でシックな内装・家具の設えとしている。

機能上は他の客室フロアと同様として、デザインのみ現代的な感覚を採り入れた。新しい試みとして、ヘッドボードに水平のスリッド照明を入れ、意匠と読書灯の両立を考慮している。

Guestroom renovations

A total of 94 rooms (single, double and twin rooms as well as suites) on 2 floors were renovated in about 2 months. Those interior and furniture accommodate urban sophistication to meet the sense of modern.

Their functions are equivalent to those of the rooms on other floors, and modern approaches are adopted for the design only. As a new technique, the headboard is provided with horizontal slit lighting to reconcile the design and reading lamp function.

改修前の客室(上：シングルルーム、下：ダブルルーム)。
Guestroom before renovation
(upper: single room, below: double room).

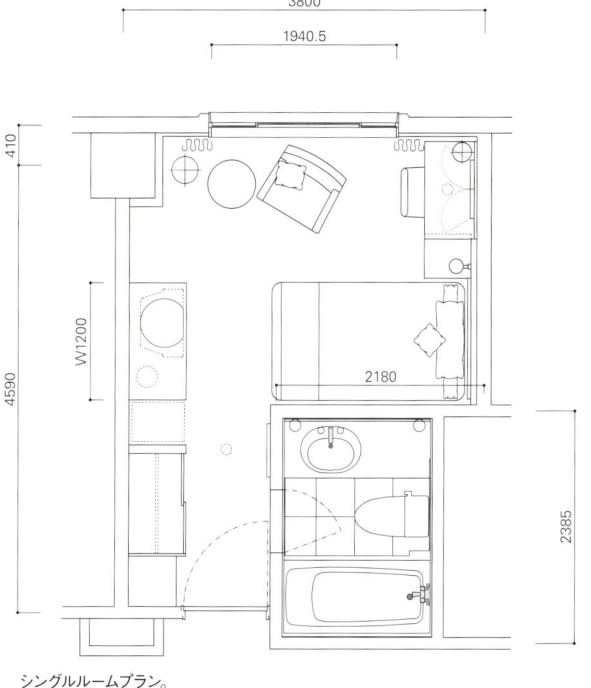

ダブルルーム。(写真:スタジオワーク)
Double room. (Photo: STUDIO WORK)

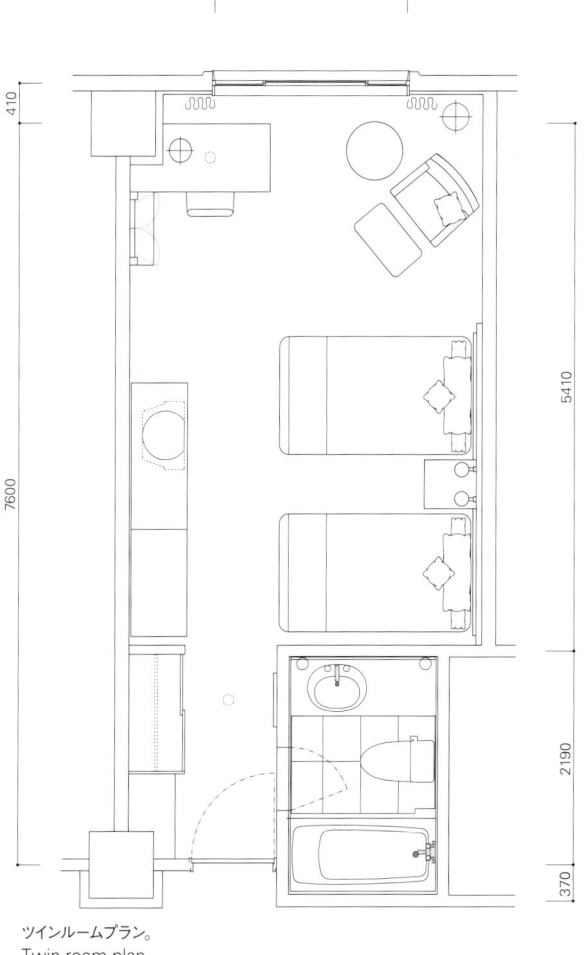

シングルルームプラン。
Single room plan.

ツインルームプラン。
Twin room plan.

名古屋東急ホテル 015

ホテルエルム札幌
構造躯体以外は全て一新したプチホテル

HOTEL ELM SAPPORO
Everything except the structural skeleton was renewed with this petit hotel

ホテルのエントランス。(写真：大麻フォトスタジオ)
Hotel entrance. (Photo: Oasa Photo Studio)

Client: Institution of Police Association Hokkaido Branch
Architect: Hokkaido Nikken Sekkei and Nikken Space Design
Designer: (Architect): Hiromu Goto
(Interior): Risa Misawa / Takayuki Nago
Construction: Itogumi Construction Co., Ltd.
Location: Sapporo-shi, Hokkaido
Site area: 1,318.45 sq m
Completion: December 2003
Original completion: 1968

改修前。(写真：大麻フォトスタジオ)
Before renovation. (Photo: Oasa Photo Studio)

改修後のファサード。(写真：大麻フォトスタジオ)
Facade after renovation. (Photo: Oasa Photo Studio)

改修前の1Fフロント。
Front desk on the first floor before renovation.

ロビー（レセプション廻り）。（写真：大麻フォトスタジオ）
Lobby (near reception). (Photo: Oasa Photo Studio)

グリル「エルムの木」。（写真：大麻フォトスタジオ）
Restaurant, ELM-no-ki (ELM tree). (Photo: Oasa Photo Studio)

改修前の1Fグリル。
Restaurant on the first floor before renovation.

昭和43年の開設以来、市民に親しまれてきた「エルム会館」が全面リニューアルにより「ホテルエルム札幌」として装いも新たに生まれ変わった。建物は躯体以外ほとんど全面的にリニューアルを行い、構造も一部は補強が行われている。デザインのキーワードは「NATURAL」。温かみを残しながら、コンテンポラリーな外観のデザインと、暖かく柔らかなインテリアとの融合をイメージし、モダンでミニマルな「邸宅」が誕生した。

The ELM Kaikan that has been popular among citizens ever since its opening in 1968 is now renewed as HOTEL ELM SAPPORO. The building was fully renovated with an exception of the skeleton, and partial reinforcements were also applied to the structure.
The design keyword was "natural". While preserving the warmth and elegance of its heritage, a contemporary exterior and a warm and tender interior are combined to establish a modern and minimal "residence".

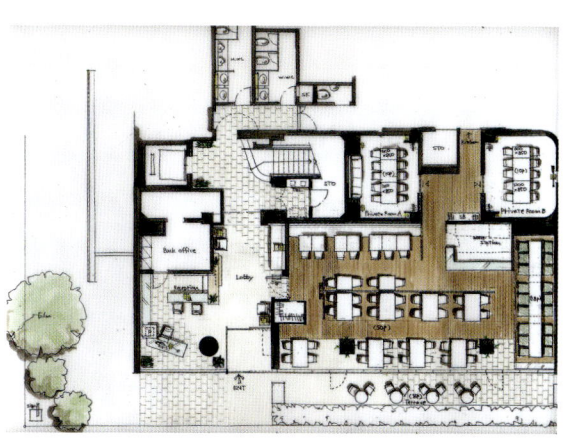

1Fロビー・グリルのスケッチとカラースキーム。
Sketches and color scheme of the lobby and restaurant on the first floor.

天井高の低さが問題であった会議室まわり。照明器具の効果や演出によりその圧迫感を取り去った。「ちょっと大きな邸宅にお邪魔した」という感じを大切にし、温かみのある明るい会議室を目指している。

洋会議室「ライラック」は全面カーペット敷きとし、木製のスタッキングチェアーを採用。旧会館のパイプ椅子からグレード感も上がり、パーティーからフォーマルな会議にも対応できる。和会議室ゾーンは、「すずらん」のみ掘りごたつを採用し、「はまなす」は間仕切り壁を移動することにより2部屋での利用が可能。親しみやすい和の空間を意識し、モダンで温かみのある和室として完成した。

Low heights of the ceilings were major issues of the old building. By carefully arranging effective lighting fixtures, a sense of enclosedness was removed. The design of the meeting rooms is warm and cheerful, giving an impression that one is casually visiting a rather big house.

The western style meeting room, Lilac, has a fully carpeted floor and wooden stacking chairs, which have been upgraded from the tubular chairs used in the old building, making the facility suitable for various uses from parties to formal conferences.

As to the Japanese style meeting rooms, Suzuran only has horigotatsu (a footwarmer fixed in a sunken floor). By removing partitions, Hamanasu meeting room may be used with an adjacent room as a single space. These rooms are designed as Japanese spaces that make one feel at home and completed as modern and warm Japanese style rooms.

2Fの会議室「ライラック」。（写真：大麻フォトスタジオ）
Meeting room on the second floor, Lilac. (Photo: Oasa Photo Studio)

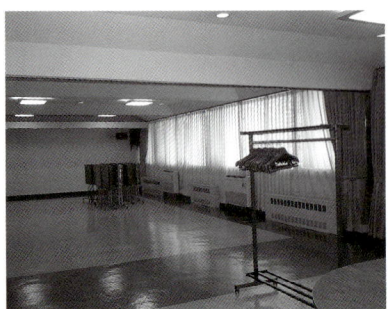

改修前の2F会議室。
Meeting room on the second floor before renovation.

改修前の2F和会議室。
Japanese style meeting room on the second floor before renovation.

2Fの和会議室「すずらん」。（写真：大麻フォトスタジオ）
Japanese style meeting room on the second floor, Suzuran. (Photo: Oasa Photo Studio)

2F会議室のスケッチとカラースキーム。
Sketch and color schemes of the meeting rooms on the second floor.

ナイトテーブルはヘッドボードと一体。
Night table integrated with the headboard.

シングルルーム。（写真：大麻フォトスタジオ）
Single room.（Photo: Oasa Photo Studio）

客室は、足元から縦長に設けた細長い窓が、狭い客室天井を高く感じさせる手助けとなり、開放感が感じられる。またヘッドボードまわりの間接照明が、柔らかく室内を包み、天井の圧迫感はなくなった。
床はフローリングを採用し、ラグマットのようにカーペットを落とし込んだ。カラースキームはシングルルームは明るい木部、ツインルームは少し赤みの入った木部を基調に、柔らかなミニマリズムを追求している。

Guestrooms give a sense of openness, thanks to a long, tall window from the floor, giving the effect of lifting the ceiling higher than it actually is. Indirect lighting near the headboard also softly illuminates the room, contributing to remove a sense of oppression because of the ceiling.
Flooring is used for the floor, which is partially covered by the carpet as if it were a rug. Flooring is used for the floor, which is partially covered by the carpet as if it were a rug. As to the color schemes, single rooms are based on light wood while twin rooms are based on slightly reddish wood in pursuit of gentle minimalism.

ツインルーム。（写真：大麻フォトスタジオ）
Twin room.（Photo: Oasa Photo Studio）

3F客室のスケッチとカラースキーム。
Sketches and color scheme of the guestroom on the third floor.

ホテルニューグランド「スカイ・チャペル」
プールの水の重さで
チャペルをつくる

Sky Chapel, Hotel New Grand
Making a chapel utilizing the weight of the water

Principal Architect: Hisao Ohyama: Shimizu Corporation
Architect: Kazuhide Sakai: Shimizu Corporation
Designer: Yoshiharu Shimura: FIELD FOUR DESIGN OFFICE
Location: Yokohama-shi, Kanagawa
Site area: 545 sq m
Structure: SRC
Completion: December, 1997
Materials: floor; karin flooring
wall; white oak plywood
ceiling; painting

トワイライトタイムのチャペルは港の光が空間に入りこむ。（写真：ナカサ＆パートナーズ）
Light from harbor entering the chapel in twilight time. （Photo: Nacása & Partners Inc.）

1927年に創設されたこのホテルは日本における最も古い本格的ホテルのひとつである。タワー型新館に設けられたチャペルは宗教性が薄く、主としてセレモニー用である。最上階という特性を利用し、水平方向として横浜港の眺望を正面に据え、さらに垂直方向の高まりとして中央の天蓋を立ち上げた。水平は日本的手法、垂直は西洋的手法とも言える。さらにホワイエとしての中庭は天空の崇さをあらわす場とも言えようか。

This hotel was founded in 1927 and is one of the oldest full-fledged hotels in Japan. Chapel built in tower shaped annex has little in religious sense and is mostly used for ceremonial purpose. Taking advantage of its top floor position, it horizontally has a view of Yokohama bay at the front, and vertically has tall canopy in the center. This horizontal sense could be traditional Japanese method and vertical could be European. And also center coat as foyer could be place for expressing highness of the heaven.

(H. Ohyama)

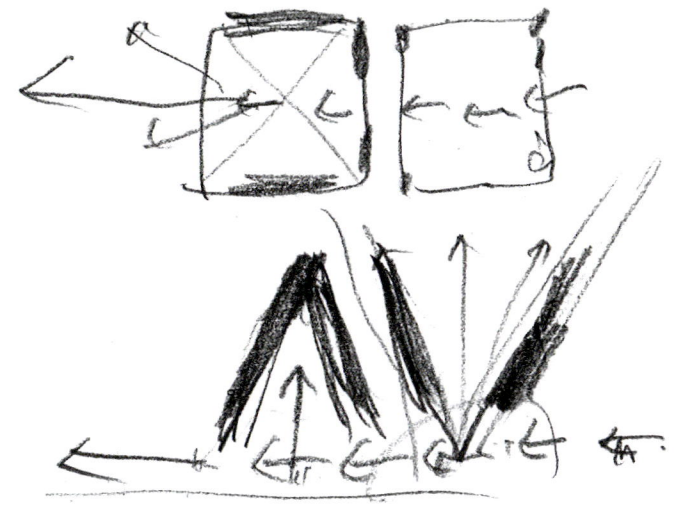

コンセプトスケッチ。
Conceptual sketch.

天井全体が光によって宇宙を演出する。(写真:ナカサ&パートナーズ)
The entire ceiling expressing the universe in light. (Photo: Nacása & Partners Inc.)

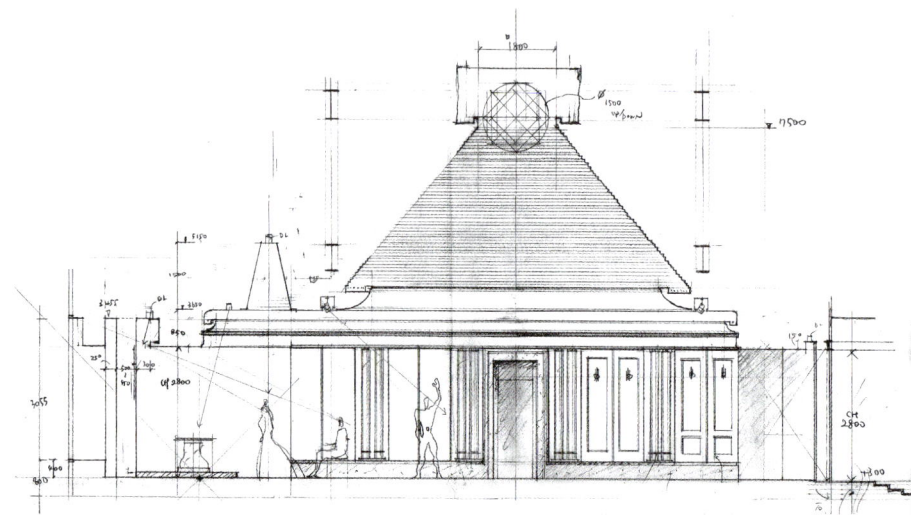

既存のスケルトンに納めるための
セクションエスキース。
Section esquisse for renovation utilizing the existing skeleton.

二つの奥行きが交差する空間を、木と漆喰の白の対比で表した。明るく透明感のある空間に、重厚なアメリカンウォールナットの扉や深みのある彫刻が施されたホワイトオークの壁が、人との暖かな関係を確かなものとする。高さ7mの方行形天井は、階段状の30mm×30mmの繊細なマチエールで、クリスタルをイメージしたオブジェがきらめく天へと昇りつめる。

A space where two different depths meet is expressed by the contrast of wood and white plaster. This well-lit space with magnificent American walnut doors and white oak walls impressively sculpted gives one a sense of warmth and familiarity as well as a feeling of transparency. The seven-meter-high ceiling is composed of delicate 30mm-by-30mm materials arranged like the inside of a stepped pyramid with the crystal-shaped object at the highest point. (Y. Shimura)

正面祭壇とベイブリッジ。(写真:ナカサ&パートナーズ)
The front alter and the Bay Bridge. (Photo: Nacása & Partners Inc.)

初期のイメージスケッチ。
Early conceptual sketch.

チャペルエントランス扉スケッチ。
Sketch of the chapel entrance.

パティオからも柔らかな自然光が入り込む。（写真：ナカサ＆パートナーズ）
Soft natural light also coming from the patio. (Photo: Nacása & Partners Inc.)

ホテルニューグランド「スカイ・チャペル」 023

ホテル日航東京「ブルー・ブリーズ」&「オーシャンダイニング」
「海・空・風・光」をテーマにした料飲施設リノベーション

hotel nikko tokyo
Bridal Salon, Blue Breeze and Mediterranean cuisine, Ocean Dining
Restaurant renovation on the theme of the sea, sky, wind and light

Client: Tokyo Humania Enterprise Inc.
Architect: Yamagi Architects & Engineers
Designer: Takashi Fujii: Nikken Space Design
Construction: JAL CONSTRUCTION CO., LTD.
Location: Minato-ku, Tokyo
Area: 250 sq m
Completion: August 31, 2004
Material: Floor: oak flooring, glass tile, and porcelain tile
Wall: Art painting wall Chloridization vinyl sheet and Paint
Ceiling: Paint and glass cloth

ブライダルサロン「ブルー・ブリーズ」

ホテル日航東京のブライダルサロンは天井高2.6m程度、四方を壁に囲まれた空間であった。また写真室・衣装室・美容室なども個々に閉じた部屋構成となっており空間の繋がりも乏しかった。今回のリノベーションでは通路やホワイエなどのパブリックスペースや、各部屋を含めた婚礼付帯施設全体として空間コンセプトを明確にすることで、このホテルブライダルに対しての新しいイメージを体感的に認識させることを狙いとしている。
サロンは既存プランの形状が不整形であったため、その形を利用し天井の高低差との組み合わせによって、ひとつの空間に異なる2つのテイストを共存することができた。客船のデッキに見立てたゾーンは天井高を既存の約2倍の高さとすることで今までにない開放感を生みだした。最も強い印象を与えるのが高さ5m、総幅30mにわたるアートウォール。コの字状になった壁の隅をR状とすることでサラウンド効果が生れ、海の上にいるかのようなフェイキーな空間をつくりだしている。一方カフェに見立てたゾーンは、天井高を4mとしその下部にガラスクロスを懸垂している。デッキゾーンよりも色温度の低い照明器具を用い、クロスを通した間接的な光とすることでゆったり落ち着いた雰囲気に仕上がっている。

既存共用部通路。サロンは写真左壁側に位置する。
Existing corridor in the common area. The salon is located to the left in the picture above.

強い印象をあたえるマリンブルーのエントランス。（写真：エスエス企画）
Highly impressive marine blue entrance. (Photo: SS Kikaku)

既存エントランス付近。
Existing entrance and its surroundings.

2つのテイストから構成されたサロン。写真手前がカフェに見立てたゾーン。奥が客船のデッキゾーン。（写真：エスエス企画）
Salon constituted by two different taste. The zone compared to a cafe terrace is in front, and the zone compared to a passenger ship deck is at the back. (Photo: SS Kikaku)

ニュートラルな印象の併設施設との共用ホワイエ。
（写真：エスエス企画）
Foyer commonly used with other facilities, giving a neutral impression. (Photo: SS Kikaku)

スケッチ。
Sketch.

爽やかさのなかに高級感を感じさせる個室。
（写真：エスエス企画）
Private room in the restaurant with a sense of both grace and quality. (Photo: SS Kikaku)

客室の甲板をイメージした打ち合わせコーナー。高さ5m×幅30mにおよぶアートウォール。
壁側の各席間には天井よりスクリーンが垂れ落ち、プライバシーを考慮した打ち合わせスペースとなる。（写真：エスエス企画）
Meeting zone having an impression of a passenger ship deck, having an artwall of 5 meters in height and 30 meters in width. Screens may be lowered for the row of tables by the wall, creating meeting spaces for visitors to find privacy. (Photo: SS Kikaku)

カラースキームボード。
Color scheme board.

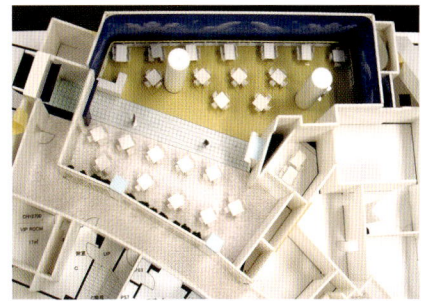

模型によるアートウォールの検証。
Examination of the artwall using a model.

Bridal Salon, Blue Breeze

Hotel Nikko Tokyo bridal salon had a ceiling height of about 2.6m, surrounded by four walls. The photo room, dressing room and beauty parlor were all enclosed, mostly independent spaces. Through this renovation, the objective was to clearly define the spatial concept of the bridal facilities including the public spaces such as the corridors and foyer as well as individual rooms in order to let clients intuitively recognize a new image of the facilities.

As the shape of the existing plan was irregular, we took advantage of this fact in combination with the different ceiling heights to establish two different tastes in one space. The zone compared to a passenger ship deck now has a ceiling height about twice as high as that before renovation, giving a sense of openness that has never been seen before. The artwall of 5 meters in height and 30 meters in width should give the strongest impression.

By changing the U-shaped corner of the wall into the R-shaped one, a tricky space is created, making one feel as if one were aboard and surrounded by the sea. The zone compared to a cafe terrace has a ceiling height of 4 meters, and glass cloths are suspended from the ceiling. Light fixtures with a color temperature lower than that in the deck zone are installed, and their light indirectly spread in the room through the cloths, completing a graceful and comfortable atmosphere.

エントランス。白と青の壁とアラビア風モチーフで構成されている。
（写真：エスエス企画）
Entrance constituted by white and blue walls and Arabian motifs.
(Photo: SS Kikaku)

「ファティマの手」というモチーフの銀細工。
（写真：エスエス企画）
Silverwork on the motif of the Fatima's hand. (Photo: SS Kikaku)

既存ブッフェコーナー。
Buffet corner before renovation.

船をイメージしたブッフェコーナー。ライティングはシーンにより変化する。（写真：エスエス企画）
Ship-like buffet corner. Lighting may be changed based on the situations. (Photo: SS Kikaku)

Client: Tokyo Humania Enterprise Inc.
Construction: Takashimaya Space Create Co., Ltd
Designer: Yuko Tsukumo: Nikken Space Design
Location: Minato-ku, Tokyo
Site area: 420 sq m
Completion: April 26, 2004
Material: (Approach Corridor) Painted plaster wall with Tunisian silver ornament,
(Buffet area) Olive wood flooring, Methacryl synthetic marble table.
(Seating area) Wenge flooring, Oak wood display cabinet,
Special finish plaster wall

地中海料理レストラン「オーシャンダイニング」

ホテル日航東京の3階、ベイエリアに向かって弧を描く細長い空間がレストランで、片面の全面ガラスからは台場の海とレインボーブリッジを一望できる。その立地から、既存店舗でも『海』というキーワードは意識されていたが、『オーシャンダイニング――"地中海とマグレブ料理のダイニング"』として改修するにあたり、そのイメージがより限定され明確に打ち出された。『マグレブ』とは北アフリカの地中海に面した国々を指す。

既存のインテリアにおける「海」のイメージは、ホテル全体の雰囲気の延長上にあるもので「ヨーロッパのリゾート」の趣であったが、新しいコンセプトから、チュニジアに代表される「マグレブの海辺の町」がイメージソースとなった。

"白とチュニジアンブルー"の色使い、陰影を生む格子パネル、アラビア風モチーフを各所に用い、洗練されたエスニックを表現している。また、エントランスを正面に変更し、中央をブッフェコーナー、その両側をダイニングとし、仕上げも分け、細長い空間に変化を与えている。

ブッフェは開孔パネルによりダイニングとは緩やかに仕切り、エントランスを入ると、船を模したブッフェテーブル"プレゼンテーションデッキ"が天井にわたされたビームと共に目に飛び込んでくる。左右のダイニングは、カウンター席を配したプライベート感の高いエリアとベンチシートを配した奥行きのあるフロア席とし、その奥に新たに格子パネルで仕切った半個室を設けた。

ホテルのオールデイダイニングとして、様々な客層・シーンに対応できる構成となっている。

店内に飾られた小物類は、実際にマルセイユ～チュニジア～シチリアの街を歩いて集めた工芸品である。店舗入口のサイン・エントランス通路の銀細工もチュニジアの工場で製作したものであるが、それら小物の持つ現地の空気感がレストランの雰囲気づくりに大きく役立っている。

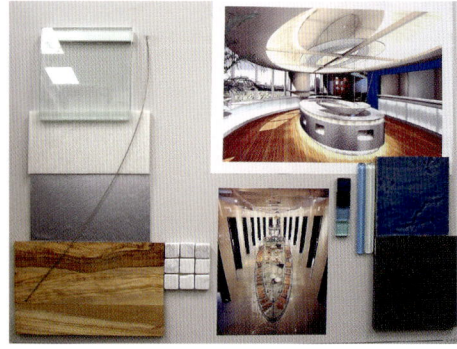
カラースキームボード。
Color scheme board.

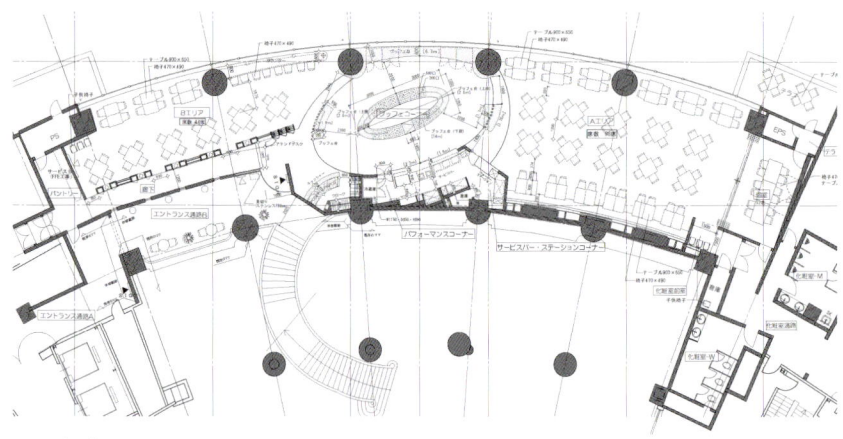
レイアウトプラン。
Layout plan.

ディスプレイ家具を背にしたダイニングエリア。(写真:エスエス企画)
Dining area with furniture for display at the back. (Photo: SS Kikaku)

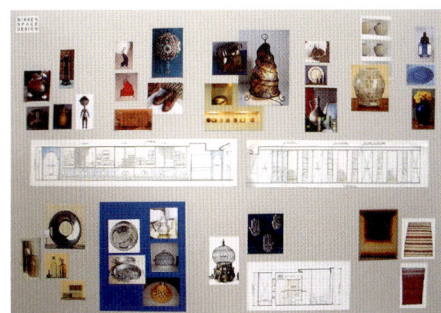
小物のディスプレイイメージ。
Display concepts of small articles.

客席イメージスケッチ1。
Conceptual sketch of seats #1.

客席イメージスケッチ2。
Conceptual sketch of seats #2.

既存店舗内部。
Interior of the restaurant before renovation.

Mediterranean cuisine, Ocean Dining

On the third floor of Hotel Nikko Tokyo is a restaurant in the long, narrow, arc-shaped space facing the bay area. The wall entirely in glass gives a bird's eye view of the sea of Odaiba and the Rainbow Bridge. Thanks to its location, the "sea" was also the keyword of the old restaurant before renovation; however, in renovating the space as "Ocean Dining: Mediterranean and the Maghreb cuisine", emphasis was put on this image more definitively and clearly. (The Maghreb means the North African countries facing the Mediterranean Sea.)

The image of the "sea" in the existing interior was an extension of the general atmosphere of the hotel: European resort. Based on the new concept, however, a "Maghreb seaside town" now serves as the source of image.

Coloring based on the "white and Tunisian blue", grilled panels to create shade and shadow, and Arabian motifs were applied here and there to express a sophisticated ethnic style. The entrance was moved to the front of the space; the buffet corner was located at the center with the dining spaces on the sides; different finishes were applied to give different impressions in the long and narrow space.

The buffet corner is loosely separated from the dining areas using holed panels. When one enters the restaurant through the endurance, one will see the standout ship-shaped buffet table, "Presentation Deck", together with beams running across the ceiling. The dining spaces to the left and right comprise of an area with counter seats suitable for private events and an area with a depth having bench seats. Behind them are semi-private guestrooms separated by grid panels.

As an all-day dining venue of the hotel, the restaurant is designed to satisfy a wide variety of guests and situations.

Small articles decorated in the interior are objects of craftwork actually purchased in towns of Marseille, Tunisia, and the Sicily. The nameplate at the entrance and silverworks found in the entrance corridor are all made in a Tunisian factory, and local properties of the articles contribute to the unique atmosphere of the restaurant.

ベンチシート席。可動の格子パネルとライティングが壁面に陰影を与える。
Bench seats. Mobile grid panels and lighting giving shade and shadow on the wall.

チュニジアで製作した入り口店舗サイン。
Nameplate at the entrance, made in Tunisia.

ベイエリアを一望できるカウンター席。(写真:エスエス企画)
Counter seats with a bird's eye view of the bay area. (Photo: SS Kikaku)

ホテル ニューオータニ高岡

スタイリッシュに変身した
高岡市民のコミュニケーションホテル

Hotel New Otani Takaoka
Takaoka citizen's communication hotel has transformed itself into a stylish place.

ロビーシーティングスペース。高岡市民のギャラリーにもなる、また人前式も行われる。（写真：北嶋俊治）
Seating space. It serves as a gallery available for Takaoka citizens as well as a space for noreligious wedding ceremonies. (Photo: Toshiharu Kitajima)

Develop:	HOTEL NEW OTANI TAKAOKA CO., LTD.
Producer:	Seiichi Nakagawa: MHS Planners' Architects & Engineers
Designer:	Mika Tomita: MHS Planners' Architects & Engineers
Location:	Takaoka-shi, Toyama
Site area:	3,880.59 squ m
Building area:	2,361.13 sq m
Total floor area:	19,640.88 sq m
Structure:	RC; SRC
Completion:	February 2000
Exterior Wall:	tile, granite
Public Wall:	painting; veneer; wallpaper
Public Floor:	marble; carpet

カフェ＆ダイニング「COO」カウンターエリア。
（写真：富田美香）
Counter area of the Cafe & Dining "COO".
(Photo: Mika Tomita)

富山県高岡市に開業したホテルニューオータニ高岡は15周年を迎えるにあたり、ホテル全体をリニューアルする計画を行った。その先駆けとして、従来の神殿での挙式、宴会場での披露宴という形のブライダルを、当時流行し始めていた一戸建て感覚のチャペルを低層部屋上に新築した。また最上階メインダイニングをレストランウエディングに対応するため、細長く見とおしがきかないプランだったものをチャペルのクラシックデザインをモダンに取り入れた広く明るいレストランに改修し、新郎新婦がオリジナルスタイルのウエディングを作り上げることが可能になった。続いてホテルの顔である1Fロビーを高岡市民のコミュニケーションの場をテーマとし、カフェテリア、ブライダルサロンを含めた大規模なリニューアルを行った。ロビー、シーティングスペースはシックな色づかいの中にコントラストを効かせて、華やかさを演出。また、カフェテリアは位置、業態も大きく変わり高岡の若者、女性に受け入れられるモダンなデザインを取り入れ、カフェゾーン、レストランゾーン、カウンターゾーンと多様なニーズに応えられるようなダイニングとなった。

Celebrating its 15th anniversary, Hotel New Otani Takaoka planned an overall renovation. In the first phase of the project, the hotel built a chapel as a stand-alone facility on the roof of the low-rise part of the building; chapel weddings were coming into fashion, and the hotel wanted to offer new bridal packages in addition to the conventional combination of a wedding ceremony at the shrine and a wedding reception at a banquet hall. The main dining at the top of the building was also renovated to meet demands for restaurant weddings. The resutaurant with a long and narrow plan with poor line of sight was updated into a wide and well-lit one whose modern design was combined with the classical design in common with the chapel. The hotel now offers custom wedding programs for newly weds. In the second phase, the lobby on the first floor as well as the cafe terrace and bridal salon was fully renewed. The theme of the renewal was to provide a communication forum for Takaoka citizens. The lobby and the sitting space of well-contrasted, chic colors offer a gorgeous atmosphere. Both the location and line of business of the cafe terrace were changed, incorporating modern design appealing to the young people and females in the city, and the dining now has a tea & coffee zone, a restaurant area, and a counter to satisfy a variety of needs.

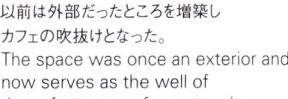

以前は外部だったところを増築しカフェの吹抜けとなった。
The space was once an exterior and now serves as the well of the cafe terrace after extension.

外観照明計画。
Exterior lighting plan.

カフェの吹抜け部分。(写真：北嶋俊治)
Well in the cafe terrace. (Photo: Toshiharu Kitajima)

カフェ＆ダイニング「COO」レストランエリア。(写真：富田美香)
Restaurant area of the Cafe & Dining "COO". (Photo: Mika Tomita)

旧ロビー。
Old lobby.

ロビー。木製のゲートが空間を引き締める。(写真：北嶋俊治)
Lobby. accentuated by the wooden gate. (Photo: Toshiharu Kitajima)

低層部屋上に建てられたチャペル「ミレニアム」。（写真：馬場祥光［サラサ］）
Chapel "Millennium" built on the roof of the low-rise part of the building. (Photo: Yoshiteru Baba[Sarasa])

ウッドデッキを敷詰めガーデンウェディングもできる。（写真：馬場祥光［サラサ］）
Wood decks, ideal setting for garden weddings. (Photo: Yoshiteru Baba[Sarasa])

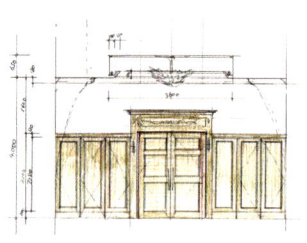

チャペル。前室より。（写真：馬場祥光［サラサ］）
Chapel. (Photo: Yoshiteru Baba[Sarasa])

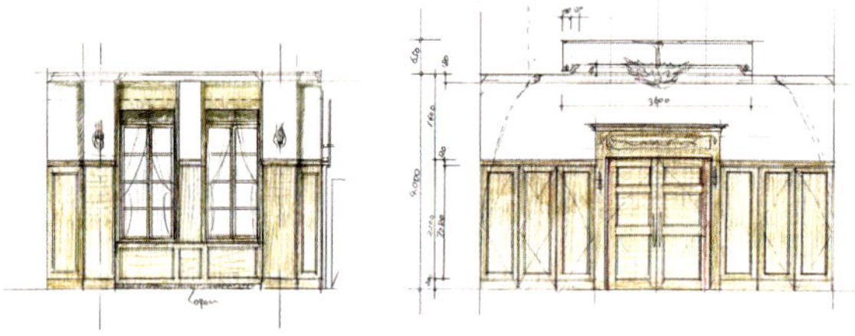

トップレストラン「フォーシーズン」。レストランウエディングにも対応可能。（写真：馬場祥光［サラサ］）
Restaurant "Four Season" meeting demands for restaurant weddings. (Photo: Yoshiteru Baba[Sarasa])

『オーク バー』（写真：馬場祥光［サラサ］）
Oak Bar. (Photo: Yoshiteru Baba[Sarasa])

ホテルグランヴィア大阪
新しい出会いを求めた
ホテルロビーの全面改修

HOTEL GRANVIA OSAKA
Full renovation of the hotel lobby for new meetings

Client: JR-West Hotels HOTEL GRANVIA OSAKA
Construction: Daitetsu Kogyo Co.,Ltd
Architect: Yasui Architects & Engineers,Inc.
Designer: Kayoko Matsuda: Nikken Space Design
Location: Kita-ku, Osaka
Site area: 1,087.3 sq m
Completion: April, 2003
Material: Lobby Floor: marble, granite
　　　　　Wall: painting, mahogany
Original completion: April, 1983

開業20周年を迎えたホテルの1階ロビーの全面リニューアル。最も重要な問題は、東玄関のイメージつくりであった。ターミナルと商業施設の近接により極めて高い利便性を有する反面、玄関へいたるアプローチの印象、ロビーとして独立した場所のイメージが希薄であった。

まず、ホテルの顔であるレセプションカウンターを移動、木目を生かしたモダンなデザインで上質感をアピールした。次に光の質が均一にならないように特化された環境イメージをつくった。南側に窓を持つラウンジは、豊かなボリューム感を生かし、ブランドショップの上質感と動きのある寛ぎを備えた明るい環境とした。

コーヒーショップは、カフェレストランとして、駅中央コンコースから直接入れる入口を新設、街に対して重要な顔をつくった。

オープンパントリーからは、焼きたてのパンの臭い、フルーツのディスプレイ、ナチュラルなカラースキームで仕上げ、清潔感、都会的センスをアピールした。

客用トイレは、移設に加えて、多目的トイレを新設した。クロークは、窓口と保管場所、宅急便受付場所と合理的な空間取りが求められたため、スペースを確保した。

豊かなヴォリューム感、寛ぎのあるロビーラウンジ。（写真：柄松 稔）
Relaxing lobby lounge with a sense of expansion.（Photo: Minoru Karamatsu）

改修前ロビーラウンジ。
Lobby lounge before renovation.

季節感を感じさせる
エレベーターホール。
（写真：柄松 稔）
Elevator hall with
a sense of the season.
（Photo: Minoru Karamatsu）

Marking 20 years of the hotel's history, the project was to completely renovate the lobby on the first floor, and the biggest challenge was to strengthen the presence of the eastern entrance.

While the entrance offered excellent convenience with its adjoined terminal and commercial facilities; neither the approach to the entrance nor the lobby gave a strong and distinctive impression.

First, the reception counter to determine a first impression of the hotel was relocated, and modern, woodgrain finish was applied to appeal the quality of the hotel.

Next, We designed a special lighting environment to avoid an even distribution and quality of light. Taking advantage of the windows to the south contributing to a sense of expansion, we designed the lounge as a place offering a quality of brand shops and positive relaxation.

The existing coffee shop was renovated as a cafe restaurant with a direct access from the central concourse of the station, giving a stronger impression of its presence to the city. From its open pantry, the fresh scent of baked bread wafts out. Fruits are displayed, and the restaurant was finished using a natural color scheme. All of these design approaches appeal the facility's cleanliness and urbanity.

The guest lavatory was relocated, and a multi-purpose toilet was newly built.

The cloakroom area was carefully designed to meet its rational functionality as a cloakroom counter, storage, and courier service desk.

ロビーレセプションカウンター。(写真:柄松 稔)
Reception counter in the lobby. (Photo: Minoru Karamatsu)

コンシェルジュカウンター。(写真:柄松 稔)
Concierge counter. (Photo: Minoru Karamatsu)

カフェレストラン「リップル」。(写真:柄松 稔)
Cafe restaurant, Ripple. (Photo: Minoru Karamatsu)

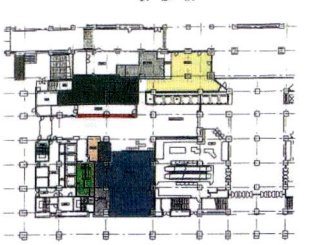
改修前のプラン。
Plan before renovation.

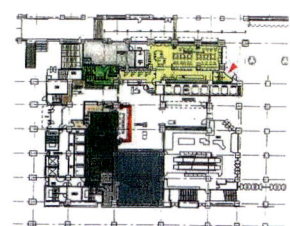
改修プラン。
Renovation plan.

改修前のカフェレストラン。
Cafe restaurant before renovation.

大阪駅中央コンコースより見た新しいエントランス。(写真:柄松 稔)
New entrance seen from the central concourse of the Osaka Station. (Photo: Minoru Karamatsu)

六甲山ホテル
昭和初期の
クラシカルなホテルを再現

Rokkosan Hotel
A classical hotel of the early Showa style recreated

Developer:	Hankyu Hotel Manegement Co., Ltd.
Cooperator maker:	Hankyu Seisakusyo Co., Ltd.
	Daiko Electric Co., Ltd. / Kurashi-no-gallery
Producer:	Seiichi Nakagawa: NEXT/m
Designer:	Mitsushi Emura:
	MHS Planners, Architects & Engineers
Location:	Nada-ku hyougo
Site area:	28,485.05 sq m
Building area:	988.8 sq m
Total floor area:	4,246.4 sq m
Renovation area:	414 sq m (banquet hall)/ 158 sq m (courtyard)
Structure:	reinforced concrete
Completion:	February 2004
Public wall:	base coat
Public Floor:	floorings and special order carpet

中庭。(写真:庄野 新/庄野 啓[フォト・ビューロー])
Patio. (Photo: Arata Shono / Hiraku Shono [Photo Bureau])

コンセプトイメージ。
Concept image.

昭和4年開業の六甲山ホテル別館。
Rokkosan Hotel Annex opened in 1929.

六甲山の緑豊かな自然の中に佇む歴史あるホテル。
本館の庭園に面した宴会場と大阪湾や淡路島が一望できる庭園内の小高い丘にあるテラスのリノベーションを計画する。

庭園に面している宴会場「フォレスト」は、昭和4年から六甲山とともに歴史を築く、クラッシックな別館のイメージを再現し、窓の外に広がる自然に溶け込み落ち着きのあるゲストハウス空間とした。

庭園にある小高い丘は「ベイビューテラス」と名づけ、ウッドデッキを設置し床を上げることにより、このホテルからしか見ることが出来ないオーシャンビュー&ナイトビューを楽しめるようにした。

宴会場と「庭園」「ベイビューテラス」を使い、様々なスタイルのハウスウエディングが出来るように計画した。

A hotel with a long history built in rich nature of Mount Rokko.
Planned are renovations of the banquet hall facing the garden of the main building as well as the terrace on the hill in the garden with a command of view of the Osaka Bay and Awaji Island.
The design of the classical style annex whose history goes back to 1929 is applied to the Forest banquet hall facing the garden. The design of this chic hall takes into account the natural setting of the garden expanding outside the window.
A small hill in the garden is named as Bay View Terrace; by building a wooden deck to make the floor higher than the ground, the ocean views and night views unique to this hotel are offered.
Various wedding styles are made available thanks to combinations of the banquet halls, gardens and Bay View Terrace.

クラシカルホテルの再現 宴会場「フォレスト」。(写真:庄野 新/庄野 啓[フォト・ビューロー])
Forest banquet hall based on the classical design of the Annex.
(Photo: Arata Shono / Hiraku Shono [Photo Bureau])

「ベイビューテラス」から神戸港をのぞむ。
(写真:庄野 新/庄野 啓[フォト・ビューロー])
Kobe Port from Bay View Terrace.
(Photo: Arata Shono / Hiraku Shono [Photo Bureau])

「フォレスト」改修前。(写真:庄野 新/庄野 啓[フォト・ビューロー])
Forest before renovation. (Photo: Arata Shono / Hiraku Shono[Photo Bureau])

「フォレスト」スケッチ。
Sketch of Forest.

「ホワイエ」スケッチ。
Sketch of Foyer.

テラスのスケッチ。
Sketch of the terrace.

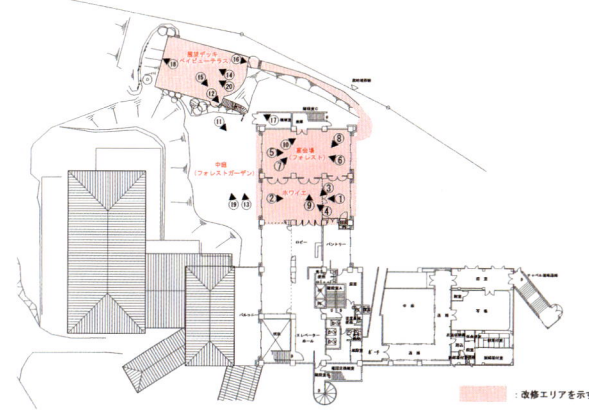

平面図。
Floor plan.

「ベイビューテラス」。(写真:庄野 新/庄野 啓[フォト・ビューロー])
Bay View Terrace. (Photo: Arata Shono / Hiraku Shono[Photo Bureau])

六甲山ホテル 035

エクセルホテル東急

「伝統・革新」をコンセプトにした
ホテルブランド再構築

EXCEL HOTEL TOKYU（Akasaka, Yokohama, Sendai, Kanazawa）
Rebranding the hotel based on the concept of the tradition and renewal

仙台エクセルホテル東急。ツインルーム。
Twin room, Sendai EXCEL HOTEL TOKYU.

仙台エクセルホテル東急。シングルルーム。
Single room, Sendai EXCEL HOTEL TOKYU.

改修前 シングルルーム。
Single room before renovation.

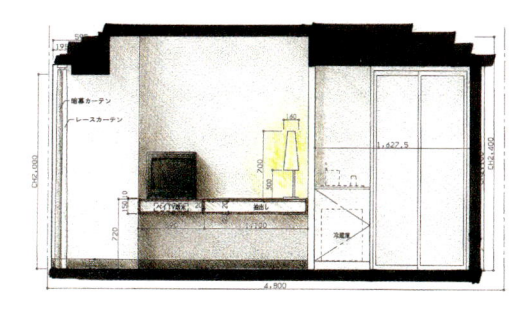

東急ホテルズの4ブランド「東急ホテル」「エクセルホテル東急」「東急イン」「東急リゾート」確立事業における「エクセルホテル東急」ブランドの一連改修工事。
仙台・金沢の客室改修以来、赤坂、横浜など各ホテルの客室まわり、エントランスロビー、宴会場、各種レストランなどの施設改修に携わった。
「伝統・革新」をコンセプトに掲げ、東急ホテルズの培ってきた伝統を大切にしながら、「エクセルホテル東急」ブランドとしての新たな革新を遂げることを念頭に置いている。各地それぞれの既存デザインに対し、ブランドキーワードである、「スタイリッシュな都会の演出」をデザイン軸として、シンプルでメリハリの利いた空間構成を展開している。

The project was one of the series of renovation works of TOKYU HOTELS to establish the group's four brands: TOKYU HOTEL, EXCEL HOTEL TOKYU, TOKYU INN, and TOKYU RESORT.
Starting with the guestroom renovations in Sendai and Kanazawa, we have been involved in renewal works including guestrooms, entrance lobbies, banquet halls, and restaurants.
The basic concept of the renovation works is "the tradition and renewal": while maintaining the long tradition of TOKYU HOTELS, the focus was on reinventing the EXCEL HOTEL TOKYU brand.
While taking the existing designs into consideration, we have developed simple yet well-defined spatial configurations, based on the concept of "creating stylish urban designs".

コンペの際に提出した資料の一部。
Some of the data submitted for the competition.

Title:	EXCEL HOTEL TOKYU （Akasaka、Yokohama、Sendai、Kanazawa）
Client:	TOKYU HOTELS CO., LTD.
Construction:	Akasaka-Tokyu Construction Yokohama-Tokyu Community Co., Ltd. Sendai-Tokyu Construction, Tokyu Amenix Corporation Kanazawa-Tokyu Construction, Tokyu Amenix Corporation
Designer:	Saburo Morishima / Nobuko Suzuki: Nikken Space Design
Location:	Akasaka (Minato-ku, Tokyo)　Yokohama (Yokohama-shi, Kanagawa) Sendai (Sendai-shi, Miyagi)　Kanazawa (Kanazawa-shi, Ishikawa)
Site area:	Akasaka: 1,856.3 sq m　Yokohama: 1,802sq m Sendai: 5,710.6sq m　Kanazawa: 2,450sq m
Completion:	Akasaka: April, 2003　Yokohama: February, 2003 Sendai: February, 2003　Kanazawa: December, 2002
Material:	Akasaka Reception + Lobby: Floor: flooring; Wall: woody panel, Sendai Guestroom: Floor: carpet; Wall: woody panel + vinyl wall covering Banquet: Floor: carpet; Wall: woody panel + wall covering
Opening year:	Akasaka: September, 1969　Yokohama: March, 1962 Sendai: October, 1980　Kanazawa: September, 1985

エクセルホテル東急

エクセルホテルブランドのフラッグシップのひとつとなる「赤坂エクセルホテル東急」。
ホテルの顔になる3階は、フロントロビーまわり、料飲施設と2期にわたって改修を行った。
料飲施設の改修は、喫茶、レストランそれぞれ独立した施設の顔を1つにすることが計画の課題であった。

One of the flagship hotels of the EXCEL HOTEL brand is Akasaka EXCEL HOTEL TOKYU.
The third floor which serves as the gateway to the hotel was renovated in two phases: front lobby and restaurant/lounge.
The goal of renovating the restaurant and lounge was to integrate these independent facilities into one.

赤坂エクセルホテル東急。レストラン「赤坂スクエアダイニング」。（写真：柴崎潤二）
Akasaka Square Dining restaurant,
Akasaka EXCEL HOTEL TOKYU. （Photo: Junji Shibazaki）

赤坂エクセルホテル東急。レストラン「赤坂スクエアダイニング」。（写真：柴崎潤二）
Akasaka Square Dining restaurant, Akasaka EXCEL HOTEL TOKYU. （Photo: Junji Shibazaki）

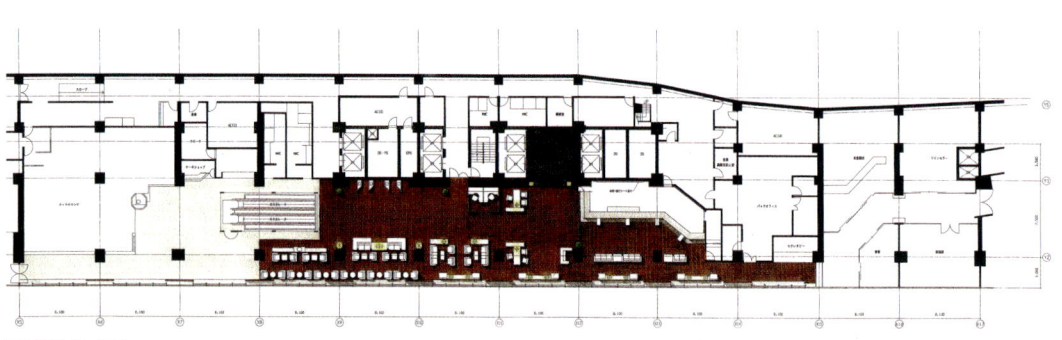

第1期改修エリア。
1st phase renovation area.

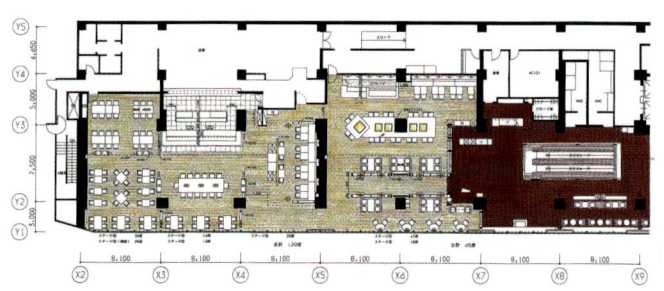

第2期改修エリア。
2nd phase renovation area.

038　第1章　ホテル

金沢エクセルホテル東急。宴会場Bは壁で覆っていた窓面をオープンにし、
明るい空間に。宴会場Aと一体空間として使用可。（写真：山下 薫）
Banquet Hall B of Kanazawa EXCEL HOTEL TOKYU. When the windows
hidden by the wall are opened, the interior becomes brighter and
more cheerful. The Hall may be used together with the adjoining
Banquet Hall A as a single space.（Photo: Kaoru Yamashita）

金沢エクセルホテル東急。宴会場Aのチャペル使用時。（写真：山下 薫）
Banquet Hall A used as a chapel, Kanazawa EXCEL HOTEL TOKYU.
（Photo: Kaoru Yamashita）

改修前。金沢エクセルホテル東急の宴会場B。
Banquet Hall B before renovation,
Kanazawa EXCEL HOTEL TOKYU.

エクセルホテルブランドにおいては宴会場をチャペルとしても
活用できるデザインとしていることがひとつの特徴である。

One of the features of the EXCEL HOTEL brand is a design
approach where banquet halls also serve as chapels.

横浜エクセルホテル東急。宴会場のチャペル使用時。（写真：柴崎潤二）
Banquet hall used as a chapel, Yokohama EXCEL HOTEL TOKYU.
（Photo: Junji Shibazaki）

横浜エクセルホテル東急。宴会場使用時。（写真：柴崎潤二）
Banquet hall used as a banquet hall, Yokohama EXCEL HOTEL TOKYU.
（Photo: Junji Shibazaki）

クラブハウス ウエディング リビエラ

さまざまな顧客のニーズに応え、
進化しつづけるウエディングハウス

Club House Wedding Riviera
Ever-evolving wedding house meeting various customers' needs

Developer:	Riviera Corporation
Designer:	Mika Tomita: MHS Planners, Architects & Engineers
Location:	Toshima-ku, Tokyo
Total floor area:	5,695.65 sq m
Structure:	W, S, and SRC
Completion:	September 2003
Exterior Wall:	Void
Public Wall:	Painting; veneer
Public Floor:	Flooring; carpet

旧宴会場。
Banqueting hall before renovation.

旧小宴会場。
Small Banqueting hall before renovation.

最上階にあった小宴会場をチャペルに改修 小屋組の形はそのまま活かした。
The small banquet hall on the top floor was turned into a chapel. The shape of the existing roof frame was used "as-is".

テラスと一体となる宴会場は明るいアジアンモダンの雰囲気とした。
The banquet hall integrated with the terrace offers a modern Asian atmosphere.

　リビエラ（旧リビエラ白雲閣）は昭和初期に創設され、専門結婚式場の草分けとして現在に至っている。増改築が何度となく行われ、今は古きよき時代の面影を残しながら、最先端のウエディングスタイルを提案できる国内でトップクラスの売上を誇る結婚式場となった。そのポジションを守るために常に時代を先取りし、顧客のニーズに敏感に応えていく姿勢を貫いている。

　それはガーデンウエディングやレストランウエディングに代表される「アットホーム」というテーマで改修がはじまった。先ず和風の中庭にテラスを増築、つづいて地下の条件の悪い宴会場を、我が家のリビングルームと設定し、友人を自分の家に招き入れるような感覚の空間を創り「ゲストハウス」と名づけた。多くの和室は、床や書院など、和のしつらえをそのままにテーブル席とし、レトロな感覚を大切に残した。また最上階の宴会場をチャペルに変身させ、ネックになっていた階段や小屋組みの構造をそのまま生かし、あたかも一軒家風の古い英国教会に生まれ変わらせた。さらに、最近の改修ではコンセプトをその年毎に変化させ、New York style、Asian Modern Styleなど、その時々の流行をいち早く察知し、取り入れ施設全体をクラブハウスと位置付け、リビエラは刻々と進化しつづけている。

Riviera (formerly "Riviera Hakuunkaku") was established early in the Showa era and has always been a pioneer in the wedding halls in Japan. After numerous additions and improvements, the wedding house proposes latest wedding styles while retaining some traces of good, old days and now is enjoys top sales in Japan. To secure the position as a forerunner, it carries the attitude to remain ahead of its time and to quickly respond to the customers' needs.

The renovation was commenced on the theme of "at-home (atmosphere)" represented by garden or restaurant weddings. First, the patio of the Japanese wedding hall was extended to have a terrace. Then, the underground banquet hall whose conditions were comparatively poor was turned into a space as if it were one's living room and built up a relaxing atmosphere to invite friends and guests. Based on the concept, it was named the "Guest House". Many of the Japanese style rooms were renovated to have tables and chairs, while maintaining the floors and studies "as-is"; this design approach gives a sense of retro fashions to the room. The banquet hall on the top floor was modified into a chapel, taking advantage of stairs and roofs that had once been obstacles; the present facility appears as if it were a detached Anglican church. In recent renovations, new concepts such as "New York Style" and "Modern Asian Style" have been adopted year by year, properly anticipating and employing the fashion of the age. Riviera positions the overall facilities as a "clubhouse" and never stops its evolution.

重たい瓦の車寄せの屋根を取払った。
The roof with heavy tiles over the porch was removed.

改修前外観(メインエントランス)。
Appearance before renovation(main entrance)

B1Fギャラリー
B1F THE GALLERY

クラシックなイメージだった地下宴会場を、光をふんだんに使いアートワークを際立たせた。
The classical underground banquet hall.

畳の個室だった部屋をバンケットの一部として、
デザートビュッフェ、待合などに使用する部屋へ改修。
A tatamized room was integrated into a banquet hall
to be used as a desert buffet or waiting room.

旧ゲストハウス。
Old guesthouse.

GUEST HOUSE アットホームのコンセプトを経て、
現在はニューヨークのクラブイメージに改修。
Based on the "at home" concept, the current guesthouse
suggests an impression of clubs in New York.

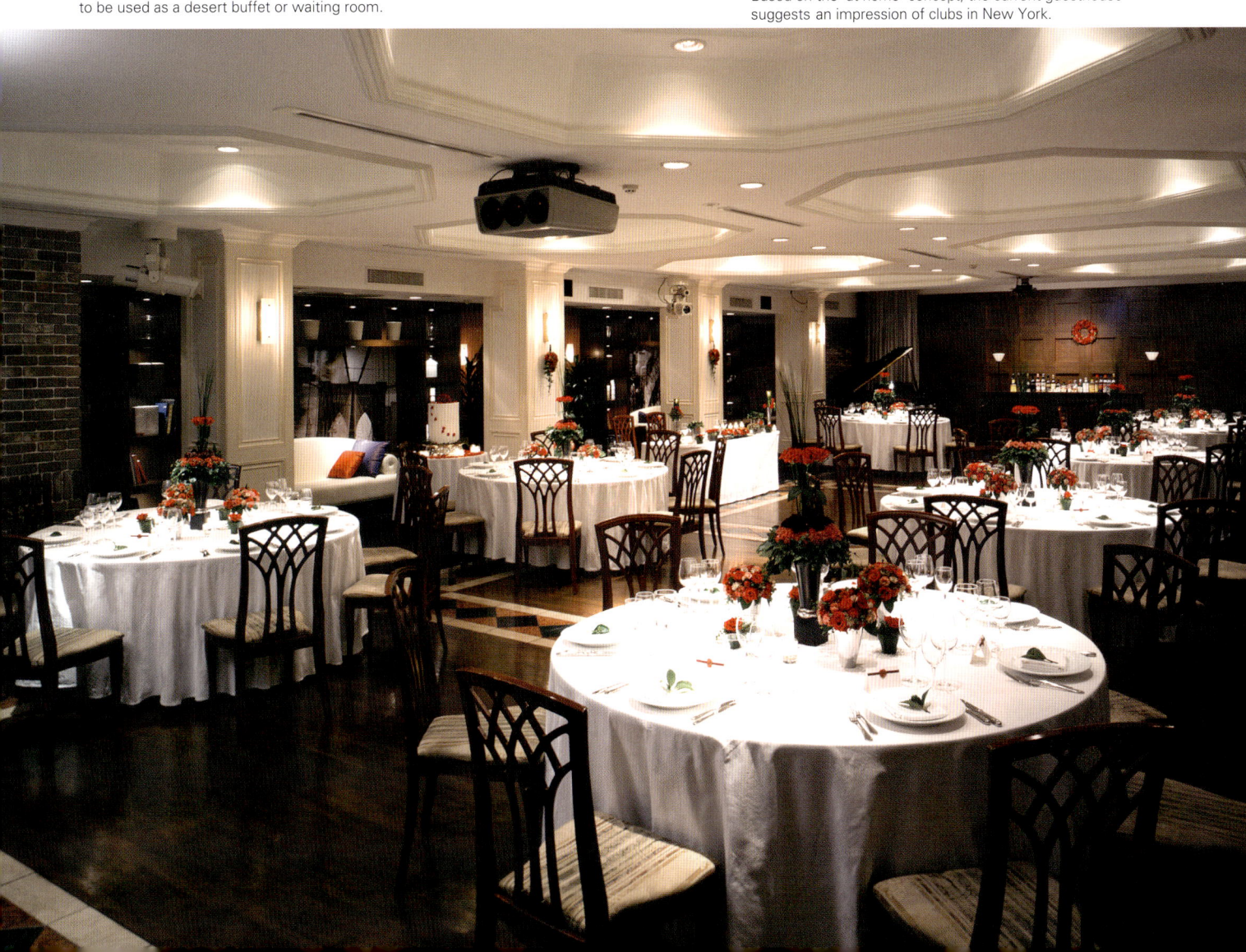

成田全日空ホテル

エアポートホテルを全面リニューアル

ANA HOTEL NARITA
A fully renovated airport hotel

Client: ANA Property Management Co., Ltd.
Designer: Setsuko Ando / Yuko Tsukumo / Noriko Suzuki: Nikken Space Design
Construction: Shimizu Corporation
Location: Narita-shi, Chiba
Site area: Guestroom area / 13,272 sq m, Banquet area / 2,105 sq m, Restaurant area / 1,338 sq m
Completion: March, 2004
Completion of the former building: June, 1989

客室

開業から15年の月日を経て、大々的な改修が行われた。1フロア約34室、計396室。全フロアの内、7フロアをスタンダードフロア、1フロアをレディース（禁煙）フロア、4フロアをエグゼクティブフロア（スイートルームを含む）として改装された。
「シンプル＆コンパクト」をコンセプトに、モノトーンカラーを主体にした内装と、シンプルな形状の家具や小物のコーディネートでモダンな現代風スタイルにインテリアを一新。
空間をできるだけ広く活用するために、家具は必要最小限のアイテム数と大きさでまとめた。
またライティングやカーテンワークで明るさ感と柔らかさを演出した。
全室には持込PC用のモジュラージャックを用意し、ビジネス対応を可能とした。
廊下はクリアガラスセードのブラケットとダークグレーのカーペットやコーポレイトカラーのブルーをアクセントの壁に用い、メリハリのある空間としている。

改修後の客室（和室→カジュアルスイート）。（写真：SS東京）
Guestroom after renovation (Japanese style room→Casual Suite). (Photo: SS Tokyo)

改修後の客室（ジュニアスイート）。（写真：SS東京）
Guestroom after renovation (Junior Suite). (Photo: SS Tokyo)

改修後の客室（スタンダードグレード）。（写真：SS東京）
Renovated standard guestroom. (Photo: SS Tokyo)

改修後の廊下。（写真：SS東京）
Renovated corridor. (Photo: SS Tokyo)

改修前の客室（パステルトーン主体の内装）。（写真：SS東京）
Guestroom before renovation (pastel-colored interior). (Photo: SS Tokyo)

Guestrooms

After 15 years since the completion, extensive renovation was performed. The hotel has a total of 396 guestrooms (about 34 rooms/floor). After the renovation, seven floors turned into the Standard Floors, one floor into the (non-smoking) Ladies` Floor, and four floors into the Exclusive Floors (including suites).
"Simple and Compact" as a concept, the refurbished interiors feature monotone colors in combination with coordinated furniture and accessories to produce sophisticated and modern images.
The lighting and curtain works offer guests well-lit and comfortable rooms.
All the rooms are fully equipped with LAN systems by installing modular jacks for business travelers.
The corridors are accentuated by bracket lightings with clear glass shade, dark-grey carpets and blue color feature walls to match the color of corporate identity, giving a lively atmosphere.

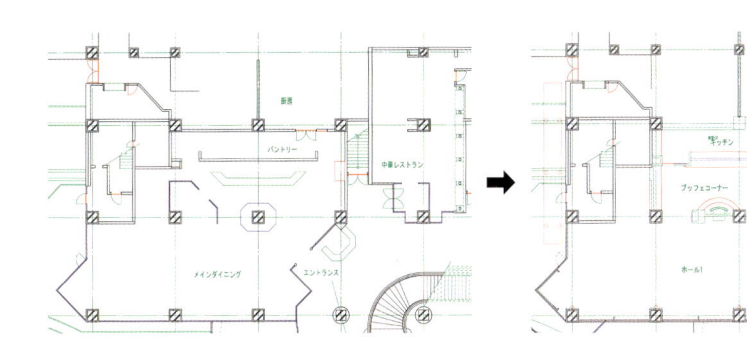

改修前平面図。(左)
Floor plan before renovation.(left)
改修後平面図。(右)
Floor plan after renovation.(right)

メインダイニング

コーヒーハウスと中華レストランの2店舗のレストランを1店舗に統合することにより、スペースを広げ、朝食時の混雑を解消し、お客様へのサービスの向上を図る目的で改修した。
また終日ブッフェ料理が主体となり、店内はブッフェコーナーを中心とし大きく3ブロック（ホール1、2、ブッフェコーナー）に分けられ、それぞれ異なった自然をテーマで演出した。
ホール1は風をテーマに、大きな窓を活かし風が抜けるような明るく開放感のある空間とし、アートフラワーや滝をイメージしたモチーフで演出した。
ホール2は光をテーマに、外光のあまり入らない空間をライティングにより演出している。
ブッフェコーナーは水をテーマに、料理のみずみずしさを引き立てるクリアなイメージの空間とした。
3ブロック全体に統一した色調や素材でまとめ、幅広い年齢層に好まれる、シンプルで心地よいゆったりしたインテリアとした。
また終日楽しめるよう昼間と夜間のイメージを変えるライティングワークとしている。

Main dining area

In designing the main dining area for renovation, two restaurants (coffee house, chinese restaurant) were integrated to a larger space for less congestion during breakfast hours for assuring improvement of services. Buffet as main style of meal offered through out the day, it arranges the buffet corner in the center of the space. The space largely divided to 3 blocks (Hall #1, Hall #2, Buffet Corner) creates each unique theme of nature.
The Hall #1 whose theme is "wind" is a well-lit space with a sense of openness and decorated with flower arts and motifs suggesting waterfalls.
The Hall #2 has the theme of "water", and this indoor space with less sunlight is dressed with carefully arranged lighting.
For the water-themed buffet corner, emphasis is on highlighting the freshness of dishes, and its transparent image of the space. The corner has a simple, comfortable and roomy interior with a totally coordinated colors and materials, preferred by all age groups.
Different lighting schemes are employed in order to maintain the activeness of the space day and night.

ホール1。(写真：SS東京)
Hall #1. (Photo: SS Tokyo)

改修前のホール1。(写真：SS東京)
Hall #1 (before renovation). (Photo: SS Tokyo)

ホール2（小団体客も収容可能）。
(写真：SS東京)
Hall #2
(capable of accommodating a small group of travellers).
(Photo: SS Tokyo)

ブッフェコーナー。(写真：SS東京)
Buffet corner. (Photo: SS Tokyo)

改修前の大宴会場。
Large banquet room before renovation.

2階 宴会場

各室のイメージは、ウェディングプランの販売コンセプトに合わせて各々の個性を明確に分けたカラースキームでデザインされている。大宴会場は「クールモダン」な空間。白とダークブラウンの構成は大空間に強いコントラストを与えている。シャンデリアを新しくし、高砂席バックのレリーフには、LED照明を組み込んでウェディングの演出にも大きな効果を上げている。中宴会場はハニーイエローを基調としたフェミニンなイメージの「邸宅風バンケット」。カーテンワークを施した窓や暖炉を設け、家具やアート・小物などの調度品を効果的に配し、自分の家のサロンにいるようなインテリアとしている。

2nd floor

Each room has a definitive color scheme to match wedding services it can offer. The large banquet room is designed to be 'cool and modern'. The combination of white and dark brown gives a strong contrast to this large space. Chandeliers are renewed, and the reliefs on the walls behind the platform for the wedding couple have additional LED lighting to provide effective illuminations and effects for a wedding ceremony. The medium-sized banquet hall has the theme of a "home-like banquet" presenting a feminine image based on a honey yellow color. Having windows with curtain work, a hearth and an effective combination of furniture, art pieces and small objects, the interior make guests feel comfortable as if they were at home.

大宴会場。(写真：SS東京)
Large banquet room. (Photo: SS Tokyo)

大宴会場前ホワイエ。(写真：SS東京)
Foyer in front of the large banquet room. (Photo: SS Tokyo)

改修前のホワイエ。
Foyer before renovation.

中宴会場。(写真：SS東京)
Medium-sized banquet room. (Photo: SS Tokyo)

改修前の中宴会場。
Medium-sized banquet room before renovation.

17階

開業当時、最上階フロアは和食・鉄板焼・フレンチレストラン、バーラウンジという構成であったが、スカイバンケットとスカイダイニング（創作料理）として大きくプランの変更を行った。バンケットは白・青・シルバーの色使いにグラフィカルな床・壁で構成されたスタイリッシュな空間とし、シャンデリアと高砂テーブルの光はウェディングの効果的な演出となっている。ダイニングは、モノトーンの中に色・光のアクセントとして和紙を配した和の小路をイメージし、客席の「顔」が変化していくよう構成とした。どちらも窓外に広がるビューを内装の重要なアイテムの一つとし、それを活かす照明計画を行っている。

改修前の店舗（スカイラウンジ）。
Restaurant before renovation (sky lounge).

スカイバンケット『イーリス』。
Sky banquet room, Iris.

改修前の店舗（和食レストラン）。
Restaurant before renovation (Japanese restaurant).

バーカウンター。（写真：SS東京）
Bar counter. (Photo: SS Tokyo)

和風レストラン→スカイダイニング。（写真：SS東京）
Former Japanese restaurant turned into a sky dining room. (Photo: SS Tokyo)

17th floor

When the hotel was first opened, the top floor had three restaurants (Japanese, teppanyaki, and French) plus a bar lounge; the floor is now reconfigured to have a sky banquet and sky dining (original dishes). The stylish banquet room is toned in white, blue and silver and decorated with graphical design and illustrations; the lights from the chandeliers and the platform for a wedding couple effectively contribute to the ceremonies. The restaurant is based on the concept of the Japanese aisle in monotones accentuated with Japanese paper, and the tables duly have different and changing expressions in light and color. For both rooms, views through the windows are employed as one of the important components for the interior design, and their lightings were planned to take advantage of the excellent views.

鉄板焼『菜里多』。（写真：SS東京）
Teppanyaki "Narita". (Photo: SS Tokyo)

成田全日空ホテル 047

京都ロイヤルホテル

古都のホテルを全面リノベーション

Kyoto Royal Hotel
Renovating a hotel in an old capital

外観。
Exterior.

エントランス。
Entrance.

Client:	ISHIN HOTELS GROUP
Construction:	Obayashi Corporation
Designer:	Manabu Nihei / Testutaro Nishida / Hiroshi Mizuhara / Yoko Ishibashi: Nikken Space Design
Location:	Nakagyo-ku, Kyoto
Site area:	11,893 sq m (public area: 3,572 sq m; guestroom area: 8,321 sq m)
Completion:	September 2001
Material:	Floors and walls of the entrance: granite
	Banquet and guest room floor: carpet
	Banquet and guest room wall: vinyl cloth
Original completion: 1972	

色を抑え、シックでモダンな印象のスイートルーム。(写真:遠山桜王[スタジオ像])
Chic and modern suite room with suppressed colors. (Sakuraou Toyama [STUDIO ZOU])

1FのCoffee shop。河原町通りより。(写真:遠山桜王[スタジオ像])
Coffee shop on the first floor seen from the Kawaracho street. (Sakuraou Toyama [STUDIO ZOU])

1FのCoffee Shop前の回廊。
Corridor in front of a Coffee shop on the first floor.

パブリックエリアは、既存インテリアの中から改修可能な要素を抽出し、費用対効果を整理した上で焦点を絞ったリファインを行った。

河原町通りに面したロケーションをもつ1階のコーヒーショップは町並みに対するホテルの顔つくりという側面から重点的に改修、オープンカフェとして通りに開放し、往来からホテルロビーへ直接人を招き入れるための中間領域的な意味合いを持たせた。

In designing the public area, attention was paid to extract factors of the existing interior that can be renovated, and in consideration of cost-effectiveness, actual renovation was performed on the factors selected with particular care.
The coffee shop on the first floor facing the Kawaracho Street was predominantly renewed as it should play an important role in the townscape as gateway to the hotel. It was thus designed as an open cafe providing free access to the street, and the cafe also serves as an intermediate territory to attract people directly to the lobby of the hotel.

フロントカウンター。
Front counter.

大宴会場。
Large banquet hall.

スイートルーム。(写真:遠山桜王[スタジオ像])
Suite room. (Sakuraou Toyama [STUDIO ZOU])

心地よさを追及したスイートルーム。
Suite room emphasizing comfort.

イメージパース。
Image perspective.

改修前。
Before renovation.

050 第1章 ホテル

ゆとりのベッドサイズを持つシングルルーム。（写真：遠山桜王［スタジオ像］）
Single room with a roomy bed. (Sakuraou Toyama [STUDIO ZOU])

客室エリアは全客室332室（23タイプ）の家具レイアウトの見直しを行った。
ベッドサイズを広げゆったりとした広がり感のある空間つくりに留意しながら使い勝手に合わせた機能性の充実を計っていった。
工事内容は建築の床、壁、天井及び扉の仕上材更新、設備の照明配置見直しといった限られた内容ではあったが、家具などFF＆E工事の全面的更新と併せ、イメージの一新につながる効果を充分に得ることができた。
「コンテンポラリーベーシック」をデザインコンセプトとし、色彩を最小限に抑え、装飾を排したミニマルなディテールにまとめ、洗練されたなかに新しい感覚と古都の伝統文化を融合、対比させることで美しい調和を図るデザインとした。
・スイートルームはコントラストの効いたモノトーンの空間をつくり出し、「あかり」を意識したスタンド類と間接照明で和み感を演出し、家具備品類は心地よさを追求している。
・スタンダードルームはナチュラルカラーの空間に「古都のイメージ」をモダンにアレンジしたパターンやモチーフによる和みとリラクゼーションの演出を随所に散りばめている。

イメージパース。
Image perspective.

和のモチーフでリラクゼーション効果を狙ったツインルーム。
Twin room designed with Japanese motifs for relaxation.

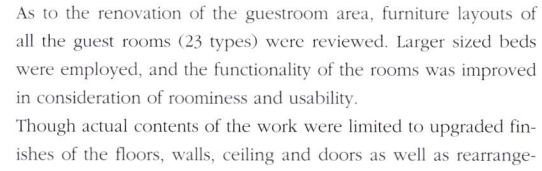

イメージパース。
Image perspective.

改修前。
Before renovation.

As to the renovation of the guestroom area, furniture layouts of all the guest rooms (23 types) were reviewed. Larger sized beds were employed, and the functionality of the rooms was improved in consideration of roominess and usability.
Though actual contents of the work were limited to upgraded finishes of the floors, walls, ceiling and doors as well as rearrangements of lighting fixtures, through a combination with full renewal of FF&E, we could completely renew the image of the guestrooms.
The design concept is "contemporary basic" where a harmony between a modern feeling and traditional culture of the old capital is created both in integration and contrast by keeping colors to minimum and eliminating decorations to realize minimal details.
*Suite rooms are well-contrasted monotone spaces; floor standing lights suggesting Japanese style lamps and indirect lighting offer soothing effects while furniture and fixtures are for comfort.
*Standard rooms are in natural colors, decorated with small articles and gadgets for comfort and relaxation taking advantage of patterns and motifs reflecting images of the old capital and finished with modern arrangements.

クレイトンベイホテル「クリスタルチャーチ」
既存の屋上に張り出した
空に浮かぶチャペル

Crystal Church, Clayton Bay Hotel
A chapel that floats in the sky, placed on top of an existing roof

発光するヴァージンロード。
Light-emitting virgin road.

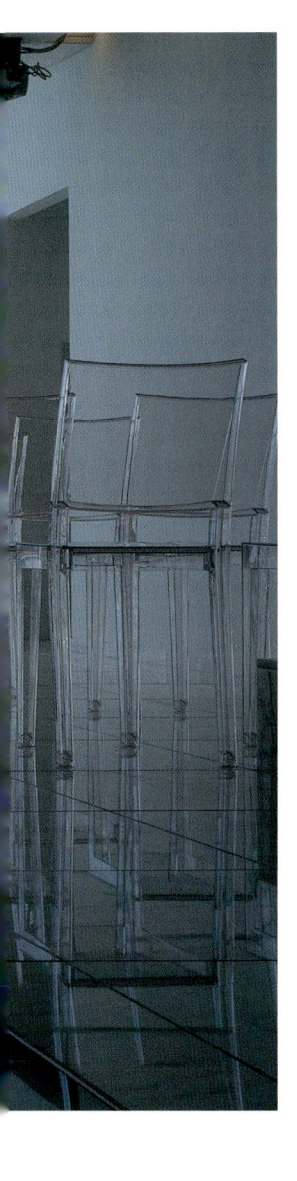

オブジェのスケッチ。
Sketch of an objet.

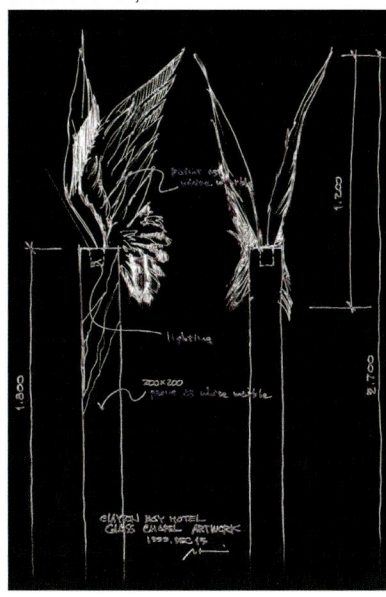

天使から授かった二人の翼。
Wings for the two gifted from angels.

One of the two Shinto-style wedding halls was extended to the roof and renovated into a non-religious hall.
The design emphasizes a sense of being separated from the ground and gravity through such features as a glass cube overhanging from the external wall, a bird's eye view of the sea of Kure, illuminating virgin road to without shadows, transparent chairs and wire-supported wedding ring board.
We thought that a sense of floating in the sky, separated from the daily life should be suitable for a place where people share a special moment of wedding.

Architect: Torii Ken-ichi: Shimizu Corporation
Designer: Uchida Atsushi: FIELD FOUR DESIGN OFFICE
Location: Kure-shi, Hiroshima
Completion: February 2000

ホテルの二つある神前結婚式場のひとつを、屋上に拡張するかたちでニュートラルな式場にリニューアルした。
外壁からオーバーハングしたガラスの立方体、前面の呉の海の鳥瞰、影が落ちない発光するヴァージンロード、透明な椅子、ワイヤーで支持された指輪台、天使から授かった二人の翼など接地感や質量感の希薄なデザインをした。
日常から切り取られて、空中にふわりと静止したかのような浮遊感がウエディングという特別な時間を分ち合う場としてふさわしいと考えた。

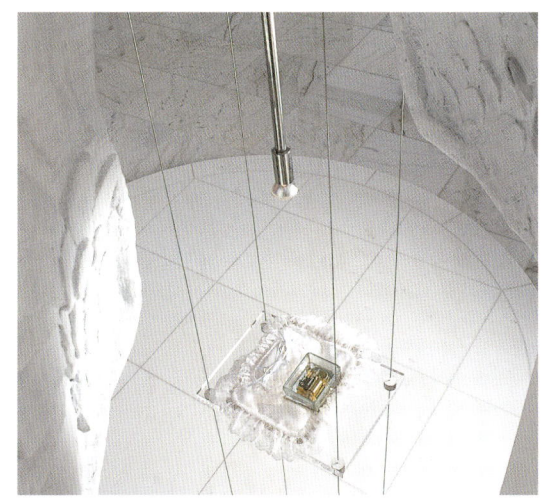

ワイヤーで支持された指輪台。
Wedding ring board supported by the wire.

クレイトンベイホテル「クリスタルチャーチ」 053

サンルートプラザ東京B棟改修計画
狭い客室を長所に変えた客室デザイン

Renovation Plan of the Building B, Sunroute Plaza Tokyo
Creating a small guest room into a charming space

Owner:	ORIX Real Estate Corporation, Plaza Sunroute Co.
Architect:	Nihon Sekkei, Inc. (formerly Nihon Sekkei Jimusho) (1986)
Designer:	Masashi Teramoto / Tohta Kasai: MEC Design International Corporation
Location:	1-6 Maihama, Urayasu-shi, Chiba
Site Area:	19,835 sq m
Building Area:	9,253 sq m
Total Floor Area:	43,060 sq m
Structure:	Reinforced concrete
Renovation Completion:	March 2005
Materials:	Tile carpet, water paint, and vinyl cloth
Project Area:	5th and 6th floor, Building B, Sun Route Plaza Tokyo
	Cruising Cabin 4: 16.5 sq m / room × 13 rooms
	Cruising Cabin 3: 16.5 sq m / room × 47 rooms
	Cruising Cabin 2: 16.5 sq m / room × 4 rooms
	Hallway / Elevator Hall: 155 sq m / floor × 2 floors

東京のウォーターフロント舞浜、東京ディズニーリゾート。一大"テーマパーク"の一角に建つサンルートプラザ東京。1986年にオープンし、ディズニーリゾート・オフィシャルホテルのパイオニアである。今回リニューアルしたのは、サンルートプラザ東京の中では最も狭い16.5平方メートルのタイプであった。しかもソファーベッド対応で3人まで宿泊可能な部屋だった。ユニットバスと入口周辺を除く客室内は約12平方メートル、所狭しと家具が置かれていた。しかしこの"狭さ"にヒントがあった。

狭い＝安い＋3人宿泊可能＝家族連れ&カップルor友達同士という明解なターゲットが形成されていた。部屋のスパンも2,500mm、これも極限まで削ぎ落とされている空間である。

今回のコンセプト"クルージング・キャビン"は客船の船室をモチーフにしている。無駄を削ぎ落とし、機能性を追求しつつも快適な居住性を兼ね備えるという船室特有のデザイン手法は、今回のリニューアル計画にフィットしたものであり、ディズニーリゾートとベイサイドという立地からも、客船をモチーフにするというアイデアは生きてくると考えた。

客室バリエーションは、2段ベッドを採用したり、リビングエリアを形成したり。アートワークやサイン等のアイテムも徹底的に"客船の演出"をしている。

C+C Room改修後（ELVを降りた瞬間から客船のデッキにいるように感じる）。
After renovation of the C+C Room (One feels as if one were on the deck of a passenger boat as soon as one has stepped out of the elevator).

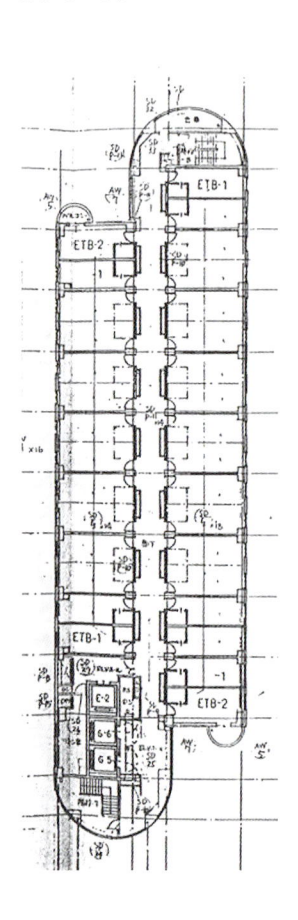

C+C Room イメージスケッチ。
C+C Room conceptual sketches.

改修前（ティピカルな印象）。
Before renovation (typical impression).

Sunroute Plaza Tokyo hotel is in a corner of a great theme park, the Tokyo Disney Resort in the Tokyo waterfront, Maihama. It is the pioneer of the Tokyo Disney Resort official hotels. Subjects of the latest renewal were the smallest 16.5-square-meter guestrooms. Despite their smallness, up to 3 persons could stay in this type of the room by using a sofa bed. When the bathroom and the entrance are excluded, the area was just about 12 square meters full of furniture.

We found the key to design in this "smallness".

The smallness means a low rate for a group of up to three persons, i.e. clear target customers of families, couples and friends. The span of the room is 2,500mm, which is functionally minimized to the limit.

The design concept of "Cruising Cabin" was borrowed from a cabin of a passenger boat. The design approach unique to a cabin where functionality as well as comfort and amenity is pursued without wasting anything fit perfectly with the renewal plan, and we also thought that using the passenger ship as a motif was suitable for the hotel's location in the Tokyo Disney Resort and bay area.

Bunk beds and provisions of living areas contribute to variations of the rooms while artworks and signs are thoroughly contributing to passenger ship impressions.

改修後。
After renovation.

イメージスケッチ。
Conceptual sketches.

改修前。
Before renovation.

C+C Room イメージビジュアル。
C+C Room image graphics.

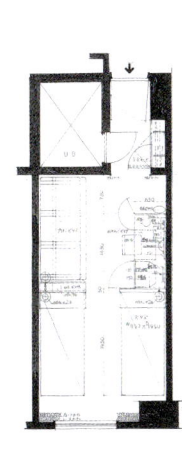

C+C Roomプラン（左より2P、ソファーベッド3P、2段ベッド4P）。
C+C Room plan (left to right: 2 persons; 3 persons with a sofa bed; 4 persons with a bunk bed).

サンルートプラザ東京B棟改修計画

デザインの目的

- 扉を開けた瞬間のサプライズを演出する。
- 今にも動きだしそうな"躍動感"を演出する。
- 客船のお客様というよりクルーになったような雰囲気を演出する。
- 壁・天井・配線ダクトをペンキで塗り込めた力強い仕上とする。
- 明暗のコントラストをより強くメリハリのある空間にする。
- 白く広い壁面を演出アイテムでバランスよく装飾する。

Purposes of the design

- Producing a surprise for one opening the door.
- Giving an impression of a 'real ship' as if one were on board.
- Letting guests feel as if they were crews of a ship rather than guests.
- Walls, ceilings and conduits are painted in dynamic colors.
- Higher contrast for a well accentuated space.
- Wide white walls decorated with a good balance, using artworks and other items.

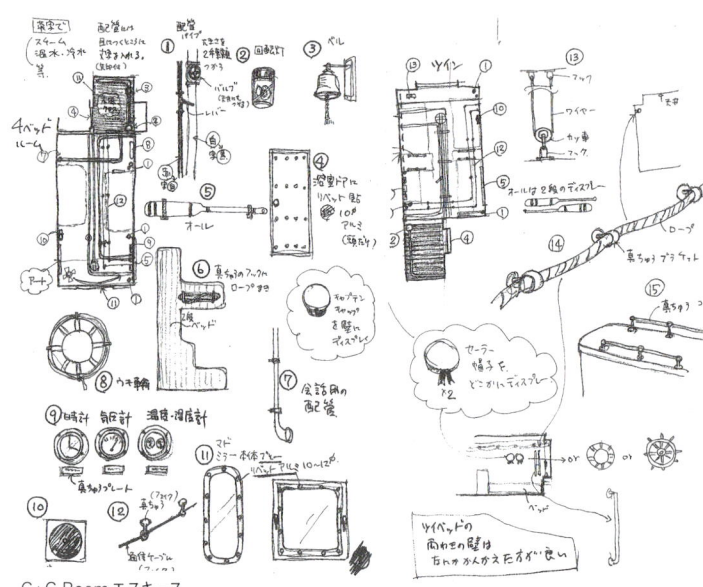

C+C Room エスキース。
C+C Room esquisse.

C+C Room マテリアルボード。
C+C Room material board.

C+C Room 演出アイテムイメージコラージュ。
Collage of decorative items for the C+C Room.

イメージスケッチ。
Conceptual sketches.

改修前。
Before renovation.

改修後。
After renovation.

イメージスケッチ。
Conceptual sketches.

改修後。
After renovation.

056 第1章 ホテル

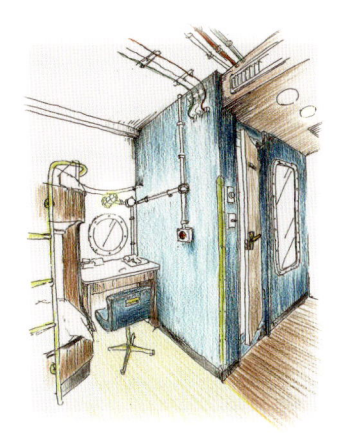

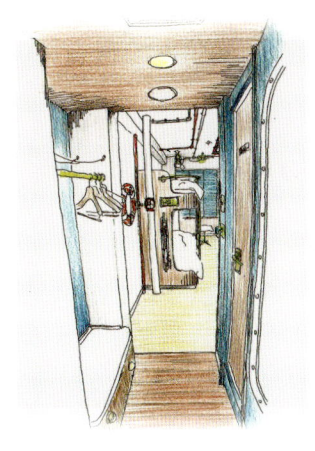

C+C Roomシーン設定スケッチ。
Conceptual sketches of the C+C Room.

改修後。
After renovation.

改修後。
After renovation.

改修後。
After renovation.

改修前。
Before renovation.

改修後。
After renovation.

改修後。
After renovation.

サンルートプラザ東京B棟改修計画

日本ユニシス伊豆エグゼクテブ・センター

耐震改修で
美しく生まれ変わった研修所

Izu Executive Center
Training center beautifully reborn after antiseismic renovation

Developer	Nihon Unisys, Ltd.
Architect	MHS Planners, Architects & Engineers
Produce	Seiichi Nakagawa: MHS Planners, Architects & Engineers
Designer	Inoue Keizou
Location	Ito-shi, Shizuoka
Site area	50,000 sq m
Building area	1,376.30 sq m
Total floor area	3,694.19 sq m
Structure	RC
Completion	August 2001
Materials	Exterior Wall: Spray paint
	Public Wall: Vinyl cloth
	Public Floor: Carpet

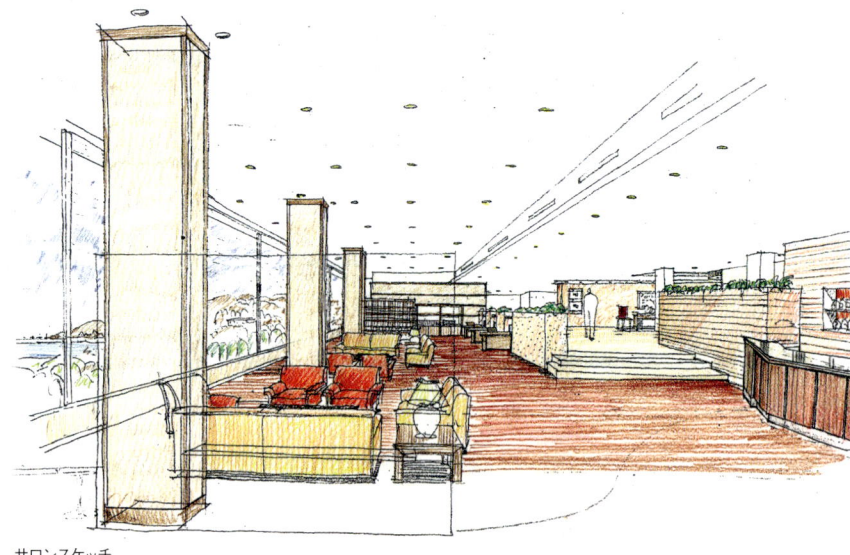

サロンスケッチ。
A sketch of the salon.

排煙トップライトを設けより明るくなったサロン。（写真：川澄建築写真事務所）
Better-lit salon thanks to a new skylight window for smoke extraction. （Photo : Kawasumi Architectural Photograph Office）

竣工後、築30年経過したこの研修所は建物本体、機械設備の老朽化と時代の変遷による機能の低下が見受けられた。企業のイメージアップを含め、継続的な利用を目的に耐震補強、機械設備の更新を実施すると共にデザインイメージの刷新、快適性の向上を目指した。

改修前は研修施設として、教育・訓練を行う場というクールなイメージの色調や家具を採用していたが、改修後は伊豆という地域性も加味し、リゾートを感じる色調や木質系の家具を配し宿泊施設としてのホテル的なイメージを前面にアピールした。

快適性の向上を肌で一番感じられるのは、設備機械のダウンサイジングにより生まれたスペースが、ツインルームの客室へと生まれ変わったことである。

30 years after the completion, this training center experienced aging of the building and hardware as well as obsolete functionality.

In addition to an upgrade of the corporate image, the renovation was carried out to give a longer life to the facilities by seismic retrofitting and replacements of hardware as well as to offer a revamping of the design and better comfort.

Before the renovation, a cool color tone was applied to the building and furniture; however, after the renovation, more emphasis was on the hotel-like function of the facility by deploying the furniture in "resort-like" or wood colors in consideration of its location in Izu as a resort peninsula.

One may find the best improvement in comfort and style by observing the space created by downsizing of hardware was turned into a twin guestroom.

旧サロン。
The salon before renovation.

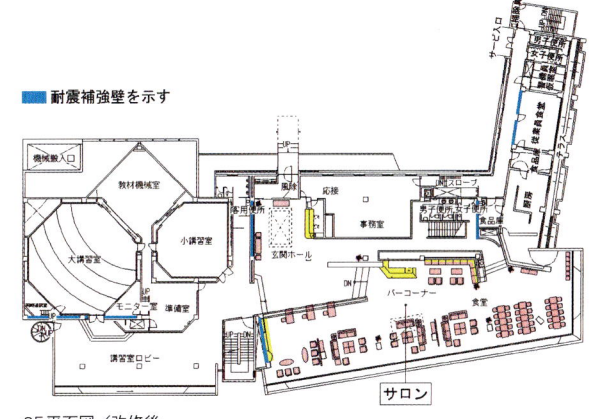

■ 耐震補強壁を示す

3F平面図／改修後。
Floor plan of the 3rd floor after renovation.

リゾート地を意識した色調や家具でホテル的なイメージへ変貌したサロン。
Salon renewed to have an impression of a hotel by employing resort-like colors and furniture.

豊かな自然の中に建つ当センター。
The Center surrounded by rich nature.

改修前（システムプラザ）。
Before renovation.(System Plaza).

耐震壁にて補強された会議室。（写真：川澄建築写真事務所）
Meeting room reinforced by the earthquake-resisting wall.（Photo : Kawasumi Architectural Photograph Office）

会議室／ラウンジスケッチ。
A sketch of the meeting room and the lounge.

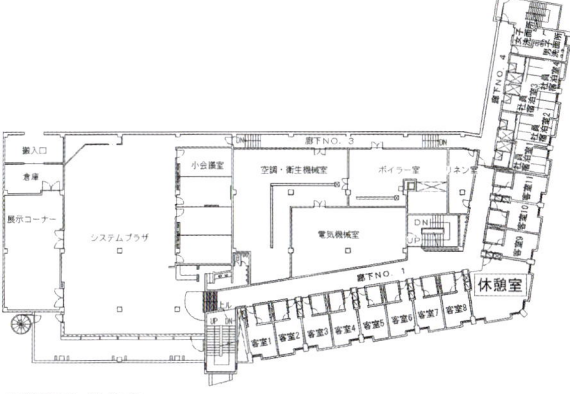

2F平面図／改修前。
Floor plan of the 2nd floor before renovation.

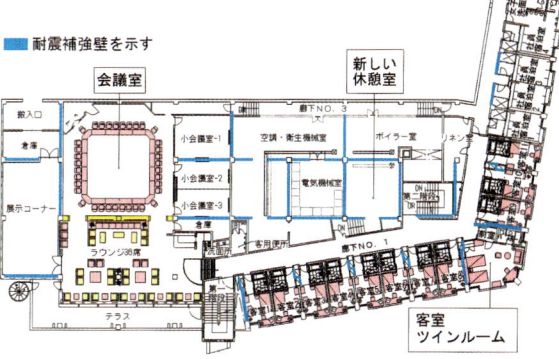

2F平面図／改修後。
Floor plan of the 2nd floor after renovation.

旧休憩室。
Lounge before renovation

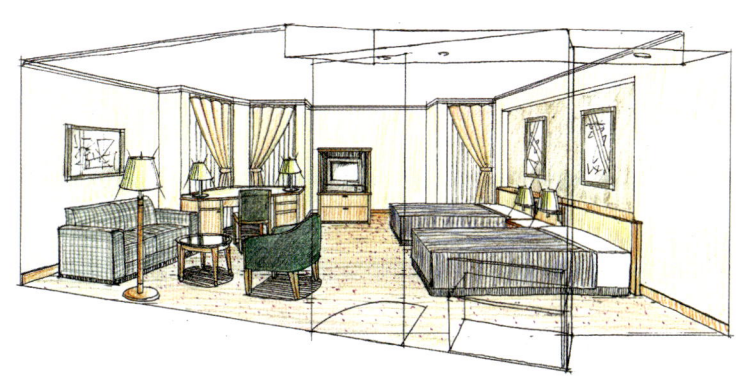

最客室（ツインルーム）スケッチ。
A sketch of a guestroom(twin).

休憩室より客室（ツインルーム）へと生まれ変わった。（写真：川澄建築写真事務所）
A guestroom(twin) created from part of lounge. (Photo : Kawasumi Architectural Photograph Office)

伊豆エグゼクティブ・センター **061**

ホテル日航茨木 大阪
リブランディングによって
生まれ変わるホテル

hotel nikko ibaraki osaka
Regeneration of a hotel through rebranding

ゲストにファーストインパクトを与えるエントランスロビー。（写真：柄松 稔）
Entrance lobby giving a strong impression on guests. (Photo: Minoru Karamatsu)

改修前のエントランスロビー。
Entrance lobby before renovation.

光壁でゲストをお迎えする
エントランス。（写真：柄松 稔）
Entrance welcoming guests
with light walls.
(Photo: Minoru Karamatsu)

Client: Asset Managers Co., Ltd.
Construction: Daimaru Design & Engineering Co., Ltd. Sogo Design Co., Ltd.
　　　　　　Mitsukoshi, Ltd. Suminoe Co., Ltd. Fujimak Corporation
　　　　　　Kawashima Textile Interior Ltd. Tobu Ryokuchi Corporation
Designer: Kenichiro Toi / Kenji Yonezawa: Nikken Space Design
Location: Ibaraki-shi, Osaka
Site area: Guest room 3,067 sq m; restaurant 620 sq m
　　　　　banquet / bridal halls: 2,238 sq m; public areas: 744 sq m; outside: 100 sq m
Completion: October 2004
Material: Lobby: floor: existing marble (partially covered with carpet); wall: existing marble;
　　　　　Sky banquette: floor: carpet; wall: vinyl chloride sheet;
　　　　　Private dining: floor: carpet; wall: vinyl cloth
Year of original completion: June 1992

吹抜けをレースで覆ったロビーラウンジ。（写真：柄松 稔）
Lobby lounge with its well decorated with lace curtains.
(Photo: Minoru Karamatsu)

大阪の中心地から約10分。竣工後10年経つベッドタウンの駅前ホテル。
リブランドのための、ホテル・リノベーション計画。
「記憶に残るもの」そして、「都市部にある洗練されたデザインが必要」というオペレーション側からのキーワードから、「マイ・フェイバリット・ネイバー（お気に入りの隣人）」をコンセプトに、地域性とブランド性を、パブリックゾーンから客室までバランスよく反映させたプロジェクト。
既存のシャンデリアを撤去し、レースカーテンで覆われたロビー空間や、ゼブラ柄のファブリックや大胆なカーペットパターンは、かつてのコミュニティーホテルの面影を残さずに、スタイリッシュな空間へと変貌した。
営業しながらの改修工事であり、工期と運用が複雑なプログラムであったことと、また「資産価値向上」を目的としたリノベーションであったため、「変わったイメージ」をいかに出せるかというポイントが重要となった。

Just about 10 minutes by train, this hotel with ten years of history stands in front of a station in a bed town.
The hotel renovation project was for the rebranding purpose.
The keywords for renovation given by the owner were "something to remain in one's memory" and "sophisticated design in the city"; in reply, we devised the concept of "my favorite neighbor" and provided the entire hotel with a sense of both familiarity and brand quality from the public zone to guestrooms.
The existing chandeliers were removed; the lobby space was decorated with lace curtains; zebra-pattern fabrics and bald carpet patterns were employed. All of these contributed to the transformation of the hotel into a stylish urban space without a trace of the old design.
The renovation work was carried out without temporarily closing the hotel, and the term of works and business operations were complicated. In addition to these conditions, assets improvement was one of the main purposes of renovation, important was how to emphasize that the hotel would have changed.

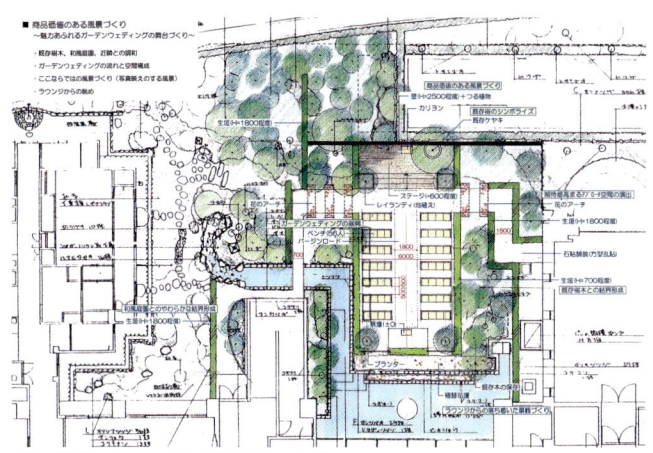

屋外の「グリーンチャペル」の計画プランニング。
Planning of the outdoor Green Chapel.

観賞用の庭を使える庭として有効活用した屋内チャペルに隣接するグリーンチャペル。
Green chapel adjacent to the indoor chapel by effectively taking advantage of the existing decorative garden.

チャペル通路のテナントだった場所にブライダルサロンを設置。（写真：柄松 稔）
Bridal salon established in a room once used by a tenant along the chapel corridor. (Photo: Minoru Karamatsu)

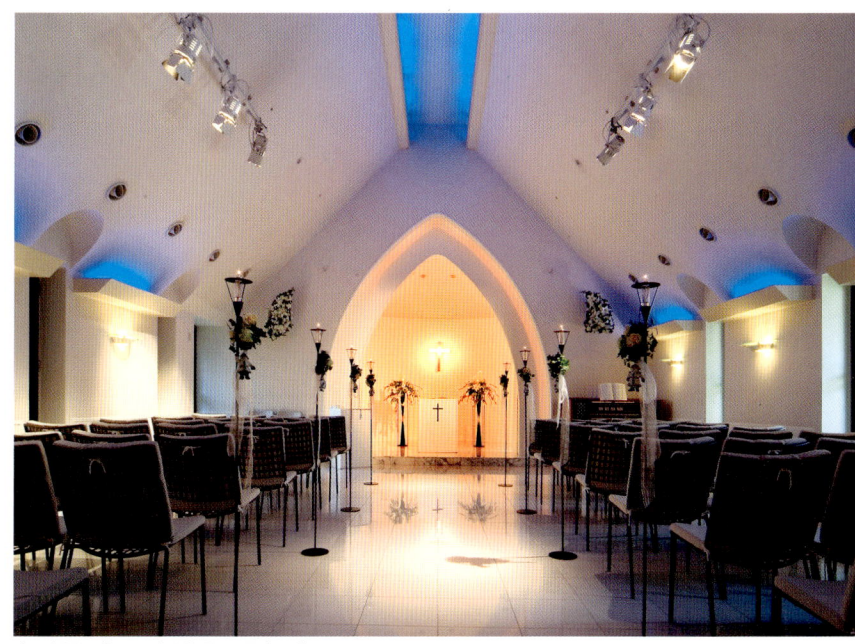

白い空間にブルーの光を強調した屋内のブルーチャペル。（写真：柄松 稔）
Blue chapel emphasizing blue lights in the white space. (Photo: Minoru Karamatsu)

EVホールから飾棚越しに中が見渡せるスカイゲストハウス「The Stage」。（写真：柄松 稔）
One can take a glance at the interior of The Stage, sky guesthouse, through display shelves. (Photo: Minoru Karamatsu)

改修後の8階スカイゲストハウス「The Stage」。（写真：柄松 稔）
The Stage, sky guesthouse on the 8th floor (after renovation). (Photo: Minoru Karamatsu)

改修前の8階ブッフェレストラン。
Buffet restaurant on the 8th floor (before renovation).

エントランス風除室には、光壁でゲストをお出迎え。
またエントランス正面の壁には来館されたゲストに「ファーストインパクト」を与える大きな鏡と赤いソファーを設置、このホテルのフォトジェニックなフォーカルポイントとした。
8階スカイゲストハウスではターゲットを婚礼に絞り、シックな色使いながら華やかに、主人公であるゲストが引き立つように計画。
またワンフロアー貸しの特徴を活かし、EVホールからガラスの飾棚越しに中の宴会場が見渡せるようにして一体感のある空間つくりとした。バーカウンターや電気暖炉、光の飾棚にはゲストのお気に入りのアイテムを置くことができ、自分流にカスタマイズできるなどプライベートな部屋にゲストを招き入れるプラスアルファの特別感を演出している。

The windbreak room at the entrance welcomes guests with light walls.
On the front wall of the entrance, a large mirror was installed, and red sofa was set in front of it to give a strong "first impression" on visiting guests. They serve as the photogenic focal point of the hotel.
Target users of the sky guesthouse on the 8th floor were defined to be bridal couples and guests, and the room was designed to highlight guests by using chic colors and gorgeous designs
Full-floor rental service was also effectively taken advantage of; one can see the interior of the banquet hall through the cabinet from the elevator hall, feeling a sense of integrity. On the bar counters, electric stove, and illuminated display shelves, guests' favorite items can be exhibited for personalized parties and ceremonies. This approach enables hosts to produce special images as if guests were invited to private rooms.

2階ロビー（改修後）。（写真：柄松 稔）
Lobby on the 2nd floor (after renovation). (Photo: Minoru Karamatsu)

2階ロビー（改修前）。
Lobby on the 2nd floor (before renovation).

バーラウンジから中国料理と和食懐石の楽しめる個室対応可能なプライベートダイニングにリニューアル。（写真：柄松 稔）
The existing bar lounge was renewed to a restaurant with private dining rooms serving Chinese cuisine and an elegant Japanese meal served in delicate courses. (Photo: Minoru Karamatsu)

ゼブラ柄のチェアカバーリングでアクセントをつけた客室。
Guestroom accentuated by zebra-pattern chair covers.

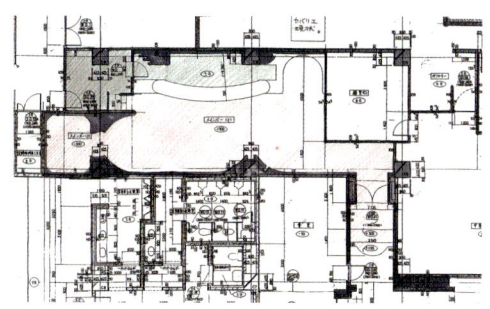

バーラウンジプラン（改修前）。
Plan of bar lounge (before renovation).

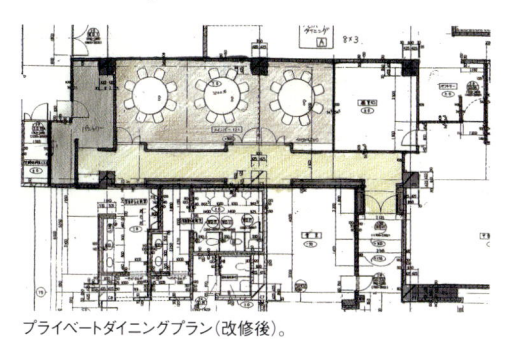

プライベートダイニングプラン（改修後）。
Plan of private dining rooms (after renovation).

渋谷東急イン

「利用者の声」を尊重した
ゲストルームのリノベーション

SHIBUYA TOKYU INN
Guestroom renovation respecting users comments

ツインルーム平面図。
Twin room floor plan.

改装前のツインルーム。
Twin room before renovation.

Client:	TOKYU HOTEL CHAIN CO., LTD. TOKYU HOTEL MANAGEMENT CO., LTD.
Designer:	Fuki Onishi / Takayuki Nago: Nikken Space Design
Construction:	Tokyu Construction Oliver Co., Ltd. (furniture)
Location:	Shibuya-ku Tokyo
Site area:	225 guestrooms
Completion:	March 20, 2004

ツインルーム。
Twin room.

スタンダードツインシングル

都心に相応しくビジネスパーソンにとって居心地の良いホテル＝「安眠追求」が要求された。
まず安眠追求の仕掛けとして"戸襖"を採用した。これにより遮光性能が高上し、カーテンのヒダがなくなったことで、窓側に大きなデスクが可能になり、ビジネスワークにも有効なものとなった。
シングルルームのデスクは2タイプあり、ツインルームは窓側にデスク・ソファ・冷蔵庫・食器等をコンパクトにまとめた。男性客だけではなく女性客の考えを取り入れアースカラーをベースとし、デザインアクセントである戸襖にオレンジ色を用いた。ビジネスパーソンをサポートする、くつろぎとシンプルで機能的な空間に生まれ変わった。

Standard twin / single

As a hotel offering comfort for businesspersons in the city center, the pursuit of quality sleep was required.
First, as a device to ensure a sound sleep, tobusuma (a sliding wooden door with thick fusuma paper on one side) was employed. This not only improved the light blocking effect but also eliminated pleats of the curtain, enabling to put a large desk useful for business use by the window.
Two types of desks are available for single rooms. Twin rooms have a desk, a sofa, a refrigerator and tableware efficiently arranged near the window.
Opinions from not only male but also female guests were taken into consideration, and the color scheme was thus based on earthy colors, accentuated by the orange of tobusuma serving as a design accent. As a result, the guestrooms turned into functional spaces with a sense of relaxation and simplicity to support businesspersons.

シングルルーム-1。
Single room #1.

シングルルーム-2。
Single room #2.

シングルルーム（アールデスク）平面図。
Single room flat plan (ergonomic writing desk).

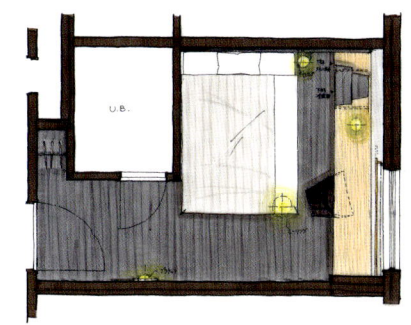

シングルルーム（窓デスク）平面図。
Single room flat plan (desk at the window).

コージールーム

「お客様の声をもっと大切にし、形にする。」という主旨で、快眠追求、自分の部屋感覚、靴を脱いで過ごすのコンセプトに基づき、今回のリノベーションにも取り込むこととなった。
270室のうち12室のシングルルームに限定し、利用者の考えを大幅にとり入れた新たなデザインで改修を行った。床はフローリングを敷き、ベッドの周りの三方にクッションを設置することにより、大きなソファとしてくつろげるものとなった。
スタンダードルームと同様、アースカラーをベースにデスクもコンパクトにまとめた。客室の扉を開け、靴を脱いで使う空間は、今までにないくつろぎ感を味わえることができる。

Cozy rooms

We addressed the renovation on the basis of the theme of "reflecting and materializing opinions of guests" and concepts of pursuing quality sleep, feeling as if one were in one's own room, and having an easier time without shoes.
New designs taking advantage of users' ideas were applied to selected 12 single rooms out of 270 guestrooms. Flooring was installed, and by arranging cushions in three directions around the bed, the combination also serves as a large sofa for relaxation.
Similar to the standard rooms, these rooms are basically colored with earthy colors, and a compact-sized desk was installed. Opening the door of a guestroom and entering the room with the shoes pulled off means an unprecedented sense of relaxation in a hotel.

コージールーム。
Cozy room.

客船"飛鳥"リド・カフェ改修計画

機能優先だったカフェテリアを
船旅が楽しめる空間にリニューアル

Renovation plan of the Lido Cafe on the passenger ship, Asuka
Renewal cafeteria from functional to cruise-ship atmosphere

イタリア・ベネチアの沖合いにリド島という世界有数のリゾート島がある。ヨーロッパの富裕層が長期休暇をとり、ゆったり寛いだり、マリンスポーツに興じたり、クルージングを楽しんだり……。本当の意味であるリゾートがそこには存在する。

その島の名前が由来となった"リド・デッキ"というフロアは多くの大型豪華客船に存在する。開放的なデッキテラスやプールに面していたり、船の航跡を一望できたり……。考え方は船によって違いこそあるが、輝く陽の光、頬をかすめる風、限り無く広がる海と空……。これこそ"船の旅"というような演出が施されている。

日本を代表する大型客船"飛鳥"においても例外ではなかった。開放的な外部デッキに面した位置に"リド・カフェ"はあった。

しかし、そこへ至るアプローチや肝心の第一印象に大きな問題が感じられた。あちこちに点在する"淀み空間"、画一的な仕上げ、広さを感じるというよりもしろ、"寂しさ"を感じるものだった。

今回のリニューアルは、就航10年を迎え、特に傷みの激しいこの"リド・カフェ"を主にリニューアルしたい。という運航会社からの依頼(コンペティション)であった。外洋航路船舶特有の国際防火基準及び、保健衛生基準によるデザイン変更や、機能改善の為の様々な要素や条件を1つ1つ検証検討し根本的に再プログラミングすることになった。

ドックにおける作業は、2週間という短期間に、船体・機関部から内装までの改修・定期チェック、国土交通省の検査まで、"戦争"の様なスケジュールだったが、リニューアルは計画通り完了した。

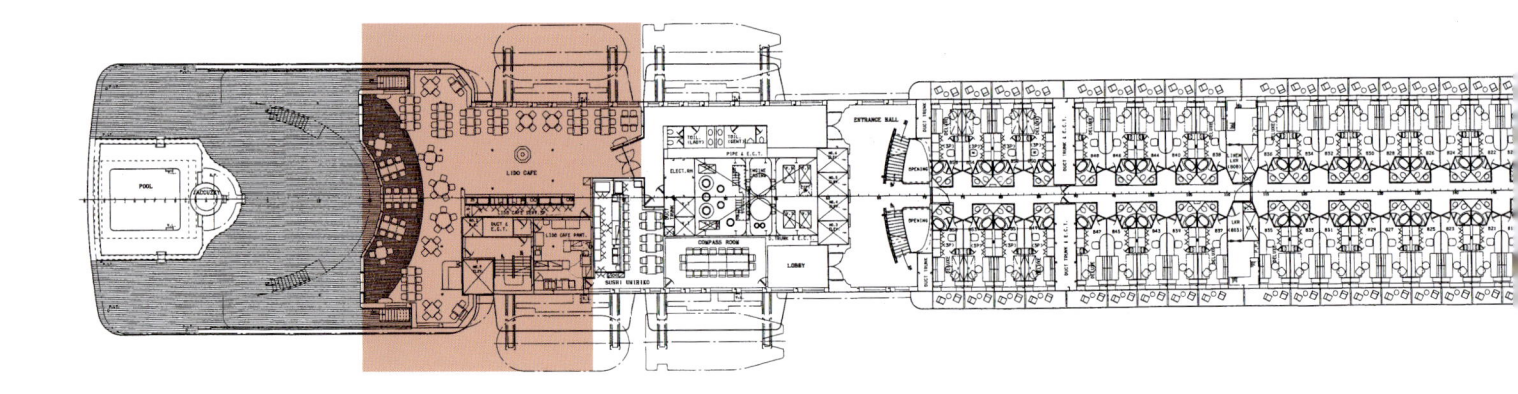

Ship's Registry:	Japan
Owner:	NYK Line
Operator:	NYK Cruises Co., Ltd.
Constructor:	Nagasaki Shipyard and Machinery Works of Mitsubishi Heavy Industries (1991)
Renovator:	Yokohama Shipyard and Machinery Works of Mitsubishi Heavy Industries
Designer:	Masashi Teramoto and Tohta Kasai: MEC Design International
Gross Registered Tons:	28,856 G/T
Length:	192.8m
Width:	24.7m
Total Floor Area:	10 decks
Structure:	Steel structure
Renovation Completion:	January 2002
Materials:	Noncombustible materials approved by the Ministry of Land, Infrastructure and Transport
Project Area:	Lido Cafe: about 260 square meters

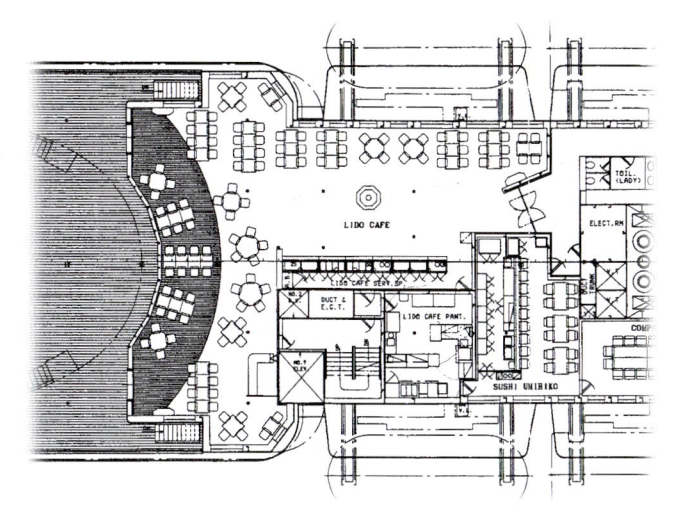

改修前プラン。必要なものをピックアップしてみる。
Plan before renovation: picking up what is needed.

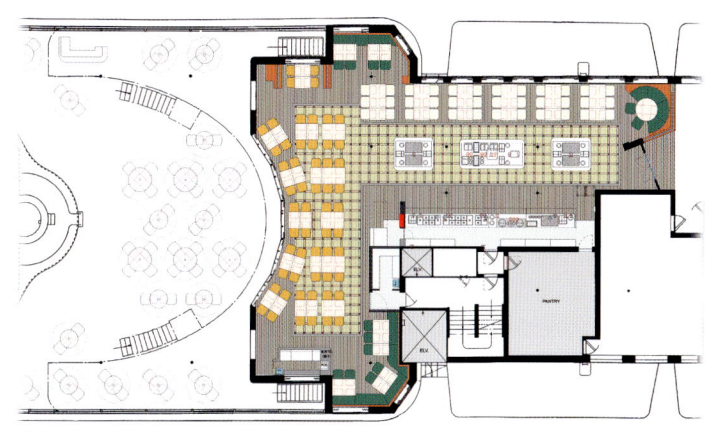

最終の改修決定プラン。
Final renovation plan.

改修前。無機質な感じの壁が問題のアプローチ。
Before renovation: a problem with this approach is inhuman and sterile walls.

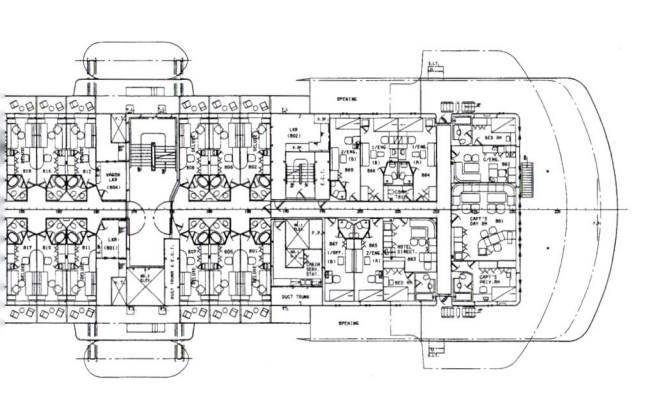

改修後。中の様子が感じられるアプローチ部分。
After renovation: approach giving a glimpse of the interior.

Located offshore Venice, Italy, is Lido Island, one of the best resort islands in the world. Rich Europeans taking a long vacation stay on the island to enjoy marine sports or cruising. It is a resort in its true sense.

Floors called Lido Deck named after the island exist on many luxurious passenger ships. They may face open deck terraces or pools or offer the command of view of the wake. Though concepts may differ from ship to ship, all of them are designed in a manner representing "travels by ships" taking advantage of bright sunlight, comfortable sea breezes, and infinite expanses of sea and sky.

Asuka, a large passenger boat representing Japan is no exception. The Lido Cafe is facing an open external deck.

We found however problems with the approach to the cafe as well as first impression it would give. There were spots creating a stagnant atmosphere here and there. The simplicity and flatness of the finish would gave one an impression of loneliness rather than a sense of expansion. The operator wanted to renew mainly this Lido Cafe with obvious wear and tear caused in a decade after its commission for service and held a competition for its design. We have carefully examined various changes in international fire prevention standards uniquely applied to seagoing vessels, design changes in accordance with safety and health regulations, and factors and conditions for functional enhancements and concluded that the design of the cafe should radically be re-programmed.

The renovation work was carried out in a period as short as two weeks. Though the schedule was very tight and we had to renovate the body, engine department and interior, perform regular examinations, and finish inspections by the Ministry, the renewal was completed on time.

改修前。食欲を感じさせないブッフェライン。
Before renovation: buffet line not stimulating the appetite.

改修前。一新したいアイランドカウンター。
Before renovation: island counter needs to be renewed.

改修後。フォーカルポイントになるアイランドカウンター。
After renovation: island counter as the focul point of the area.

改修後。人気席のベンチシートコーナー。
After renovation: popular bench seats.

改修前。客席はさらに味気ない!。
Before renovation: seats are less inviting!.

改修後、人気席となったエントランス側。
Popular seats near the entrance after renovation.

改修後。人気席のデッキカフェテリア。
After renovation: popular cafe terrace on the deck.

デッキカフェテリアイメージ。
Image of the cafe terrace on the deck.

ベンチシートコーナーイメージ。
Image of the bench seats.

ブッフェカウンターイメージ。
Image of the buffet counter.

エントランス側イメージ。
Image of the entrance side.

コンペ提案段階イメージパース。
Conceptual perspective proposed for the competition.

1. アプローチ側から中の様子が伺えること。
2. 入った瞬間のフォーカルポイントを考慮。
3. コーナーごとにキャラクターを与える。
4. 不人気席をなくす。
5. 衛生的かつ魅力的に演出する。
6. 毎日来ても飽きない空間にする。

1. Permitting glimpses of the interior from the approach.
2. Consideration given to the focal point at the moment one enters the room.
3. Characterizing each area.
4. Eliminate unpopular seats.
5. Sanitary and attractive settings.
6. Space where everyday visit doesn't lead to boredom.

改修後ドリンクステーション(バーカウンター)。
Drink station (bar counter) after renovation.

千里阪急ホテル「パオーレ」

プールサイドの休憩所が
ウエディングヴィラに大変身

Paole, Senrihankyu Hotel
A resting place by the pool is dramatically transformed into a wedding villa

改修前。
Before renovation.

プールサイドより見た「パオーレ」全景。(写真：時空アート)
Paole seen from the poolside. (Photo: Jiku Art)

外観CGパース
CG perspective drawing of the exterior.

バンケットのスケッチパース。
Perspective sketch of the banquet area.

千里阪急ホテル「サンシャインテラス」のリノベーションに引き続きブライダル施設のバリエーションを増やし更なる施設力の強化を目的とすると共に、エリア内に競合する他のホテルやゲストハウス系のウエディングに対抗すべく個性的で魅力あるホテルウエディングを打ち出すことをコンセプトとした。

改修前の既存施設は広々としたガーデンのプールサイドに建つ柱と屋根だけの完全なオープンエアー仕様であり、暖かい時期はバーベキューなどを楽しめるが、冬の寒い時期には使用できず収益を生むことのできない施設であった。改修内容は開放的なオープンエアーの雰囲気はそのままで、ブライダルの演出を考慮した建具、四季を通じて快適な空調設備と、ゲストハウスウエディングにはない十分な音響、照明設備を新たに完備した。中規模ではあるがフルスペック仕様のバンケットへと改修した。

先にリニューアルオープンした「サンシャインテラス」の斜め向いに位置し、プール付の広々としたガーデンに面している。夏は小粋なビアガーデンスポットとしても活用できる、「サンシャインテラス」のデッキテラスが舞台やステージとなり、プールサイドでジョッキを傾けながらコンサート等のイベントも楽しめる。

デザイナーの役割は単なる設計者としてではなく、クライアントの利益を守るためのリノベーションであり、老朽化した施設の資産価値を高め、利益を新たに生み出す再生計画を行った。

「新郎・新婦の入場シーンはプールサイドをゆっくりと歩きガーデンから入場してくる、緑の庭に白いドレスが更に美しく映える、ゲストは光が降りそそぐ明るい室内で拍手と共に二人を迎える……」。

Developer:	Hankyu Hotel Management Co., Ltd
Architect:	Mori-Gumi Co,. Ltd.
Producer:	Seiichi Nakagawa: NEXT/m
Designer:	Toshiyasu Nishio: NEXT/m
	Naofumi Yamashita: MHS Planners, Architects & Engineers
CG perspective:	Chida Takashi: C-design
Location:	Toyonaka-shi, Osaka
Total floor area:	172 sq m

トップライトの光をやわらげ、四季を通じて利用される
バンケット「パオーレ」に生まれ変わった。（写真：ラヴィファクトリー）
Villa renovated to be a banquet facility, Paole,
that can be used for all seasons. (Photo: La-vie Factory)

水に映った「パオーレ」。（写真：時空アート）
Paole reflected on water. (Photo: Jiku Art)

Following the renovation of the Sunshine Terrace, Senrihankyu Hotel decided to offer an increased number of wedding facilities for better serving its customers and to compete with other hotels and guesthouses in the area by proposing unique and attractive hotel wedding packages.

The existing facility before renovation was of a complete open-air design and was comprised of columns on the poolside and a roof only. Though it could offer the enjoyment of barbeque cooking in a warm season, it was useless in the cold wintertime, leaving no profit. In the renovation, while maintaining the spaciousness of the original open-air design was maintained, a complete range of facilities was newly added including fixtures for bridal arrangements and decoration, air-conditioners to assure comfort through all seasons, a sound system rarely seen with the guesthouse wedding, and lighting facilities. It turned into a medium-sized yet complete banquet facility.

Paole stands catercorner to Sunshine Terrace that was renewed earlier, facing a wide garden with a pool. In summer, it can also be used as a beer garden. The deck terrace of Sunshine Terrace may be used as a stage for performance to hold concerts and other events while the audience drink beer on Paole.

The role of the designer was to propose renovation for creating additional benefits for the client, not just to propose another design; thus we planned the renovation in order to increase assets value of obsolete facility and to generate additional profits.

"The bride and bridegroom slowly walk on the poolside and come into the banquet hall through the garden. Her white dress looks more attractive in the green garden. Guests welcome the couple in the bright hall full of light."

改修前。
Before renovation.

カラースキームボード。
Color scheme board.

千里阪急ホテル「サンシャインテラス」
老朽化が進んだ喫茶室を
バンケットホールに再生

Sunshine Terrace, Senrihankyu Hotel
A dilapidated coffee shop revitalized as a banquet hall

サンシャインテラスの全景。(写真:時空アート)
Sunshine Terrace Overview. (Photo: Jiku Art)

Developer:	Hankyu Hotel Management Co., Ltd
Architect:	Mori-Gumi Co,.Ltd. (construction contractor)
Producer:	Seiichi Nakagawa: NEXT/m
Designer:	Toshiyasu Nishio: NEXT/m
	Naofumi Yamashita:
	MHS Planners, Architects & Engineers
Lighting Designer:	Takahiro Muranishi:
	TACT Daiko Electric Co., Ltd
Location:	Toyonaka-shi, Osaka
Total floor area:	banquet: 75 sq m (terrace: 55 sq m)

「千里阪急ホテル」は、「大阪万国博覧会」が開催された1970年3月に開業した、緑豊かな落着いた環境を誇り、南欧を意識したアーバンリゾートタイプのホテルである。

近年増えているブライダル特化型施設や周辺の他ホテルとの競合などを踏まえ市場のニーズの変化を見据えたリノベーション計画を行った。

開業以来あまり手を掛けられていない状態だった75平方メートルの施設を改修の対象とした。同ホテルは大小複数の婚礼・宴会場を有するがすべて開業当時のイメージを引き継いでおり、新たなバリエーションの小宴会場の利用ニーズを考えて施設の強化を目指した。35年の時が経ち老朽化が進んでいた既存のティーラウンジを「モダンでスタイリッシュ」なバンケットホールに再生、小ぶりな空間だが開放的な窓の外にはプール付の広々としたガーデンが拡がる。ウッドデッキテラスとオーニングを新設し、バンケットから外部デッキへとつながり、さらにプールサイドの庭へも容易に出られる空間構成とした。

最近人気のある少人数対応のレストランウェディングでホテルならではの質の高いサービスが受けられ、大人の雰囲気を求める若年層世代の婚礼客に好まれるイメージの空間とした。

またデザートブッフェもできる外部のウッドデッキに800平方メートルの広大なガーデンも取り込みプライベートに使うこともできるパーティースペースとした。

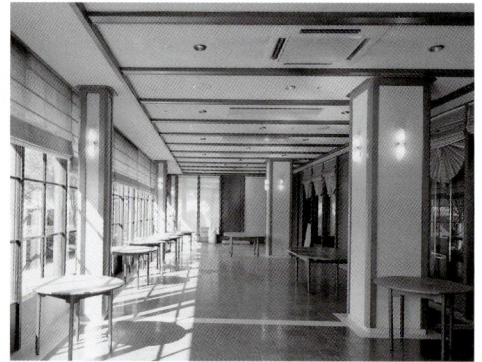

改修前(旧サンラウンジ)。(写真:時空アート)
Before renovation (old Sun Lounge). (Photo: Jiku Art)

スタイリッシュにリノベーションされた「サンシャインテラス」。(写真:ラヴィファクトリー)
Stylish Sunshine Terrace after renovation. (Photo: La-vie Factory)

スケッチパース。
Perspective sketch.

平面図。
Floor plan.

テラス改修前。
Terrace before renovation.

プールに面したテラス。（写真：時空アート）
Terrace facing the pool. (Photo: Jiku Art)

プールサイドのステージにもなるテラス。（写真：時空アート）
Terrace that can be used as a stage on the poolside. (Photo: Jiku Art)

Opened in March 1970 when EXPO Osaka Japan 1970 was held, Senrihankyu Hotel is an urban resort hotel in a relaxing natural green environment and with a Mediterranean atmosphere.

In consideration of competitions with increasing wedding halls/facilities and other hotels in the neighborhood, the renovation project was planned to respond to future changes in market needs.

A 75-square-meter facility that had remained untouched since the opening of the hotel was the subject of the renovation. The hotel has multiple large and small wedding and banquet halls; however all of them had succeeded the original design concepts at the time of completion. We planned to enhance the facility by renovating a small tea lounge into a "modern and stylish" banquet hall in order to meet new and different needs for the facility. Though the space was rather small, there was a large garden with a pool expanding outside the windows. We proposed a design to newly build a wooden deck-terrace and install awnings; the banquet hall was directly connected to the external deck and was provided with access to the poolside garden.

The spatial concept of the project is based on small-group restaurant weddings with quality services and appeals to young wedding couples.

The wooden deck that can also provide a dessert buffet is integrated with a large 800-square-meter garden and made available for private parties.

スタイリッシュにリノベーションされた「サンシャインテラス」。（写真：ラヴィファクトリー）
Stylish Sunshine Terrace after renovation. (Photo: La-vie Factory)

FFEのプレゼンテーション。
FFE presentation.

FFEのプレゼンテーション。
FFE presentation.

バー。（写真：時空アート）
Bar. (Photo: Jiku Art)

カラースキームボード。
Color scheme board.

076　第1章　ホテル

第2章 オフィス

Chapter 2
Offices

日本財団ビル

設計者・吉村順三氏の設計コンセプトを継承したオフィス

The Nippon Foundation Building
Office building, Designed by the late Junzo Yoshimura's concept was described as follows

日本財団ビルは、1962年日本ナショナル金銭登録機械株式会社の新社屋として、虎ノ門に誕生した。故・吉村順三氏の設計によるもので、洗練された外観はこの時代の代表作である。
竣工当時の建築雑誌を開けば必ず掲載されており、そこには……
1、入居者の理念を表現できるオフィスビルであること
2、威圧感を与えないスマートなデザインであること
3、オフィススペースはオープンであること
といった設計者の考えが語られている。
また、技術的にもダブルスキンサッシに組み込まれた給排気のシステム、可動間仕切り、光天井等々、オフィスビルにおいて、今日の先駆けとなる試みに溢れたビルであった。古くとも良質なものを大切に使っていく事や、公共性の高いロビー空間とする事は、公益法人であるクライアントの日本財団の理念に適うものであり、オープンなオフィスづくりもスタッフ間の協調性が必要なクライアントのオフィスワークに適したものであった。元設計を活かし、コンセプトを理解し継承する形で行ったリノベーションである。

The Nippon Foundation Building was built in Toranomon as the office building of Nippon National Cash Resistor Company in 1962. Designed by the late Junzo Yoshimura, its sophisticated exterior represented the architectural design of the era.
At the time of its completion, the building was carried in every architectural magazine, and the designer's concept was described as follows:
1. The office building must represent the ideal of an occupant.
2. The design must be sophisticated and should not be intimidating.
3. The office space must be open.
In terms of technology, it was full of pioneering approaches to an office building such as air intake and exhaust incorporated in the sashes of the double-skin system, mobile partitioning, and luminous ceiling.
Using old yet quality things with care and providing a lobby space with emphasis on publicness met the ideal of the public-service corporation client, the Japan Foundation, and creating open offices was suitable for office works of the client in which collaborations are often required. In designing the renovation, we took maximum advantage of the original design, understanding and carrying on its concept.

日本財団ビル・外観。(写真：川澄建築写真事務所)
The Japan Foundation Building (exterior). (Photo : Kawasumi Architectural Photograph Office)

Developer:	The NipponFoundation
Designer:	Masato Watanabe
Location:	Minato-ku, Tokyo
Site area:	1,519.52 sq m
Building area:	2,084.12 sq m
Total floor area:	18,329.45 sq m
Structure:	SRC
Completion:	October 2003
Material:	〈Lobby〉Floor: Granite (partial tile carpet)
	Wall: Marble
	Ceiling: Luminous ceiling (partial plaster substrate/EP paint)
	〈Office〉Floor: Tile carpet (partial flooring)
	Wall: Stucco finish
	Ceiling: Acoustical absorption board with plaster substrate and EP finish

竣工当時の旧・日本NCRビル。
The Japan NCR Building at the time of completion.

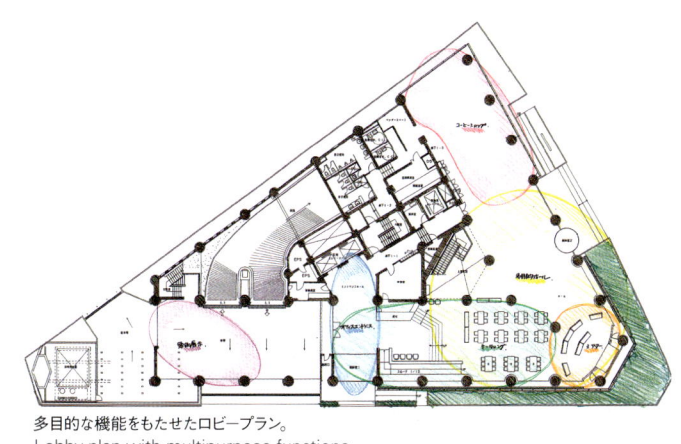

多目的な機能をもたせたロビープラン。
Lobby plan with multipurpose functions.

ショールーム機能を持っていたロビー。
Lobby serving as a showroom.

ロビーの中心にある階段。
Stairway in the middle of the lobby.

定期的にコンサーホールやギャラリーになるロビー。（写真：川澄建築写真事務所）
Lobby used for regular concerts and exhibitions. (Photo : Kawasumi Architectural Photograph Office)

オリジナルの姿を残した階段。（写真：川澄建築写真事務所）
Stairway maintaining its original structure. (Photo : Kawasumi Architectural Photograph Office)

ロビーホール・エントランス。（写真：川澄建築写真事務所）
Lobby entrance. (Photo : Kawasumi Architectural Photograph Office)

オフィス・エントランス。（写真：川澄建築写真事務所）
Office entrance. (Photo : Kawasumi Architectural Photograph Office)

日本財団ビル 079

オープンなオフィスのイメージスケッチ。
A sketch of an open office.

改修前のオフィス・スペース。
Office space before renovation.

ワーキングエリア。(写真：川澄建築写真事務所)
Work area. (Photo : Kawasumi Architectural Photograph Office)

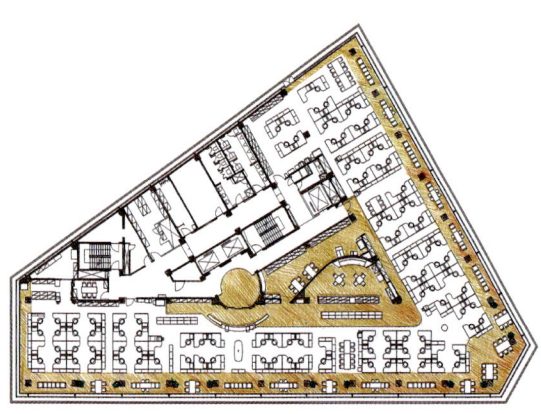

自由に回遊できるオフィスプラン。
Office plan offering freedom of movement.

オフィスづくりは、「オープン」をキーワードとした。開かれた窓側のスペース全てをミーティングなどの共用部とする事により、快適なミーティングスペースが得られ、オフィスに回遊性が生まれる。また、柱スパンに縛られない自由なワーキングレイアウトも可能になった。

仕上材は、木の床、土の壁などできるだけ自然素材を用い、間接照明、明るいカラーリング、自由曲線などを積極的にデザインに取り入れる事で、働く人、訪れる人にとって優しいオフィスとなった。

The keyword of the office design was "openness". By making open areas on the window side available for meeting and other public activities, the office can offer comfortable meeting spaces with freedom of movement. Column spans do not restrict the workspace layout.

With regard to finishing materials, natural ones such as wooden floor and earthen walls were employed as much as possible, and by positively employing indirect lighting, bright coloring and free-form curves, the office became friendly for both office workers and visitors.

自由曲線を使った役員フロア。（写真：川澄建築写真事務所）
Executive floor taking advantage of free-form curves. (Photo : Kawasumi Architectural Photograph Office)

個室。
Private room.

応接室。
Reception room.

NCRビル時代の役員フロア。
Executive floor during the NCR days.

EVホール。
Elevator hall.

日本財団ビル **081**

菱化システム

オフィスの生産性を
より高めるためのリノベーション

Ryoka Systems Inc.
Renovation to elevate the spirit and thereby increase office productivity

Designer: Yayoi Ogo: Mec design International Corporation
Location: Tokyo Daiya Bldg., 1-28-38, Shinkawa, Chuo-ku, Tokyo
Completion: March 2003
Materials: （Major interior materials: light-gauge steel frame with PB finish; AEP; non-organic cloth; tile carpet; reinforced glass）
Project Area: 900 sq m
Photo: Nacása & Partners Inc.

画一的なデスクを必ずしも必要としない部署。
Department not always in need of uniform desks.

営業部。
Sales Department.
自由な雰囲気の中、組織を越えた知識が飛び交うハブとなるスペース。
外部・顧客現場から得た知識を、各グループ間と共有し将来の戦略に生かす場。
A space serving as a hub of information and knowledge beyond departments in a free atmosphere. Place to share knowledge acquired from the outside and clients and to apply it to future strategies.

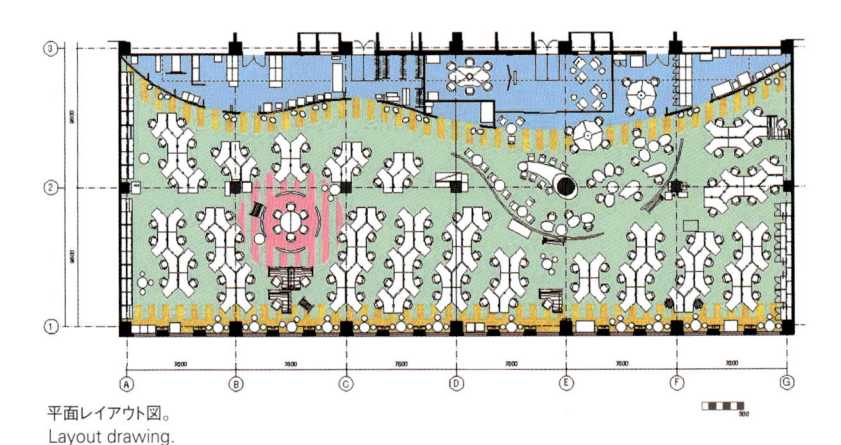

高度成長期の量的生産性が最重視された日本経済が大きな転換期を向かえている。
企業の源動力を経営と知財の統合に求める動きが高まる中、知財創造の担い手である財としての人材の有効性を最大限に支援する独自の働き方と環境の設計をこのプロジェクトの目的としている。
様々な知識の相互作用を支援する、総合的な対話環境を創る為に多様な場の仕掛けを試みた。
情報通信技術に関しては、営業職のフリーアドレス化や、随所にちりばめられた打ち合わせスペースを有効活用するためにフロア全体に無線LANを導入し、営業職はデスクトップからノートパソコンに移行している。

The Japan economy that has put first priority to quantitative productivity in its days of high growth is now facing a great turning point.
As a combination of management and intellectual property has become increasingly important as the main corporate driving force, the goal of this project is to design a unique way and environment of working to assist valuable human resources or supporters of intellectual property creation.
We devised many mechanisms to establish a comprehensive and interactive environment to support interactions of various knowledge elements.
As to information technology, wireless LAN is introduced to cover the entire floor, and salespersons are now using laptop PCs instead of desktop machines in order to promote their mobility and effective use of meeting spaces.

平面レイアウト図。
Layout drawing.

新しい働き方の概念図。
Conceptual diagram of a new way of working.
©Fuji X-erox Co., Ltd. 1995-2005 all rights reserved.

打ち合わせラウンジ。
Meeting lounge.
カジュアルな打ち合わせに設けられたハイカウンターは、
通りすがりの飛び入り参加を積極的に促進。
High counters for casual meetings positively permitting
open-participation by all interested persons.

閉鎖的な打ち合わせコーナー。
Exclusive meeting corner.

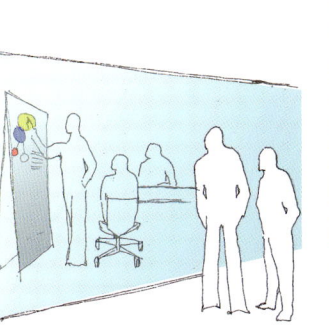

議論やプレゼンを支援するツールの無い応接室。
Reception room without tools to
support discussions and presentations.

プレゼンルーム。
Presentation room.
情報の双方向性の一貫としてガラス張りにし、
見られる事で会議の質を上げる心理効果を狙っている。
Glass-paned and see-through as part of bi-directional information
exchange in order to improving quality of meetings by
promoting psychological effect on participants.

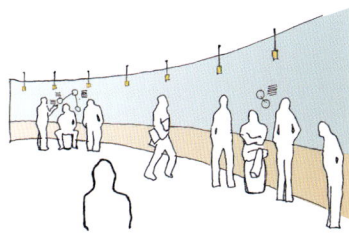

対話による問題解決の場が少ない。
Few places for problem solving through dialogues.

戦略企画スペース。
Strategic planning space.
誰でも参加が出来る360°開かれた、
独創性や企画力を支援するブレーンストーミングブース。
Brainstorming booth to support originality and
planning capability permitting fully open participation.

ホワイトボード壁。
White board wall.
フロアを横断するホワイトボードで出来た壁に書き残された
議論の痕跡を共有し、内部の連携強化。
In-house collaboration enforced through sharing traces of discussions
left written on the wall made of white board running across the floor.

対話による問題解決の場が少ない。
Few places for problem solving through dialogues.

菱化システム 083

丸紅東京本社
自然光を取り入れて
威圧感をなくしたオフィスエントランス

Marubeni Corporation Tokyo Headquarters
Non-intimidating office entrance taking advantage of natural light

景観を取入れ、明るく生まれ変わったロビー。（写真：北嶋俊治）
Bright renovated lobby incorporating the landscape. (Photo: Toshiharu Kitajima)

東京本社のリノベーションは、21世紀に向けて、国際的に活躍する総合商社の拠点としてふさわしい機能を備えたオフィスビルとするべく計画された。

エントランスロビーは、企業イメージを最初に印象づける重要なスペースである。外部の床や壁や軒天井が同じマテリアルで構成されていたロビー空間の質を高め、威圧感の無い明るいロビーとするため、床と壁を白い石に張り替えた。天井の形状を格子とし、レセプションカウンターのある正面の壁を木のパネルとする事でさらに雰囲気を和らげた。加えて西側の公開空地を親しまれる緑の歩道に造り替え、その景観をロビーの借景とした。また、北に面していた従来の外来者用のレストランも緑の庭に面して配置させ、景色もインテリアに取り入れた。

地下にある社員食堂のリノベーションでは、明るいカラーリング、壁面の間接照明、グリーンによる間仕切り等により、地下という閉塞感を和らげるようにした。好きなメニューをオープンキッチンカウンターから取り、カードで清算するカフェテリアスタイルとする事で、人の流れを整理した。

カウンター席、ベンチシート席、テラス席など、幾つかのエリアを作り、座席にバリエーションをもたせる事でニーズの幅を広げ、女性社員の利用を促した。

Developer:	Marubeni Corporation
Designer:	Masato Watanabe
Location:	Chiyoda-ku Tokyo
Renovated area:	5,256 sq m
Structure:	SRC
Completion:	October 1998
Material:	〈Lobby〉Floor: granite
	Wall: Marble; some veneered natural wood (rosewood)
	Ceiling: Plaster board + artificial wood substrate finished with EP paint

木パネルと格天井で構成されたレセプションカウンター廻り。（写真：北嶋俊治）
Reception counter area constituted by the wooden panels and coffered ceiling. (Photo: Toshiharu Kitajima)

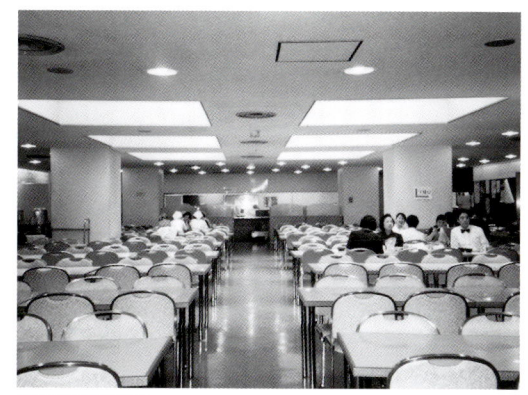

改修前の社員食堂。
Staff canteen before renovation.

座席にバリエーションをもたせた社員食堂。（写真：北嶋俊治）
Staff canteen with varied seats. (Photo: Toshiharu Kitajima)

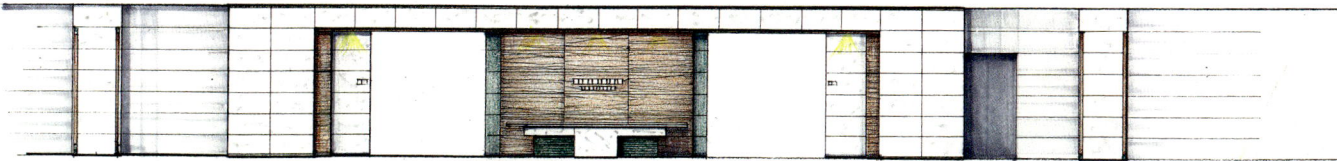

展開スケッチ。
A developed view.

緑の庭に向けた
外来者用のレストラン。
（写真：北嶋俊治）
Visitor's restaurant
facing the garden.
(Photo: Toshiharu Kitajima)

The purpose of the renovation of the Tokyo Headquarters was to convert the existing structure into an office building appropriate for a trading company engaged in international business activities toward the 21st century.

The entrance lobby is the important space that determines the first corporate impression. In order to upgrade the lobby space made of materials same as that of the exterior floors and eave soffits and to make it bright and non-intimidating, white stone was applied to the floor and wall. By employing coffered ceiling and wooden panels on the wall behind the reception counter, the atmosphere was more relaxed. In addition, the vacant lot to the west that was open to the public was turned into a sidewalk, and the landscape was used to enhance the lobby. The existing visitors restaurant to the north now faces the garden in green, taking advantage of the scenery as part of interior design.

In refurbishing the staff canteen in the basement, such design techniques as bright coloring, indirect lighting on the wall, and flower pots as partitions contributed to lessen a sense of confinement. Human traffic flow was better controlled, thanks to employment of the self-service concept where one picks up one's favorite dish from an open-kitchen counter and pays by card.

The canteen was divided into several areas having a variety of seats such as counters, benches, or seats on the terrace to meet different needs and to attract female employees.

陶山國男記念室
スケルトンを残す理由、インフィルをつくりこむ理由

Dr. Kunio SUYAMA Memorial
Reasons for leaving the skeleton, reasons for building in the infill

Designer: Yoshiharu Shimura / Eriko Izitsu: FIELD FOUR DESIGN OFFICE
Client: OYO Corporation
Location: Tsukuba-shi, Ibaraki
Site area: 50 sq m
Structure: SRC
Completion: March 2000
Materials: floor: Carpet
wall: painted board and wood panel
ceiling: painted board

部屋全体を見る。手前の像はThe Doodlebugger、その奥は当時使われていた計器など。（写真：川澄建築写真事務所）
A view of the room: The figure in front is the Doodlebugger. Behind it are instruments Dr. Suyama used. (Photo: Kawasumi Architectural Photograph Office)

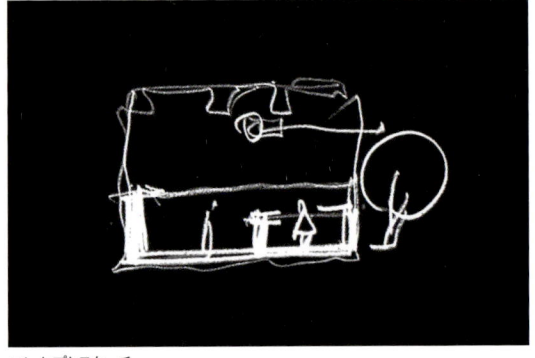

コンセプトスケッチ。
Conceptual sketch.

既存。
Existing.

右手は執務エリア。
窓の開口H2200にあわせて
木パネルを設置、インフィルをつくる。
(写真：川澄建築写真事務所)
Office area to the right.
Wooden panel matching the window
opening (H: 2,200mm) to make infill.
(Kawasumi Architectural Photograph Office)

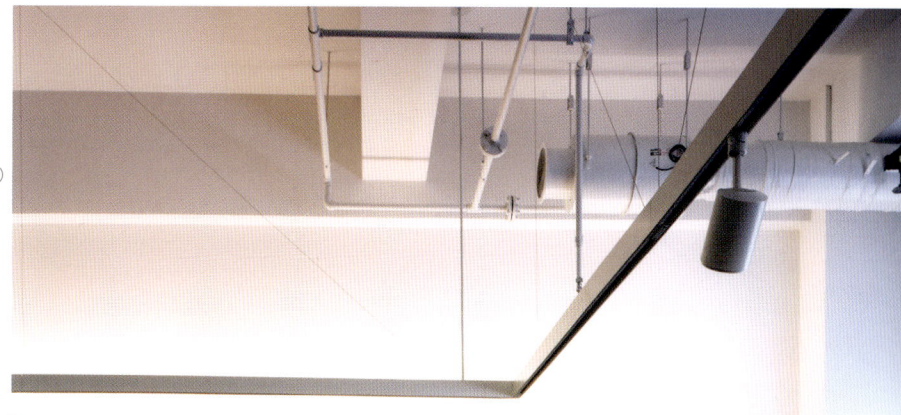

プラン。
Plan.

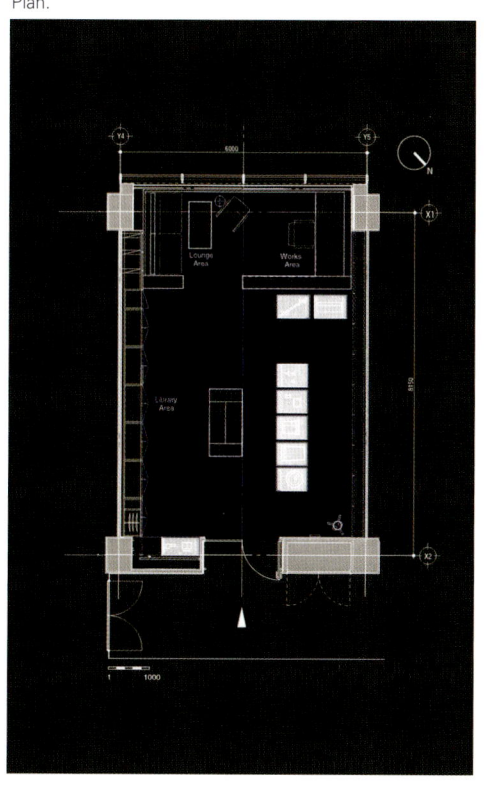

地質学者として研究所の創立に関わり、わが国最大の地質コンサルタント会社を育てた偉大なる足跡と、教訓を残された陶山國男博士の記念室である。

その部屋はつくば市の研究室群の中にひっそりと佇んでいる。現在も稼動している研究室の中にスペースを見つけて、「場」を作ることにより、今も若い研究者へ日々、博士の思想と夢とを語り続けている。

記念室は展示のみではなく執務・ラウンジ・閲覧コーナーを設け、人と建築の間にあるべきエレメントの明確化をおこない、人とのコミュニケーションの中で、新しい何かが生まれる可能性を秘めた大事な「場」となっている。

身近で機能的なスケルトンは「開発された技術」をあらわし、インフィルは「博士のひととなり」をあらわしている。またインフィルは人に近いディメンションと素材を設定し、全て家具工事とすることでスケルトン工事とは分離して施工できるように計画をした。

This is a memorial room for the late Dr. Kunio Suyama who accomplished great achievements and gave lessons through his involvement in the establishment of a research center as a geologist, which has grown into the biggest geological consulting company in Japan.

The serene aspect of the memorial is found in a group of research rooms in Tsukuba city. By finding a space and setting up a 'field' in a currently used research room, it has become possible to convey thoughts and dreams of Dr. Suyama to young researchers.

The Memorial accommodates not only exhibitions but also an office, a lounge and a reading corner. By clearly defining the elements that exist between humans and the architecture, it serves as an important 'field' with possibilities to create something new through interactions between them.

The familiar and functional skeleton represents the 'technologies developed' while the infill stands for the 'personality of Dr. Suyama'.

The infill has size and materials like a human, and it was planned that by preparing it all as furniture, construction work could separately carried out from the skeleton works.

日建スペースデザイン 大阪設計室

スケルトンを顕わした
オフィス空間

Nikken Space Design Osaka Office
Office space with exposed skeleton

外観。（写真：柄松 稔）
Exterior. (Photo: Minoru Karamatsu)

Construction: Touzai Kenchiku Service Co., Ltd
Designer: Tetsutaro Nishida: Nikken Space Design
Location: Chuo-ku, Osaka
Site area: 472 sq m
Completion: October 2004
Material: Floor: tile carpet; Wall: AEP on concrete; Ceiling: skeleton (AEP on concrete)
Year of original completion: 1959

自社オフィスの移転に伴う改修事例。築40年の8階建ペンシルビルの1～3階を改修、デザイン事務所として入居している。

改修にあたって、躯体と基幹設備以外の構成物をいったん取り除き、スケルトン化した上で最適化されたインフィルを再構築。ファクトリー的執務空間を志向した結果、ほぼスケルトンに近い内部空間となった。

またオフィスと建物外部の連続性を確保するため、2階床スラブを一部撤去。吹抜けで1階と一体化し、そこに接客スペースを設けている。

近畿ニューオフィス推進賞受賞。

This is a case of renovation along with a relocation of the corporate headquarters. This design office renovated the first to third floors of an 8-story urban small building with 40 years of history.

To implement renovation program, all the existing elements with exceptions of the skeleton and basic facilities were removed, and infill was recreated. Based on the concept of factory-like office space, the interior space was very close to the skeleton.

In addition, to provide continuity between the office and the exterior, part of the second floor slab was removed to form a well in which a receiving space was built.

Awarded: Kinki New Office Promotion Award.

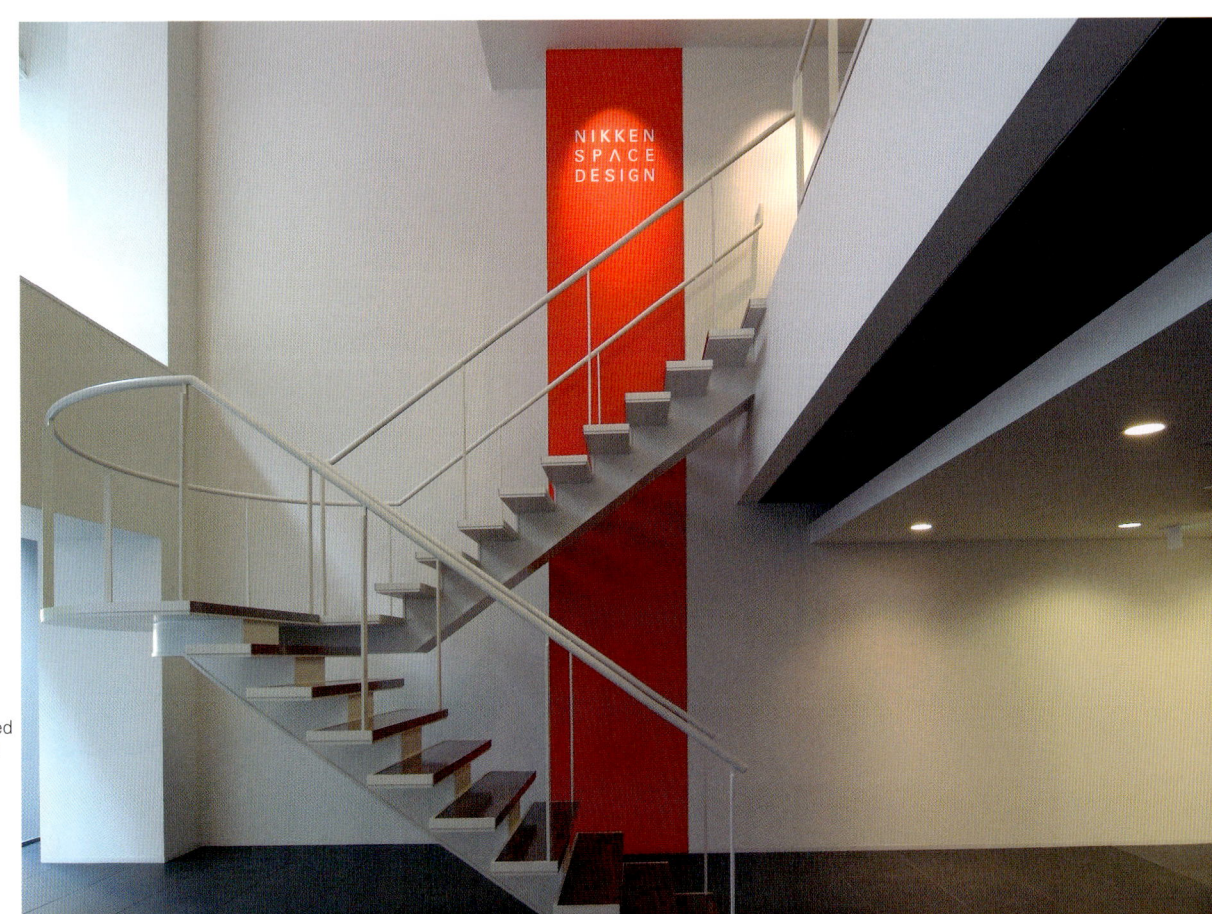

2階の床スラブを撤去して生まれた吹抜け空間と階段。
（写真：柄松 稔）
A well and stairway created by removing the floor slab on the second floor.
(Photo: Minoru Karamatsu)

2階の接客スペース。(写真:柄松 稔)
Receiving space on the second floor. (Photo: Minoru Karamatsu)

改修前の外観。
Exterior before renovation.

改修前の内観。
Interior before renovation.

3階のライブラリー。(写真:柄松 稔)
Library on the third floor. (Photo: Minoru Karamatsu)

日建スペースデザイン 大阪設計室 **089**

執務スペースは天井高3.5m。あえてOAフロアを採用せず、ケーブルラックを用いた吊下げワイヤリング方式をとった。
中央通路を軸にしたコミュニケーションのあり方など、独自の手法を数多く取り入れている。

Office spaces have a ceiling height of 3.5m. We dared to employ no OA floor system and instead, used cable racks for suspended wirings.
Communications focused around the central corridor and other unique measures and approaches are also employed.

コミュニケーションの取り易いワークステーション。(写真:柄松 稔)
Workstations for easy communications. (Photo: Minoru Karamatsu)

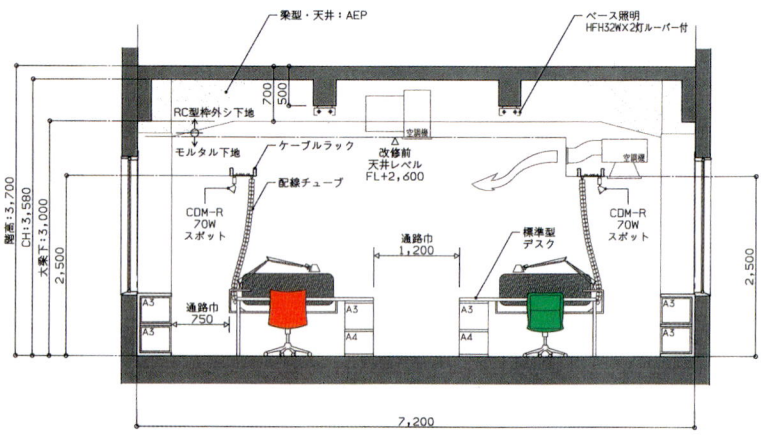

3階執務スペースの断面。
Section of the office floor on the third floor.

3階の執務スペース。(写真:柄松 稔)
Office space on the third floor. (Photo: Minoru Karamatsu)

3階の執務スペース。(写真:柄松 稔)
Office space on the third floor. (Photo: Minoru Karamatsu)

第3章 病院

Chapter 5
Hospitals

ふれあい横浜ホスピタル・シニアホテル横浜

ホテルの居心地をそのまま病院にコンバージョン

Fureai Yokohama Hospital/Senior Hotel Yokohama
Comfort of a hotel converted to that of a hospital

ふれあい横浜ホスピタル・シニアホテル横浜は関内駅前の高層ホテルを新たに病院と高齢者用ホテルとして用途変更する手法（コンバージョン）によって、既存建物を再生させた大変ユニークな事例である。

そもそも、ホテルとホスピタルはその語源を同じくしていることより類似点も多い。ここで、ホテルと病院の建築としての空間構成を比較してみると、ホテルでの不特定多数の方がアクセスしかつゆっくり集う「エントランスロビー」は病院での「総合待合ホール」に類似している、ホテルでの「各種テナントスペース」は病院の「外来・中央診療部門」に、又静かに宿泊する「客室部門」は「病棟部門」にと、ハード面においての類似点が多い事に気がつく。そして、このように建物の空間構成に類似点が多くあったことが、病院へのリニューアルを実現しやすくしてくれた。

また、インテリアデザインにおいても既存内装をできるだけ再利用し、改修工事にお金をかけなければかけないほど……その結果として、『病院らしくない病院・ホテルのような病院』が出来あがるという、とてもユニークな結果となり、まさにその事が今回のリニューアルにおける最大のメリットとなった。

外観（改修後）。
Exterior (after renovation).

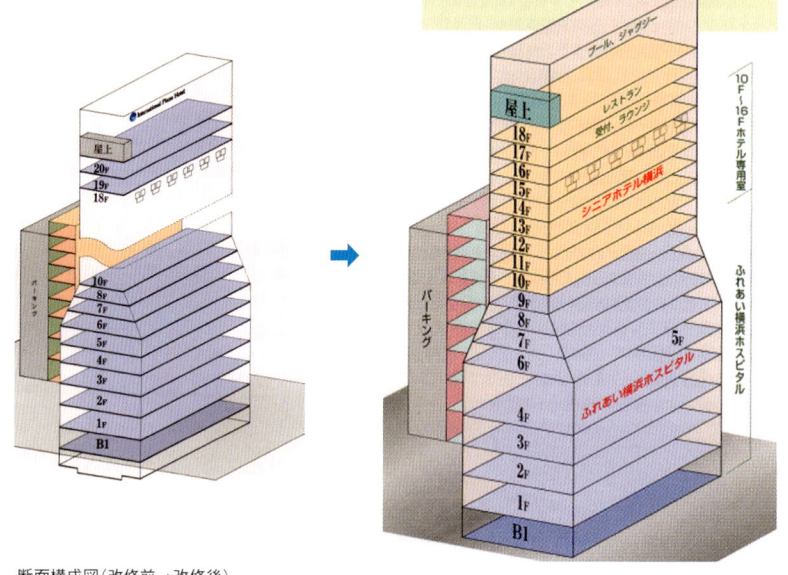

断面構成図（改修前→改修後）。
Section (Before and after renovation).

Owner:	Medical Corporation Koshinkai
Main use:	Hospital / hotel
Location:	2-3-3 Bandaicho, Naka-ku, Yokohama, Kanagawa
Design / supervision:	K. Ito Architects & Engineers Inc.
Construction:	Shimizu Corporation
Design period:	October 2000 to April 2001
Construction period:	July 2001 to February 2002
Site area:	2,385 sq m
Building area:	1,550 sq m
Total floor area:	18,409 sq m
Structure:	SRC structure, partially S structure; 1 basement-level floor, 18 floors above ground
Exterior finish:	precast concrete/porcelain tiles
Basic interior finish:	Waiting hall: floors / walls: marble; ceiling: vinyl cloth
	Patients' rooms: floors: vinyl sheets; walls / ceiling: vinyl cloth

Fureai Yokohama Hospital/Senior Hotel Yokohama is a unique example of renovation of an existing building by converting a high-rise hotel in front of JR Kannai station to a complex of a hospital and a hotel for senior citizens.

As the terms hotel and hospital are derived from the same origin, they also have many things in common. When we compare architectural spatial structures of hotel and hospital, we notice that the entrance lobby where many and unspecified persons come and gather is similar to the waiting hall. In terms of hardware, we may compare tenant spaces of the hotel to medical clinics for outpatient/central consultation facilities and guestrooms where guests stay quietly to patients rooms. Many of these similar spatial structures facilitated us to design this renewal/conversion to hospital.

In terms of interior design, the existing elements were recycled as much as possible to reduce the cost of renovation, and, as a result, built was a non-hospital-like and very hotel-like hospital, which became a largest advantage of this renewal project.

1階総合待合ホール（改修後）。
General waiting hall on the 1st floor (after renovation).

1階ホテルロビー（改修前）。
Hotel lobby on the first floor (after renovation).

高齢者ホテル専用エントランス（改修後）。
Entrance exclusive for the hotel for senior citizens (after renovation).

病院1階の総合待合ホールはホテル時代の趣をそのまま残すため、内装は出来るだけ既存を利用した。また、新たな機能として追加する診察室は木質系の柔らかな材質を基調として採用した。

In order to preserve the atmosphere of the days as a hotel, the interior of the waiting hall on the first floor of the hospital was recycled wherever plausible. For clinics as a new function, soft and woody materials were selected as the basis of design.

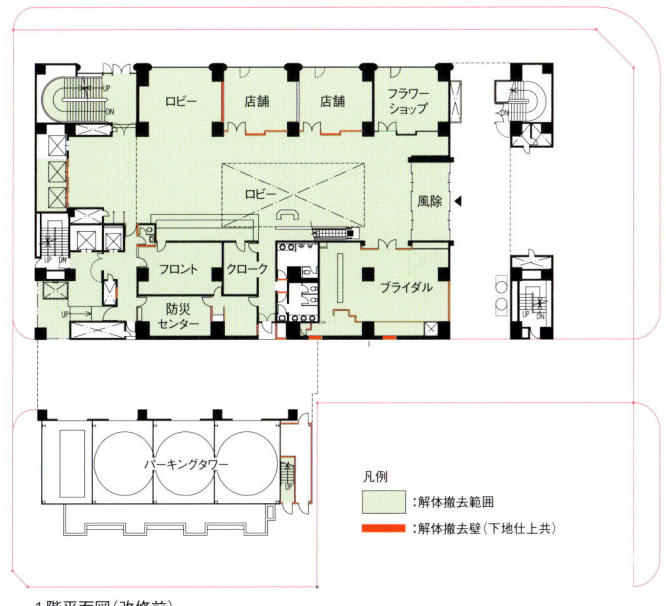

1階平面図（改修前）。
Floor plan of the 1st floor (before renovation).

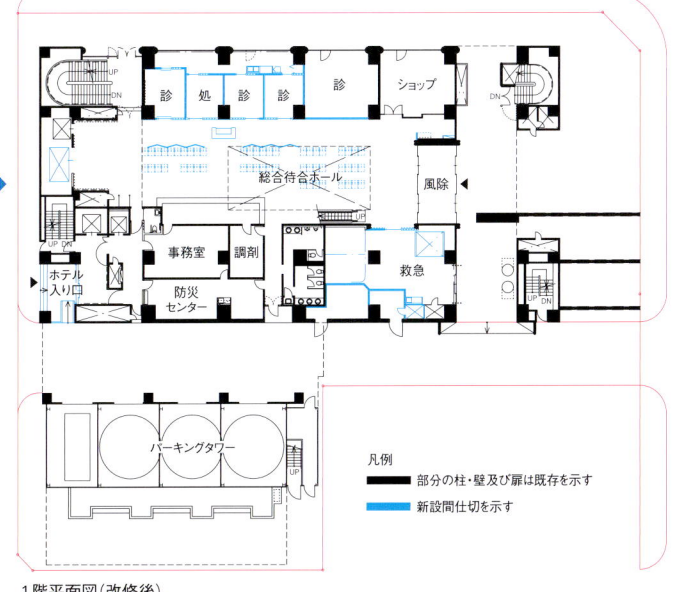

1階平面図（改修後）。
Floor plan of the 1st floor (after renovation).

ふれあい横浜ホスピタル・シニアホテル横浜　093

2階外来待合ホール(改修後)。
Waiting hall for outpatient on the 2nd floor (after renovation).

吹き抜け空間で連続された2階も病院の外来診療部としてリニューアルされた。インテリアは1階と合わせ明るい木質系の仕上げで統一した。

The 2nd floor connected to the 1st floor with a well was also renewed as medical clinics for outpatient. To keep the integrity in design with the fist floor, light, woody finishes were adopted.

2階ロビー(改修前)。
Lobby on the 2nd floor (before renovation).

外来診察室(改修後)。
Medical clinics for outpatient (after renovation).

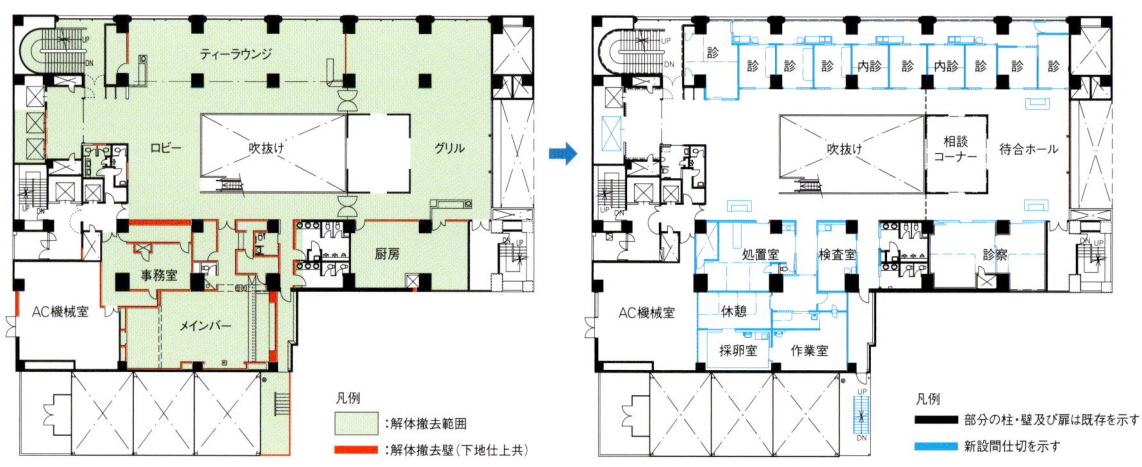

2階平面図(改修前)。
Floor plan of the 2nd floor (before renovation).

2階平面図(改修後)。
Floor plan of the 2nd floor (after renovation).

094 第3章 病院

大宴会場の床はフローリングに、建具は引戸に改修したが、天井のデザイン照明は既存をそのまま利用することにより、天井が高く明るい開放的なリハビリテーションの部屋が完成した。

Though the floor of the banquet hall was changed to flooring and fixtures were changed to sliding doors, design and lighting on the ceiling were used as-is to realize a rehabilitation room with a high, well-lit ceiling with a sense of openness.

リハビリ前ロビー（改修後）。
Lobby in front of the rehabilitation center (after renovation).

4階大宴会場（改修前）。
Banqueting hall of the 4th floor (before renovation).

4階リハビリテーションセンター（改修後）。
Rehabilitation center on the 4th floor (after renovation).

4階平面図（改修前）。
Floor plan of the 4th floor (before renovation).

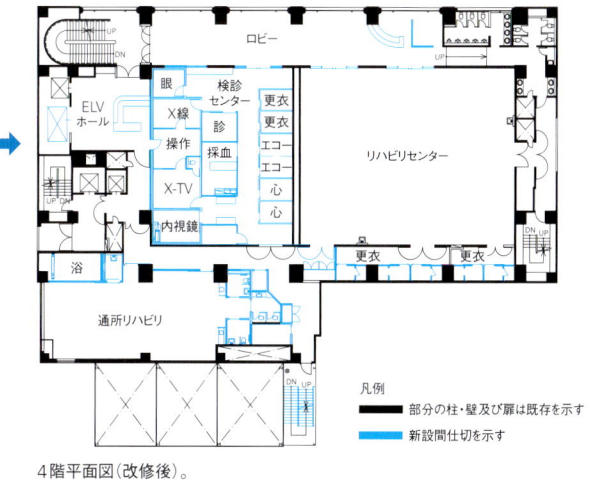

4階平面図（改修後）。
Floor plan of the 4th floor (after renovation).

二人の愛を誓った式場は手術室にリニューアルされ、現在はその場所で多くの生命を救命するための手術がおこなわれている。

The bridal hall where once couples pledged their love is now a place for operations to help many lives.

6階結婚式場（改修前）。
Bridal hall (before renovation).

6階チャペル（改修前）。
Chapel on the 6th floor (before renovation).

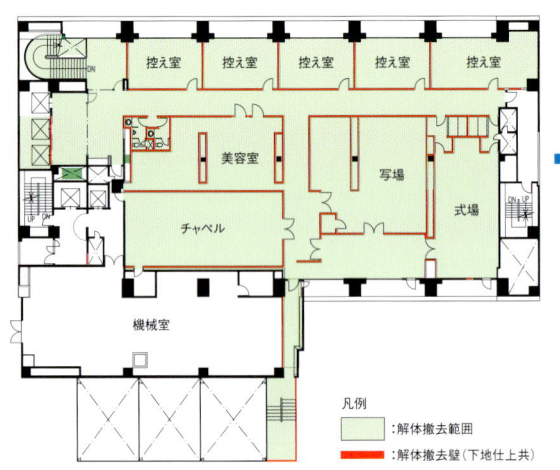

6階平面図（改修前）。
Floor plan of the 6th floor (before renovation).

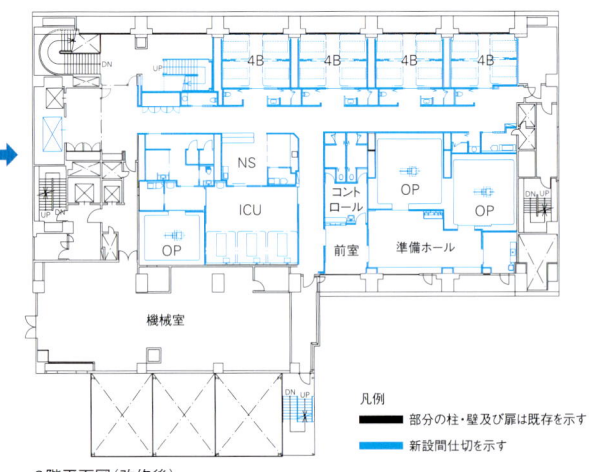

6階平面図（改修後）。
Floor plan of the 6th floor (after renovation).

6階手術室（改修後）。
Operation room on the 6th floor (after renovation).

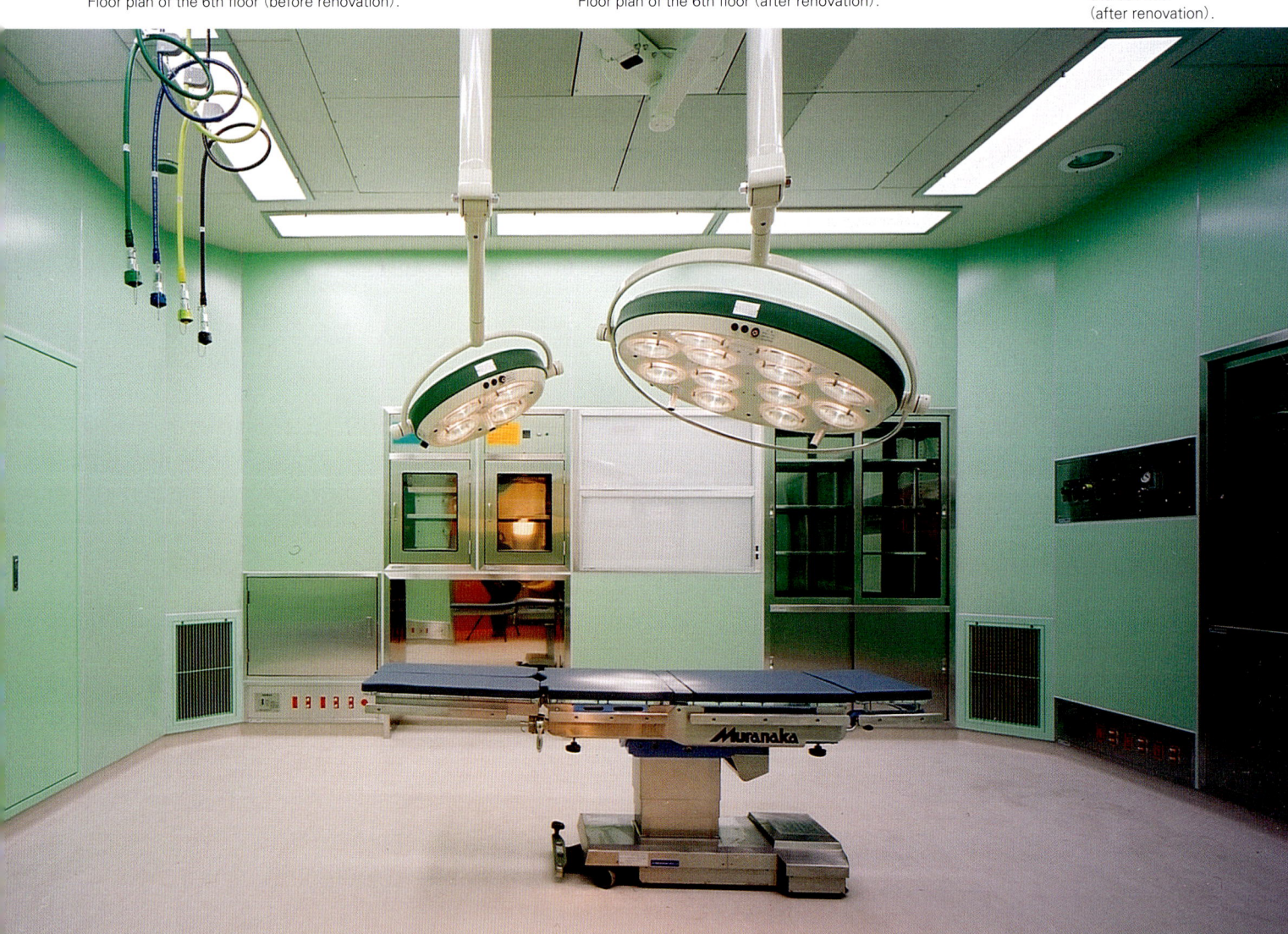

18階高齢者ホテルラウンジ（改修後）。
Hotel lounge on the 18th floor of the hotel for senior citizens (after renovation).

ぐるりと360°横浜市内を見渡せるスカイラウンジは高齢者ホテル用のラウンジとして使用されている。ダンスが踊れるように床をフローリングに張替え、雰囲気づくりのデザイン照明を追加している。

The sky lounge with a panorama view of Yokohama city is used as a lounge for the hotel for senior citizens. Flooring is applied to the floor for dancing, and designed lighting is added for livening up the atmosphere.

18階スカイラウンジ（改修前）。
Counter bar on the 18th floor (before renovation).

18階平面図（改修前）。
Floor plan of the 18th floor (before renovation).

18階平面図（改修後）。
Floor plan of the 18th floor (after renovation).

18階カウンターバー（改修後）。
Counter bar on the 18th floor (after renovation).

17F

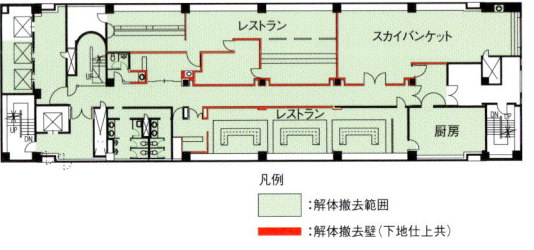

17F改修前平面図
Floor plan of the 17th floor before renovation.

17階ロビー(改修後)。
Lobby on the 17th floor(after renovation).

7F

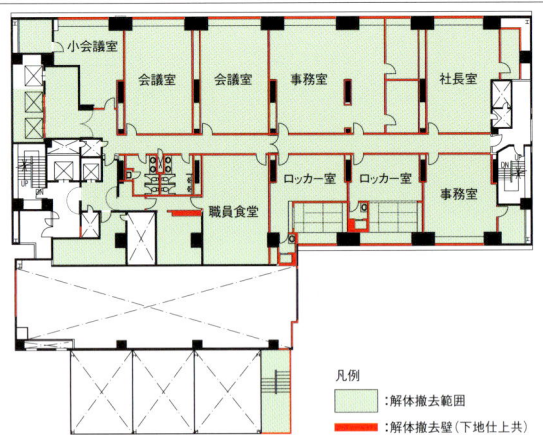

7F改修前平面図
Floor plan of the 7th floor before renovation.

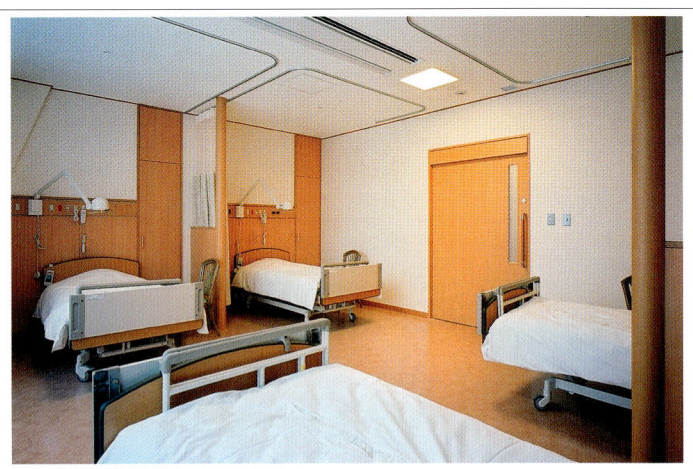

7階4床室(改修後)。
4 bedroom on the 7th floor(after renovation).

3F

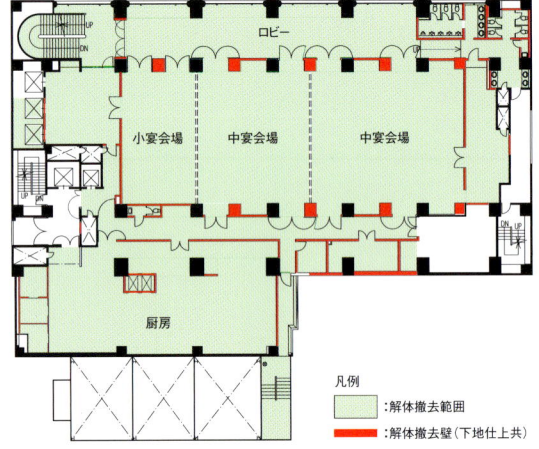

3F改修前平面図
Floor plan of the 3rd floor before renovation.

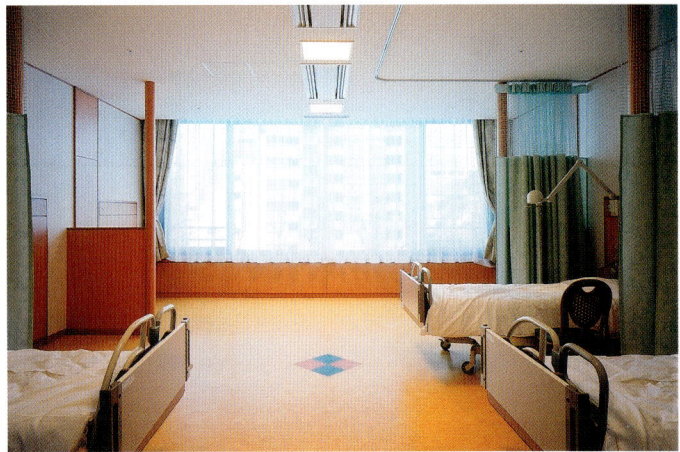

3階6床室(改修後)。
6 bedroom on the 3rd floor(after renovation).

B1F

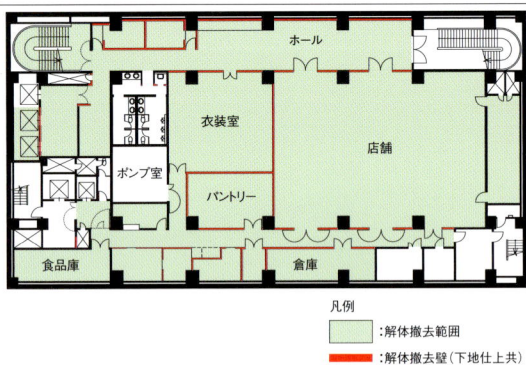

地下1F改修前平面図
Floor plan of the basement before renovation.

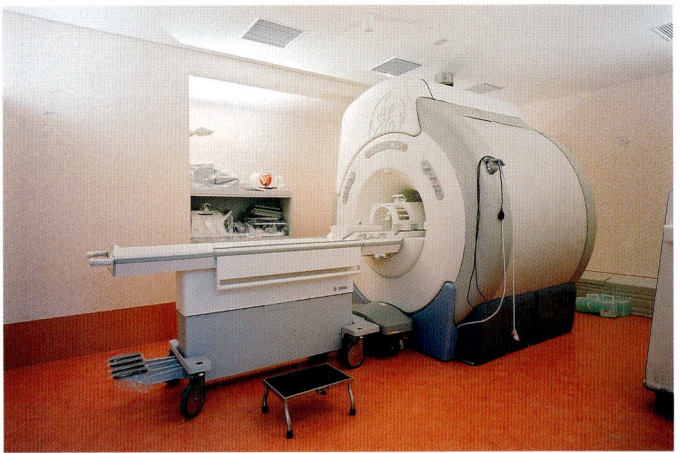

地下1階MRI室(改修後)。
MRI room on the basement(after renovation).

高齢者ホテル。
Hotel for person of advanced age.

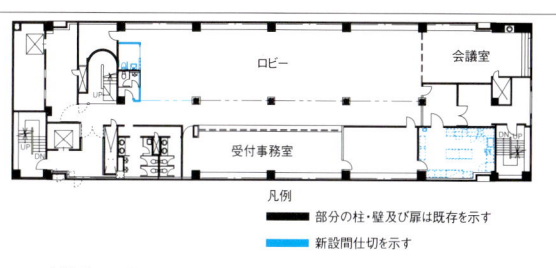

17F改修後平面図
Floor plan of the 17th floor after renovation.

個室病室。
The Private room.

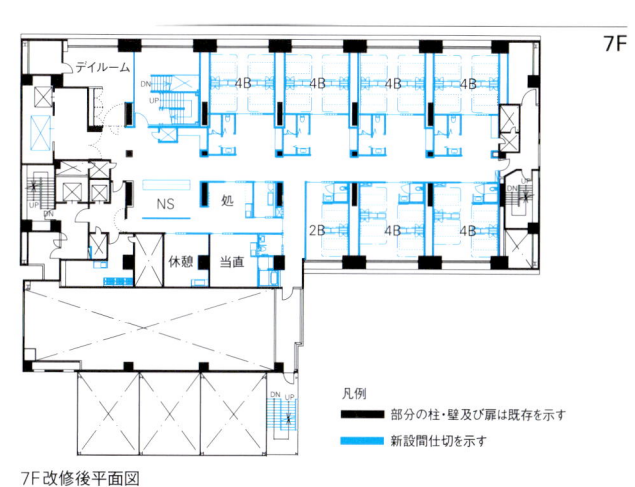

7F改修後平面図
Floor plan of the 7th floor after renovation.

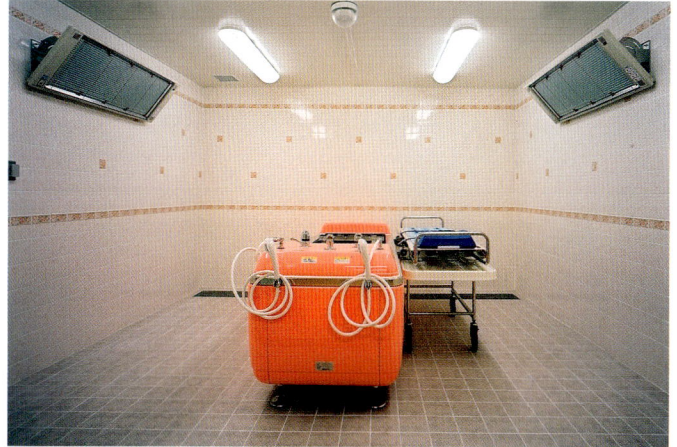

3階特殊浴室。
Specific bath on the 3rd floor.

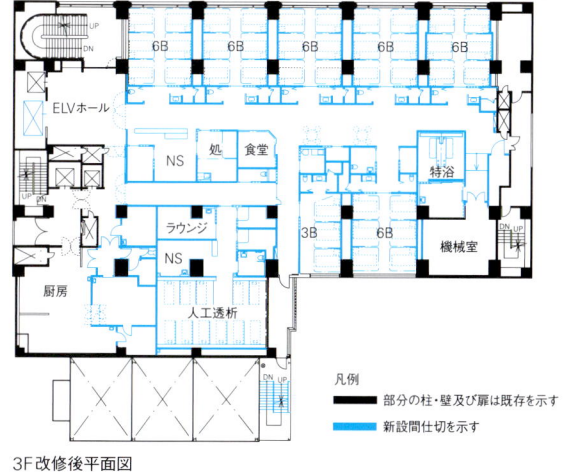

3F改修後平面図
Floor plan of the 3rd floor after renovation.

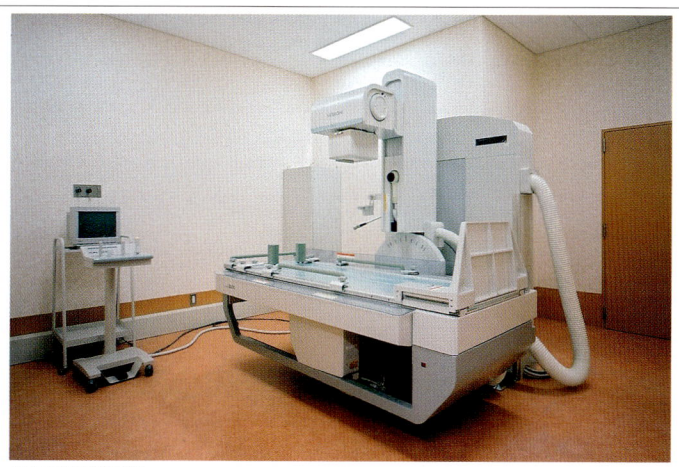

地下1階X線TV室。
TV room Roentgen ray of the basement.

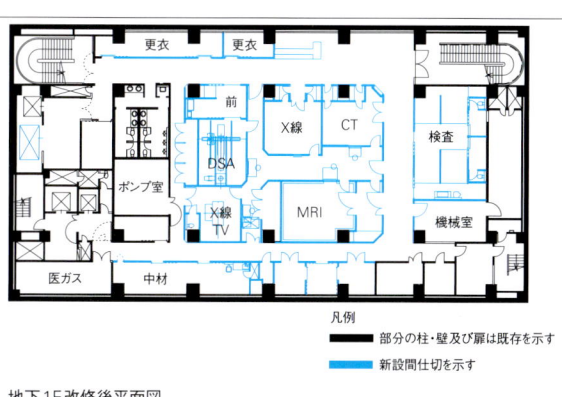

地下1F改修後平面図
Floor plan of the basement after renovation.

ふれあい横浜ホスピタル・シニアホテル横浜 099

福井県済生会病院 外来診察部門
スタッフの顔が見える外来診察部門に改修

Out-patient Department, Fukui-ken Saiseikai Hospital
Renovation of outpatient department to promote face-to-face communications between staff and patients

写真:中村幹生[アルプスカメラ]
Photo: Mikio Nakamura [ALPS CAMERA]

Client: Fukui-ken Saiseikai Hospital
Architect: Hideo Kubota, Hiroshima International University
Designer: Akira Yoshikawa: Nikken Space Design
Practice Design / Construction: Kumagaigumi Co., Ltd
Location: Wadanaka-machi, Fukui
Site area: 9200 sq m
Completion: November 2004 (1st period) /
 May 2005 (2nd period) /
 under construction (3rd period)
Year of original completion: March 1993

病院は絶えず変化する。医療の進歩、医療内容や対象患者の変化と増減、それに法律の改正など、様々な要因がある。この病院の外来診療部門は、診察室を診療科で特定しない方式として、将来の変化にフレキシブルに対応できるようにした。並行して、内科、外科などの診療科目の、総合外来、生活習慣病センター、女性診療センターなどへの組み替えも行なわれている。

また大きな特徴として、看護師などのスタッフ動線を患者側に一本化するために、従来から一般的な診察室後方のスタッフ通路をやめている。

スタッフカウンターを診察室前に配置することで、患者とスタッフの接点が大きく拡がり、患者にいつもスタッフの顔が見える患者への気配りが行き届く待合となった。

Hospitals are ever changing. Behind this, there are a variety of factors including medical progress, changes in diseases and increase/decrease of their patients, and amendments of laws. The outpatient department of this hospital decided to fix the use of clinics based on clinical departments so that flexibility should be secured for future changes. In parallel with this, clinical departments have also been reorganized into Outpatient Clinic, Lifestyle-related Illness Center, Female Clinics, etc.

One of the unique features of the hospital is elimination of conventional staff corridors behind clinics in order to integrate patients' traffic line with that of nurses and other staff. By establishing a staff counter in front of each clinic, contacts between patients and staff have greatly been promoted, and patients can always have opportunities to communicate with the staff in the waiting rooms.

写真:中村幹生[アルプスカメラ]
Photo: Mikio Nakamura [ALPS CAMERA]

待合いには肘掛け椅子も用意されている。生活習慣病センター付近。
Waiting area of the Lifestyle-related Illness Center offers armchairs.

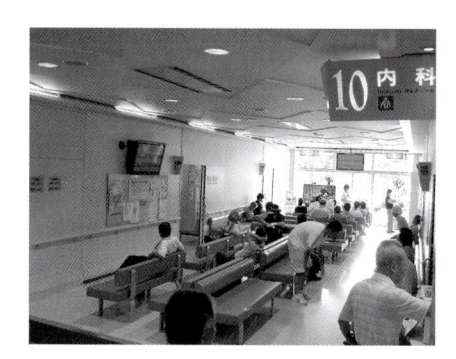

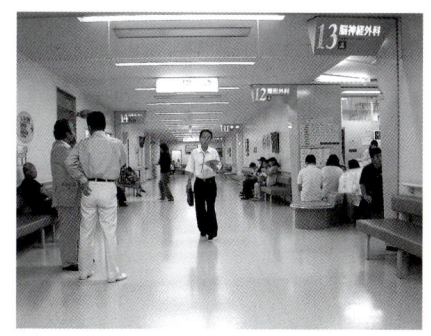

改修前の診療室前待合い。
Waiting area in front of a clinic before renovation.

診察室の前にスタッフカウンターが設置されている。(写真：中村幹生［アルプスカメラ］)
Staff counter in front of the clinic.
(Photo: Mikio Nakamura [ALPS CAMERA])

窓のある診療室。
Clinic with windows.

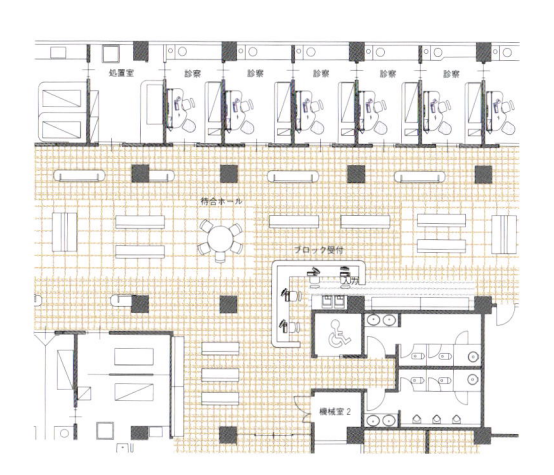

待合室はガラス扉で仕切られている。床は患者の安全と騒音の吸収のために、診察室を含めて、可能な限りタイルカーペット敷きとした。家具も長椅子ばかりでなく、一人用の肘掛け椅子も増やして居住性を高めている。

The waiting rooms are separated using glass doors. Wherever appropriate, tile carpets are laid on the floors including those of clinics in order to secure safety of patients and to absorb noises. Regarding the furniture, armchairs are located in addition to benches for better comfort.

ブロック受付カウンター。(写真：中村幹生［アルプスカメラ］)
Reception counter of the block. (Photo: Mikio Nakamura [ALPS CAMERA])

小児科ブロックの入口ゲート。(写真：中村幹生[アルプスカメラ])
Entrance gate of Pediotics block. (Photo: Mikio Nakamura [ALPS CAMERA])

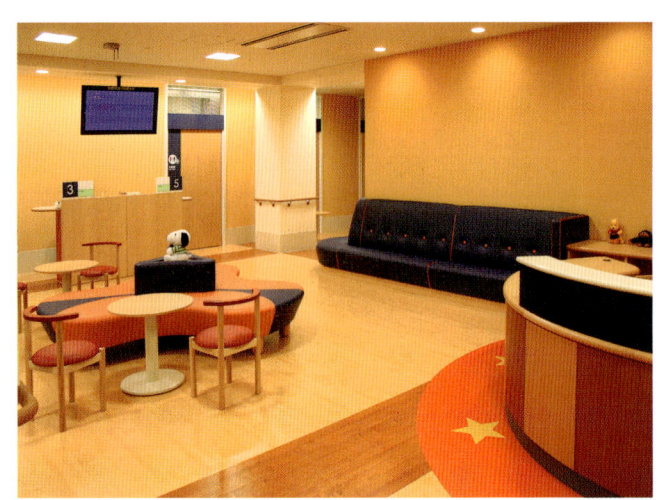

小児科待合い。
Waiting room of Pediotics Department.

女性診療センター・廊下。
Corridor of the Female Clinics.

産科待合いロビー。(写真：中村幹生[アルプスカメラ])
Waiting lobby of the Obstetris.
(Photo: Mikio Nakamura [ALPS CAMERA])

改修前の受付。
Reception before renovation.

総合受付は相談形式のローカウンターを主体に椅子に座って受付をする配置に改修された。

In the renewed general reception, patients can sit at the low counter, face-to-face with the staff.

改修後の総合受付ロビーイメージ。
Sketch of the reception lobby after renovation.

新患受付は相談デスクスタイル。
New patient is received in a "consultation desk" style.

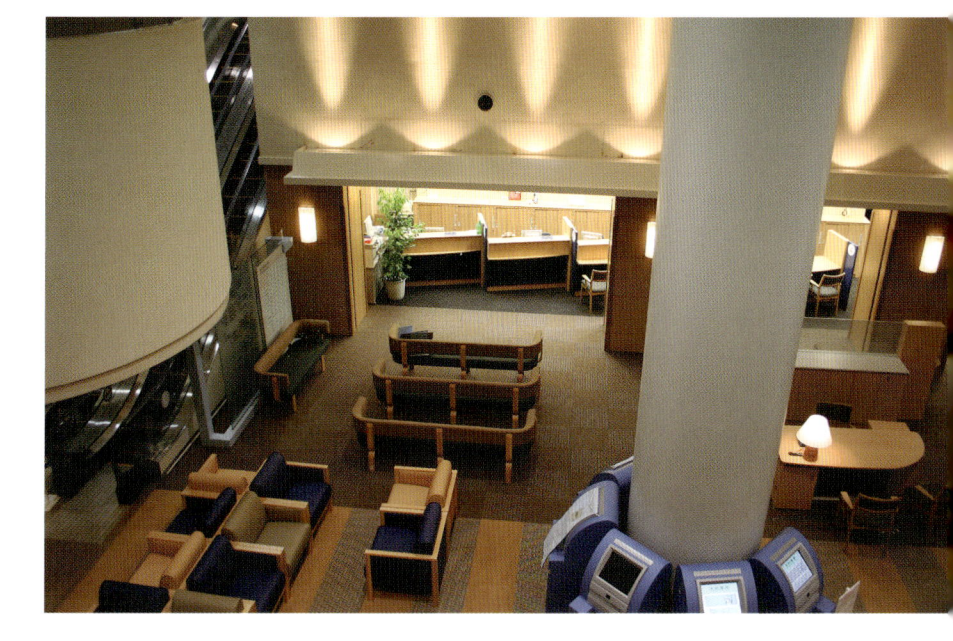

福井県済生会病院 外来診察部門　**103**

楠樹記念クリニック

装飾性の強いサロンから、リラックスできるラウンジへ

Nanjyu Memorial Clinic
From a highly ornate salon to a lounge where you can relax

改修後のレセプション。（写真：馬場祥光［サラサ］）
Reception after renovation. （Photo: Yoshiteru Baba［Sarasa］）

改修前。
Before renovation.

改修前。
Before renovation.

改修後の待合。（写真：馬場祥光［サラサ］）
Waiting room after renovation. （Photo: Yoshiteru Baba［Sarasa］）

Developer:	Medical corporation SEIZAN-KAI
Architect:	Archibest CO., LTD
Designer:	Masako Suzuki
Location:	Shinjuku-ku, Tokyo
Total floor area:	587.86 sq m
Completion:	May 1998

高層ビルの中にあり、人間ドック、定期健診などの検査が主なクリニックである。
ここには健康な状態で来る人がほとんどで、患者ではなく、お客様という形で、普段と変わらずいかにリラックスした状態で、気持ちよく検査をうけてもらえるかを考え計画を進めた。
初めて訪れた人はサロンのようなエントランスは少し戸惑うかもしれない。
検査部分は、中央に待合ラウンジを広く取り、そのまわりに各検査ルームを配置し、検査・検診時の動線を短くした。天井壁画については院長のアイデアで、オアシスのイメージで描かれている。
家具については、ゆったり座れるソファータイプとし、フロアスタンドやラグなどを置き、目線などに配慮し自分の居場所を解かりやすく、待合時の不安感、ストレスを極力なくすようレイアウトをした。
内装材では、フローリングや左官材など素材感のある材料を使用し、グリーンをアクセントとしたやさしくナチュラルなカラーで全体をまとめ、病院の持つ無機的な表情を感じさせないよう配慮した。
グリーン、アート、サイン、備品など細部にわたり、このクリニックの持つ"らしさ"にこだわり少し気が重くなるような雰囲気と不安感を取り除き、穏やかで気持ちの良い空間作りを心掛けた。

改修前。
Before renovation.

改修後の廊下。(写真:馬場祥光[サラサ])
Corridor after renovation. (Photo: Yoshiteru Baba[Sarasa])

検査室。(写真:馬場祥光[サラサ])
Examination room. (Photo: Yoshiteru Baba[Sarasa])

アートとグリーンで癒される。(写真:馬場祥光[サラサ])
Comforting arts and the color of green. (Photo: Yoshiteru Baba[Sarasa])

This clinic is in a skyscraper, and its main focus is thorough physical examinations and periodic checkups.

Most of the visitors are healthy, so in planning its renovation and are not patients. Planning thus emphasizes the fact that they are guests and how to let them comfortably experience examinations, feeling relaxed.

First-time visitors may be a little taken aback at the entrance that looks like a salon.

For the examination area, a wide waiting lounge is located at the center, surrounded by individual examination rooms so that traffic lines should be kept short.

Suggested by the director, the ceiling murals give an image of oasis.

As to the furniture, comfortable sofa-type chairs are employed; floor stands and rugs are carefully arranged in consideration of eyes; and layout is made in a way that one can easily find one's place and minimize a sense of uneasiness or stress while waiting.

As interior materials, flooring, plastering and other materials with a sense of rawness are used, and the general tone is based on gentle natural colors with an accent color of green so that non-organic impression found in hospitals should be avoided.

Such details as the color of green, artworks, signs and equipment creates the ambience unique to this clinic. Its design puts emphasis on establishing a quiet and comfortable space, removing a little depressing atmosphere and a sense of uneasiness.

IVFなんばクリニック

やわらかな光で包むクリニックに
コンバージョン

IVF Namba
Conversion into a clinic surrounded by soft radiance

おおらかなエントランスロビー。
Entrance lobby with a sense of serenity.

1／50スタディモデル。
1／50-scale study model.

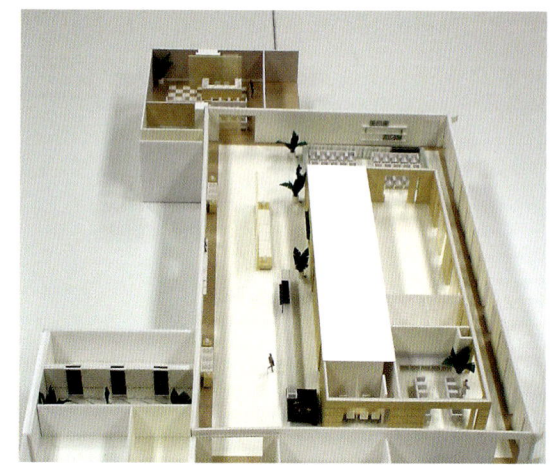

1／50スタディモデル。
1／50-scale study model.

改修前の倉庫。
Warehouse before renovation.

Architect: Shimizu Corporation
Designer: Harada Yasuyuki: FIELD FOUR DESIGN OFFICE
Location: Namba, Osaka-shi, Osaka
Site area: 1,000 sq m
Structure: RC
Completion: September 2003

ゲストを最初に迎える飾り台と一体となったレセプションカウンター。
Reception counter to welcome guests.

大阪難波にある倉庫を改修し、新たに誕生した不妊治療クリニックである。
倉庫という広く天井の高い空間の持つポテンシャルを最大限に生かすため、廻りに診察ゾーンを設け中央に広いホールを配置した。
ベージュの色合いで統一されたホールは、四周を取り囲む間接光でやさしく全体が照らし出され、これらはその広さと高さを強調し、格子天井や発光するカウンター、壁面に設置された飾り棚はやさしく一様に広がる空間の中で、アクセントとしての役割を果たす。
ここで生み出された空間は、都会の喧騒の中を期待と不安をいだきながらこのクリニックにやってくるゲストに対して、心地よい安らぎとくつろぎを提供する。

This is a newly completed infertility treatment clinic by renovating an existing warehouse in Namba, Osaka.
In order to take maximum advantage of a potential offered by the warehouse with a large floor and a high ceiling, a large hall is established at the center, surrounded by examination rooms.
The beige-toned hall is lit up by the soft, indirect lighting around it, which emphasizes the area and height of the structure. The coffered ceiling, illuminating counter, and display shelves on the wall serve as accents in the gentle, uniform space.
This designed space provides guests visiting the clinic with expectations and uneasiness in the bustle and hustle of the city with the comfortable serenity and relaxation.

発光するガラスカウンター。
Illuminating glass counter.

やさしい光がまわる診察廊下。
Corridor leading to examination rooms filled with mellow light.

IVFなんばクリニック

大阪府済生会中津病院
記憶に残る
デザインの継承

Saiseikai Nakatsu Hospital
Inheriting design to remember

関西の中心梅田駅近くに位置するこの病院は、交通の便もよく都心にあるため、救急から通院患者まで様々な形で利便性が高い。設計コンセプトは、病院の顔として長年親しまれてきたレンガ造りの旧本館（設計：中村與資平）正面部分を新病院の玄関棟として復元再生し、低層部デザインへ継承することであった。

旧本館のイメージを忠実に再現するために、解体前に詳細の写真撮影、実測を行い、記念碑的な部位（マントルピース、シャンデリア、吐水口、レリーフなど）は原物を保存し復元に役立てた。現在もそのいくつかは玄関棟やメモリアルルームに組み込まれ、展示公開されている。

メモリアルルームの空間設計は、まさにそのマントルピースから始まっているといっても過言ではない。

新玄関棟のボールド天井のレリーフや彫刻などは、石膏で型取りしたものをGRCで復元、シャンデリアについても照度計画に合わせて改良修理し、一部については実測し複製を製作した。

内装材についても旧館のイメージ通り、ウォールナット材の羽目板やレンガタイルの壁面、珪藻土の塗り壁を多用し、玄関棟の木部繰型については、旧本館院長室のディテールを実測しバランスを守りながら徹底的に引用した。

最新の電子医療システムが導入されていても、愛着のある顔には変わりがない。多くの人々に親しまれ今でも記憶に残る病院として復元は必要なことであったと思われる。来院した人々は全て、この玄関棟を通って目的の場所に向うことになる。

吹き抜けに設けられた喫茶コーナーでは、誰でもコーヒーを飲み、くつろぐこともできる。

Client: Social Welfare Organization Saiseikai Imperial Gift Foundation Inc.(Osaka Saiseikai Branch)
Architect: Nikken Sekkei
Construction: Takenaka Corporation
Cooperation Designer: Kenji Yonezawa: Nikken Space Design
Location: Kita-ku, Osaka
Site area: 24,227.21 sq m
Completion: March 2002
Material: Entrance building: walnut, brick tile, diatomite, etc.
Year of original completion: 1935

旧玄関棟のデザインを踏襲した、アメニティホール。（写真：柄松 稔）
Amenity hall following the design of the old entrance building.
(Photo: Minoru Karamatsu)

外来ロビー。（写真：柄松 稔）
Lobby for outpatients. (Photo: Minoru Karamatsu)

This hospital near Umeda station at the center of Kansai area offers facilities for communication and is convenient located for a wide variety of patients from emergency ones to outpatients. The design concept was to renovate and renew the front section of the old main building (designed by Yoshihei Nakamura) made of bricks that had long been familiarized as the gateway to the hospital.

In order to adhere to and reproduce the image of the old main building, we took photographs and measured the building in details before disassembly and preserved monumental components (mantelpiece, chandeliers, spouts, and relief) for later restoration. Some of them are now incorpo-

済生会中津病院の顔として、長年親しまれてきたレンガ造りの旧本館（竣工：昭和10年（1935年）、設計：中村與資平：1880年浜松生まれ。東京帝国大学工科大学建築学科卒業。主な代表作：浜松市公会堂（1925年）、静岡市庁舎（1934年）、静岡県庁舎（1937年）等）の正面部分を新病院の玄関棟として復元再生し、低層部のデザインへと継承した。

低層の外来部門は、エスカレータ動線を兼ねた吹き抜けを中心に各診療科がわかりやすい平面構成とし、待合空間に中庭などを設けることにより、診療待ち環境の快適性に配慮した。

Old main building made of bricks as the gateway to Saiseikai Nakatsu Hospital familiarized by people for many years (completed in 1935; designed by Yoshihei Nakamura (born in Hamamatsu in 1880; graduated from Tokyo Imperial University; major works: Hamamatsu City Auditorium in 1925; Shizuoka City Hall in 1934; Shizuoka Prefecture Municipal Government Facilities)

The front section was reproduced and renewed as the entrance building of the new hospital, and the design is also reflected upon the lower part of the new building.

The low-rise part of the building serving as medical clinics for outpatients has a layout centered on the well which is also serving as escalator traffic so that the clinics should be easy to identify. A patio is established in the waiting area in consideration of comfort when outpatients are waiting.

玄関棟と雁行平面型の高層病棟。（写真：東出清彦）
High-rise ward in a staggered formation. (Photo: Kiyohiko Higashide)

旧玄関棟1。
Old entrance building #1.

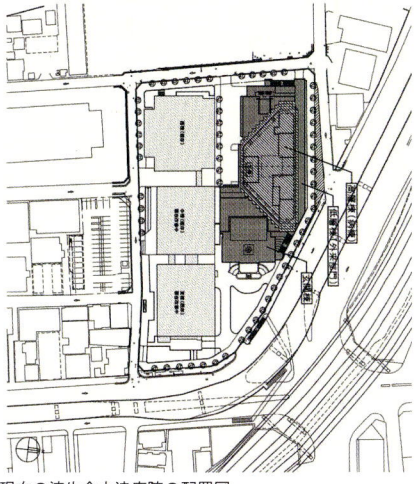

現在の済生会中津病院の配置図。
Layout plan of the current Saiseikai Nakatsu Hospital.

旧玄関棟2。
Old entrance building #2.

rated and exhibited in the entrance building and the Memorial Room open for public.

We may well say that the spatial design of the Memorial Room started with the mantelpiece.

We plaster-casted the relief, sculptures, etc., and reproduced them on the arched ceiling or installed in the new entrance building as appropriate by using GRC (Glass fiber Reinforced Cement). The chandeliers were also improved and repaired in accordance with the illumination plan. Some of them were reproduced after actual measurements.

The interior materials were also carefully selected to maintain the image of the old building. Walnut sidings, brick-tile walls, and diatomite plastering were heavily used; the wooden moldings in the entrance building were thoroughly quoted by measuring details of the director's room of the old main building and preserving the original design.

Even though the latest electronic medical systems have been introduced, the familiar appearance of the building remains the same. This restoration seems to be natural as the hospital has been loved by many people and staying in their hearts. All the visitors go through this entrance building to their destinations.

The coffee room in the well is open for everyone to have a cup of coffee and take a relax.

旧院長室のマントルピースからデザインを始めた嘉門記念館。(写真:柄松 稔)
Design of the Kamon Memorial Hall started with the mantelpiece in the old director's room.
(Photo: Minoru Karamatsu)

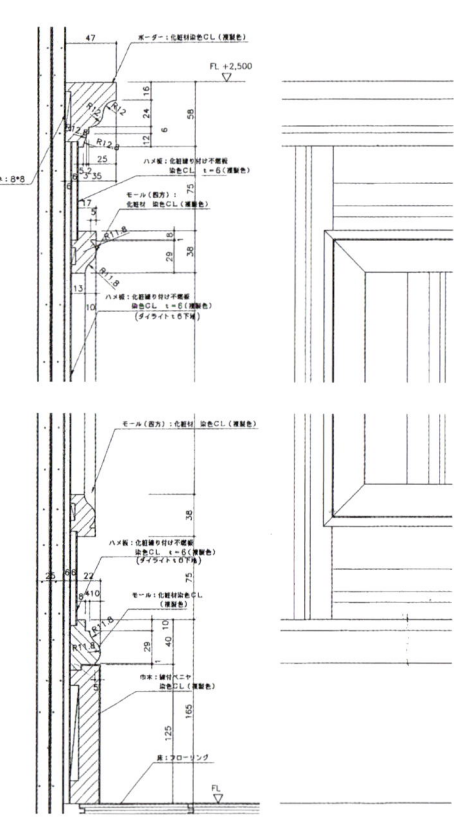

実測された旧院長室の繰型断面詳細。
Detailed section of the measured molding of the old director's room.

旧院長室。
Old director's room.

解体前に詳細の写真撮影、実測を行い、解体後も記念碑的な部位(マントルピース、シャンデリア、窓枠、吐水口、レリーフなど)は原物を保存し、復元に役立てた。
現在もそのいくつかは玄関棟の前庭や「嘉門記念館」というメモリアルルームに組み込まれ、展示公開されている。
玄関棟の木部繰型については、旧本館院長室のディテールを全て実測しバランスを守りながら徹底的に引用した。

We took photographs and measured the building in details before disassembly and preserved original monumental components (mantelpiece, chandeliers, spouts, and relief) for later restoration. Some of them are now incorporated and exhibited in the front garden of the entrance building and in the Kamon Memorial Room open for public. The wooden moldings in the entrance building were thoroughly quoted by measuring details of the director's room of the old main building and preserving the original design.

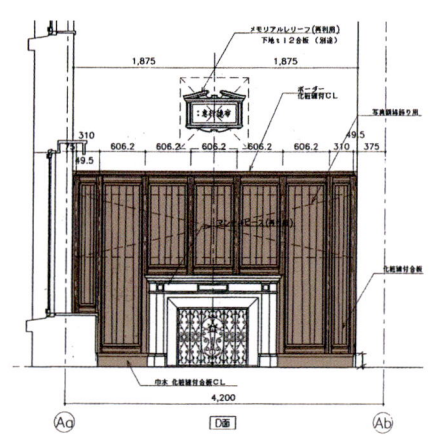

嘉門記念館のマントルピース。
Mantelpiece in the Kamon Memorial Room.

旧院長室のマントルピース。
Mantelpiece in the old director's room.

第4章 商業施設

Chapter 4
Commercial Facilities

資生堂パーラー 銀座4丁目店
記憶に残る「心の高まり」をつなぐフォルムと光

Shiseido Parlour, Ginza 4-chome Branch
Form and light to produce "the rising of emotion" to remember

明治の時代から続く「資生堂パーラー」は今でもファッショナブルな銀座のシンボルである。その歴史性を表すことと、パーラー（応接室）として独自の流麗さを保つことを目指した。賑やかな銀座通りに面した小さな扉を開いたところから、静かに階段を下り、脇のサロンを垣間見ながら席につくまでの"心の高まり"を演出しようと考えた。
仮店舗であったが7年間営業は続けられ、近年惜しまれつつ閉店した。

"Shiseido parlor" which exists from Meiji era is still a symbol of fashionable town "Ginza". Our aim in this project was to express its history and maintain its unique elegance as parlor, and to produce "the rising of emotion" in its sequence, such as opening the small door facing bustling Ginza street, walking down the stairs calmly, and finally sitting on the seat with catching the glimpse of salon on side. Though it was makeshift store, its operation lasted for seven years and closed recently with much regret. (H. Ohyama)

Principal Architect: Hisao Ohyama: Shimizu Corporation
Designer: Yoshiharu Shimura: FIELD FOUR DESIGN OFFICE
Location: Chuo-ku, Tokyo
Site area: 455 sq m
Structure: SRC
Completion: June 1997
Materials: Floor: marble and carpet
Wall: limestone and painted board
Ceiling: painted board

銀座教文館ビル（昭和8年）外観。
（写真：銀座文化史学会編集・発行／泰川堂書店発行
「震災復興〈大銀座〉の街並みから」清水組資料写真より。）
Ginza Kyobunkan Building exterior (1933).
(Photo: Ginza Cultural History Society (Ed.), "From the Townscape of Dai-ginza in the Process of Reconstruction from the Great Earthquake" (photographs from Shimizu-gumi Archives, Shinsendo Books))

銀座教文館ビル（昭和8年）内観。
（写真：銀座文化史学会編集・発行／泰川堂書店発行
「震災復興〈大銀座〉の街並みから」清水組資料写真より。）
Ginza Kyobunkan Building interior (1933).
(Photo: Ginza Cultural History Society (Ed.), "From the Townscape of Dai-ginza in the Process of Reconstruction from the Great Earthquake" (photographs from Shimizu-gumi Archives, Shinsendo Books))

ファサード。（写真：ナカサ＆パートナーズ）
Facade. (Photo: Nacása & Partners Inc.)

ボールト天井のやさしい光で迎えるエントランス。（写真：ナカサ＆パートナーズ）
Entrance welcoming guests with soft light from the vault ceiling. (Photo: Nacása & Partners Inc.)

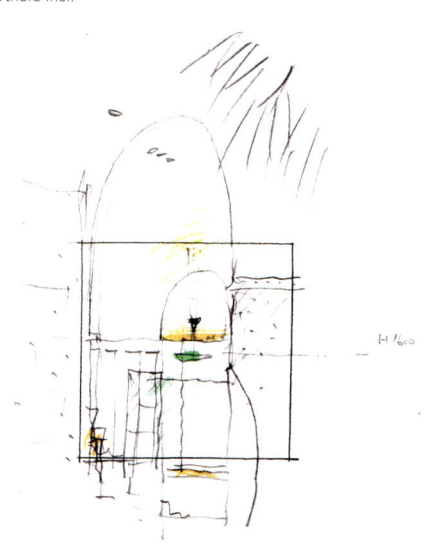

客席から見たレセプション。
（写真：ナカサ＆パートナーズ）
Reception seen from a seat.
(Photo: Nacása & Partners Inc.)

資生堂パーラー 銀座4丁目店 **113**

アプローチの途中に格子とガラスで仕切られたコンパートメントが見え隠れする。(写真:ナカサ&パートナーズ)
One can glimpse compartments partitioned by grids and glass, led to the seat.
(Photo: Nacása & Partners Inc.)

各エリアのゾーニングと空間の関わり方を検討する
コンセプトモデル(1/200)。
Concept miniature model to review area zonings and interrelations with spaces (1/200 scale).

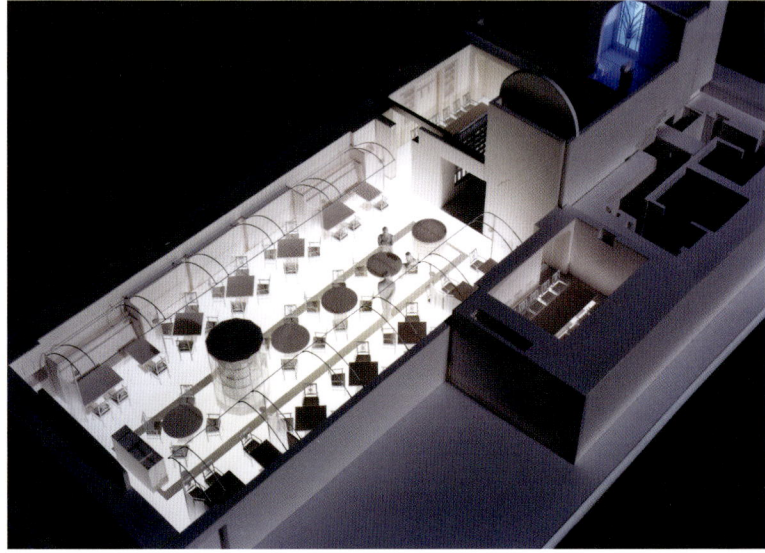

光のシークエンスを検討(1/50)。
Reviewing the light sequence (1/50 scale).

育んできた長い時間を表すために、包容力のあるフォルムと浄化された「白」を記憶の中の空間のように表現した。光が廻り込むライムストーンとイタリアンスタッコは、黒いハイバックソファーと対比して女性を美しく見せる。客席中央のガラスシリンダーは、構造柱を隠す解決法であったが、お客様同士の視線を適度にコントロールし、華やかな食事を演出するという二つの役目を果たしている。

To express the long period of time the building has passed through, an embracing form and cleansed white are expressed as if they were a space remembered. The limestone and Italian stucco works enhance contrast with black high back sofas, accentuating the beauty of women. The glass cylinder in the middle of the seats is primarily a solution to hide the structural column; however, it also modesty controls lines of sights of guests and offers a top notch dinner in a gorgeous atmosphere. (Y. Shimura)

レストラン全景。手前で数段下りるので、このシーンは突然やってくる。
（写真：ナカサ＆パートナーズ）
A general view of the restaurant: this scene appears out of the blue because one should come down several steps before that.
(Photo: Nacása & Partners Inc.)

WC。（写真：ナカサ＆パートナーズ）
W.C.. (Photo: Nacása & Partners Inc.)

客室中央にはシンボリックなガラスシリンダー。（写真：ナカサ＆パートナーズ）
Symbolic glass cylinder in the middle of the seats. (Photo: Nacása & Partners Inc.)

資生堂パーラー 銀座4丁目店 115

ポーラミュージアムアネックス
1、2階を開放した銀座の古いビル

POLA Museum Annex
An old building in Ginza renovated with a sense of openness

築45年のポーラ銀座ビルは箱根に同時期オープンしたポーラ美術館の情報発信の基点として再生された。1階は60席のカフェ、2階は講演会や催事を行なうことができる多目的スペースから成る。

天井内に隠されていたＲＣ造の構造体を露出させることによる、新旧の対比表現を試みている。

ファサード側は2階の床を撤去し吹抜けをつくり、外装はリブガラスに取り替え、青い大きな扉と黄色い壁による明るくダイナミックな空間に替っている。

仕上げには美術館の工事で廃棄処分とするはずであったコンクリート型枠の杉板を利用、光壁や家具も美術館と同じものを採用することによって、ミュージアムアネックスとしての役割を果たしている。オープンキッチンはステンレスの素材感を強調している。

外観もインテリアイメージを伝えるため、ワイド8ｍの引き戸を開け放つことで、半屋外のエントランスホールとして銀座中央通りにスタイリッシュなオープンスペースを提供している。

Client: POLA COSMETICS, INC.
Architect: Nikken Sekkei
Construction: Takenaka Corporation
Designer: Sadao Nakayama: Nikken Space Design
Location: Chuo-ku, Tokyo
Renovation area: 612.98 sq m
Completion: July 2002
Material: Cedar wooden panels for concrete form; direct ceiling, mortar floor, etc.
Year of original completion: December 1960

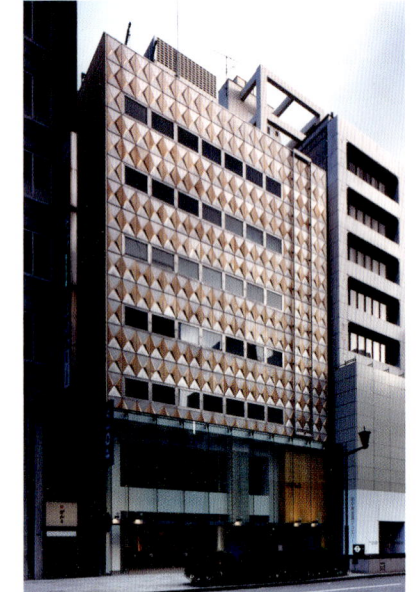

ポーラ銀座ビル。（写真：石黒 守）
POLA Ginza Building.（Photo: Mamoru Ishiguro）

ポーラミュージアムアネックス。（写真：石黒 守）
POLA Museum Annex.（Photo: Mamoru Ishiguro）

1Fカフェサロン TUNE
壁際にはゆったりくつろげるソファーとイタリアンカラーの小さなクッションが置かれている。中央には白いテーブルと椅子を配置し、カジュアルで洗練されたスペースと知的で高品位な空間が調和している。

Coffee salon on the first floor, TUNE
Comfortable sofas and small Italian-colored cushions are found by the wall while at the center are white tables and chairs, creating a harmony between the casual, sophisticated space and the intelligent, high quality space.

1Fカフェサロン TUNE。(写真:石黒 守)
Coffee salon on the first floor, TUNE. (Photo: Mamoru Ishiguro)

The 45-year-old POLA Ginza Building was renovated as the information base of POLA Museum opened in Hakone in the same period. The first floor has a 60-seat cafe terrace, and the second floor offers a multi-purpose space for lectures and events.
By exposing the RC structure once hidden in the ceiling, we attempted to emphasize contrasts between the old and new designs.
As to the facade, the existing second floor was removed to create a well, rib glass panels were employed for the external facing, and large blue doors and yellow walls contributed to give a dynamic impression.
As a finishing material, we took advantage of cedar wooden panels for concrete form that were to be disposed of during the construction work of the museum. Light walls and furniture identical to those at the museum were employed for representing the building's role as annex to the museum. The open kitchen features the stainless materials.
By opening 8-meter-wide sliding doors, the semi-outdoor entrance hall can be realized as a stylish open space for Ginza Chuo Street, enabling people to have a glimpse of the interior.

2Fアートギャラリー。(写真:石黒 守)
Art gallery on the second floor. (Photo: Mamoru Ishiguro)

三木サービスエリア

お土産コーナーから脱皮した
ベーカリーショップ

Miki Service Area
A bakery that was originally just a small souvenir shop

改修前。(写真:庄野 新/庄野 啓[フォト・ビューロー])
Before renovation. (Photo: Arata Shono / Hiraku Shono[Photo Bureau])

CGパース。
CG perspective.

リノベーションされた外観。(写真:庄野 新/庄野 啓[フォト・ビューロー])
Renovated facade. (Photo: Arata Shono / Hiraku Shono[Photo Bureau])

山陽自動車道三木サービスエリアにベイク―オフスタイル(パン専用厨房を持つショップ)のベーカリー&ケーキショップを計画する。高速道路・サービスエリア施設に求められる要素の1つは、休憩をとるために訪れた人が、短い時間で、楽しむことができることである。そのためには、初めて訪れた人にわかり易いブロックプランとしなければならない。

もともとベイク―オフスタイルのベーカリーショップが棟内の土産物コーナー奥にあったが、アピール度が低く、宝塚ホテルのパンのうまみが伝わりにくかった。そこで、ベイク―オフスタイルのベーカリーショップを建物前面に移設し、他のコーナーと離すことにより棟内外からの存在感をアピールした。また、パン厨房に大きなFIXガラスを設け活気のある厨房内を、訪れたれた人々に見てもらい、『パンのうまみ』が伝わるような焼きたてパンを売るショップとして、話題性を高めた。

It was planned to build a bakery and patissier having its own baker room at the Miki service area of Sanyo Highway. One of the requirements for highway service areas is that visitors coming to take a break can enjoy the facilities in a short period of time. For this goal, a block plan easy to understandfor visitors should be prepared.

There was a bakery at the back of the gift shop in the building; however, it was not so attractive and didn't appeal the genuine taste of bread from Takarazuka Hotel. In the renovation, the bakery with its own baker room was moved to the front of the building and separated from other shops to emphasize its presence when seen from outside. The baker room has large fixed glass so that visitors should see lively activities inside and that the good taste of bread should be appealed; the bakery became popular for its freshly baked bread.

Developer:	Hankyu Hotel Manegement Co., Ltd.
Cooperator maker:	Hankyu Seisakusyo Co., Ltd.
	Daiko Electric Co., Ltd.
Producer:	Seiichi Nakagawa: NEXT/m
Designer:	Toshinori Nisio: NEXT/m
	Mitsushi Emura:
	MHS Planners, Architects & Engineers
Location:	Miki-shi, Hyogo
Site area:	34,487.10 sq m
Building area:	1,825.597 sq m
Total floor area:	1,985.995 sq m
Renovation area:	94 sq m
Structure:	Reinforced
Completion:	March 2004
Public wall:	Wallpaper
Public Floor:	Resilient flooring

改修前のショーケース。(写真：庄野 新／庄野 啓[フォト・ビューロー])
Showcase before renovation.
(Photo: Arata Shono / Hiraku Shono [Photo Bureau])

ショーケース。(写真：庄野 新／庄野 啓[フォト・ビューロー])
Showcase. (Photo: Arata Shono / Hiraku Shono [Photo Bureau])

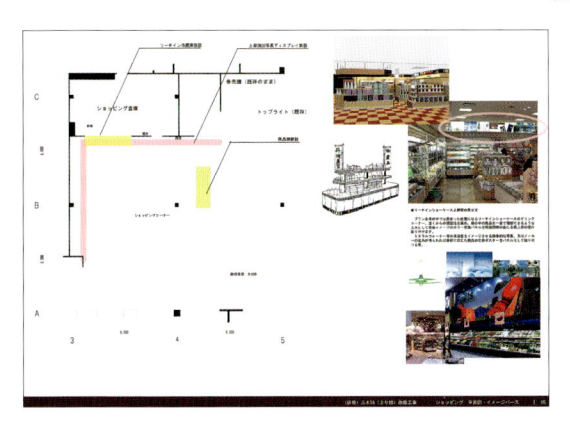

新しくなった
ベーカリー＆ケーキショップ。
(写真：庄野 新／庄野 啓
[フォト・ビューロー])
Renovated
bakery & patissier.
(Photo: Arata Shono /
Hiraku Shono
[Photo Bureau])

セラトレーディング乃木坂ショールーム
ショーウインドウに入る感覚の
ショールームつくり

CERA TRADING Nogizaka Showroom
A show room designed so that you feel as if you are entering a show window

Client: CERA TRADING CO,. LTD.
Designer: Sadao Nakayama / Noritaka Umemura: Nikken Space Design
Construction: Takenaka Corporation and Zeniya Co, Ltd.
Location: Minato-ku, Tokyo
Site area: Basement floor: 180 sq m; 1st floor: 200 sq m
Date of Completion: September 30, 2003
Year of original completion: October 1983

改修前。
before renovation.

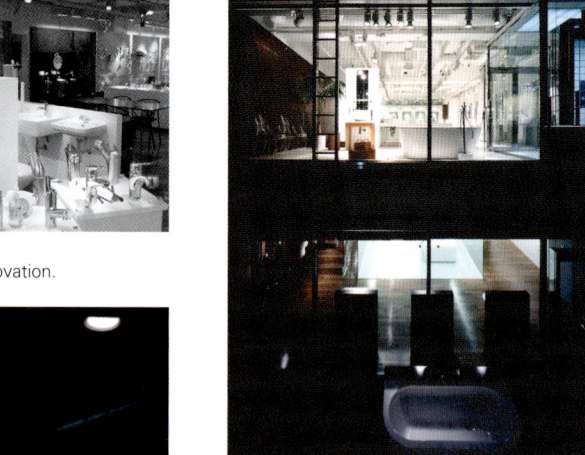

外観。(写真:ナカサ&パートナーズ)
Exterior. (Photo: Nacása & Partners Inc.)

階段(増設)。(写真:ナカサ&パートナーズ)
Stairs (extension). (Photo: Nacása & Partners Inc.)

B1 ショールーム。(写真:ナカサ&パートナーズ)
B1 Showroom. (Photo: Nacása & Partners Inc.)

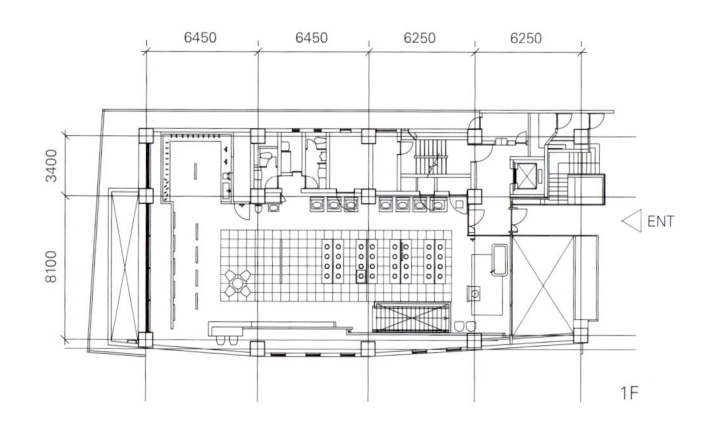

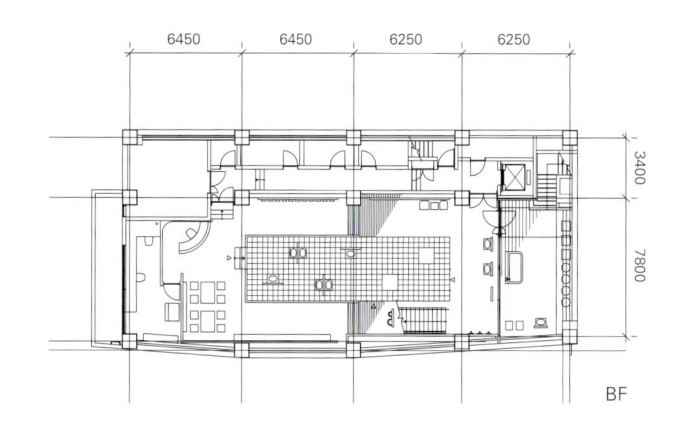

1F ショールーム。（写真：ナカサ＆パートナーズ）
1F Showroom.（Photo: Nacása & Partners Inc.）

B1 ショールーム。（写真：ナカサ＆パートナーズ）
B1 Showroom.（Photo: Nacása & Partners Inc.）

B1ドライエリア。（写真：ナカサ＆パートナーズ）
B1 Dry area.（Photo: Nacása & Partners Inc.）

B1 ショールーム ギャラリー内部。（写真：ナカサ＆パートナーズ）
B1 Showroom inside.（Photo: Nacása & Partners Inc.）

古いオフィスの1階だけにあったショールームの床の一部を撤去して階段を設置、2層のショールームとして再生した。地階にはガラススクリーンで囲われた「浮床」状のステージを設け、単なる器具の展示ではなく空間そのものを見るような環境デザイン展示を実現している。

ショーウインドウは外から眺めて楽しむものであり、ショーケースも同様である。

しかしここでは、人気の高いデザイナーズモデルとしての商品を鑑賞するのではなく、ショーケースの中に入って商品に触れ、人と商品の関わりを展示する空間を表現している。

光とガラスは空間を切り取るための透明なマテリアルとして使用し、限られた展示空間のランドスケープを開放的に間仕切っている。既存のスケルトン空間に浮かぶ光のフローティングステージ。この象徴的なショーケースは訪れる客の好奇心や高揚感を高める。

古い建物の表層を覆い隠し、新築のような空間をつくるのではなく、時を経たスケルトンと新しいインフィルの興味深い出会いを実現させている改修工事ならではの表現となっている。

The floor of the existing showroom on the first floor of the office building was partially removed to build a stairway and a two-story showroom. In the basement, a "floating floor" stage surrounded by the glass screen was built, and realized was a design display environment where one looks at the space itself, not a simple display of equipment.

Usually, one thinks that show windows are something to enjoy from outside and so are showcases.

In this showroom, however, this space offers opportunities where instead of appreciating popular designers' model products, one actually enters in the showcases and touches products, participating in the process of exhibiting relations between man and products.

Light and glass are used as transparent materials to separate the space and partition the landscape of the limited exhibition space in an open manner. The floating stage is highlighted in the existing skeleton space. This symbolic showcase stimulates curiosities and excitements of visitors.

Instead of an approach of hiding the surfaces of an old building to create a space that appears to newly be built, presented is a design expression unique to renovations where aged skeleton and new infill meet in an interesting manner.

はん亭
100年を生き抜く商家
HANTEI
Shop house surviving a century

Client: HANTEI Corporation
Architect: Unknown (original building);
　　　　　　Nikken Space Design / Studio As (renovation)
Construction: Serita Koumuten (1st to 4th phase);
　　　　　　　Mizusawa Koumuten (5th phase)
Designers: Kazuya Ura and Akiko Ura
Location: Nezu, Bunkyo-ku, Tokyo
Site area: 279 sq m
Completion: 1978 (1st phase); 2001 (5th phase)
Materials: Floor: slate; wall: citta;
　　　　　　ceiling: Japanese cedar and pine
Year of original completion: 1909 / 1917

不忍通側外観。（写真：堀内広治）
Exterior seen from Shinobazu Street.（Photo: Koji Horiuchi）

改修前の明治期に建てられた部分。
Section built in Meiji Era before renovation.

明治、大正、昭和、平成を生き抜いてきた木造商家の改築、改装。
明治42年頃、東京不忍池の奥に下駄の爪皮を商う商店ができ、主人は富を得て大正6年頃根津の町を見下ろすような三階家を建てた（最近東京都の文化財に指定された）。
商店と三階家の間には「蔵」があった。昭和の終わりになって現オーナーが三階家を入手、串揚げの店としてよみがえらせ、その後蔵部分の改修を経て表通りの店を改築し、現在にいたったという5期にわたるスーパーリノベーション。最後の改築は前面通りが拡幅されるため、建物が痛ましくも切り取られたが、法の措置に異議を唱えるように切断面を鉄格子のファサードにしている。室内は人気の串揚げ料理を供する多くの部屋から成る部分と茶房部分に分かれているが、漆、紙、木、竹、石などを適所に使って懐かしさもある日本の空間としている。時代を超えた一画は根津のシンボルとなった。

大正期の三階家と路地前。（写真：堀内広治）
3-story house facing an alley.（Photo: Koji Horiuchi）

4人席の個室、漆和紙を使用。(写真:堀内広治)
4-seat private room. Japanese lacquer paper used. (Photo: Koji Horiuchi)

三階家の1階、長円のテーブル席。(写真:堀内広治)
1st floor of the 3-story house with an oval-top table.
(Photo: Koji Horiuchi)

蔵を見る客席。(写真:堀内広治)
Seats toward the warehouse. (Photo: Koji Horiuchi)

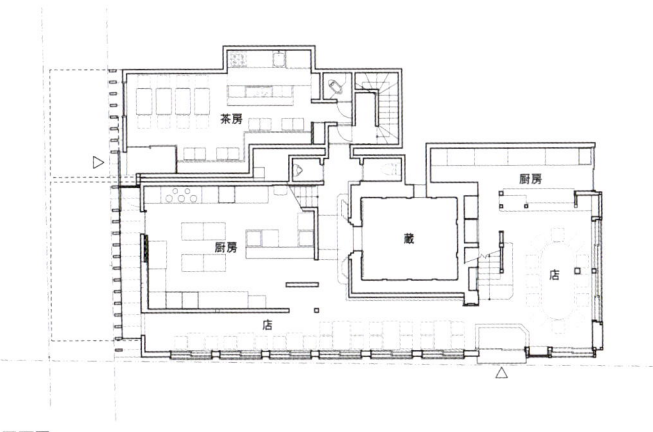

平面図。
Floor plan.

入口を別にする茶房。彩色和紙を使用。(写真:堀内広治)
Tearoom with a different entrance. Colored Japanese paper used. (Photo: Koji Horiuchi)

Renovation and renewal of a wooden shop house surviving the Meiji, Taisho, Showa and Heisei eras

In 1909, a shop selling parts of wooden clogs was opened at the rear of the Shinobazuike Pond in Tokyo, and the owner became rich enough to build a three-story house with a view of Nezu town seen below one's eyes in 1917. (The house recently has been designated cultural asset by the Tokyo Metropolitan Government.)

There was a warehouse between the shop and the three-story house. At the end of the Showa era, the present owner bought the three-story house, renovated it as a restaurant of kushiage (deep-fried delicacies on bamboo skewers). Later the owner also renovated the warehouse, then the shop facing the main street. The facility has been renovated in as many as five phases in the end.

Because of the road-widening plan, part of the building was to be cut off, to our regret. As if to raise a voice in protest, the section is covered with grid. The inside of the building are separated into the area with many rooms to serve popular kushiage and a tearoom. Japanese lacquer, paper, wood, bamboo, stone and other materials are effectively used to establish a Japanesque space. This place beyond time has become a symbol of Nezu.

上野精養軒
鹿鳴館の香りを残した
次世代レストラン

Ueno Seiyoken
Next-generation restaurant with the ambience of the Rokumeikan

Architect: Shimizu Corporation
Designer: Shimura Yoshiharu / Okubo Toshiyuki / Takita Tomomi: FIELD FOUR DESIGN OFFICE
Location: Ueno, Taito-ku, Tokyo
Site area: 7,775.83 sq m
Structure: RC
Completion: September 2003

明治のころの精養軒。
Seiyoken in the Meiji era.

改修前の外観。
Facade before renovation.

性格の違う2つの入口を明確にするため、既存グリルを利用した「光壁」の左右に、「明るい光壁」と「優しい炎」で迎えるエントランスとを創りました。
Two entrances welcoming guests with "bright light wall" and "gentle fire" were established on the left and right of the light wall taking advantage of the existing structure in order to clearly define the two entrances with different

緑を映すサイン。
Name plate reflecting the green of the surroundings.

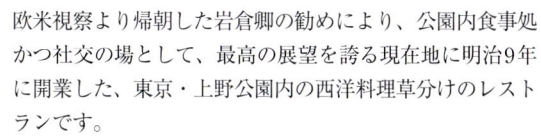

欧米視察より帰朝した岩倉卿の勧めにより、公園内食事処かつ社交の場として、最高の展望を誇る現在地に明治9年に開業した、東京・上野公園内の西洋料理草分けのレストランです。

当時は内外王侯貴族名士達が馬車で駆けつけ、鹿鳴館時代の華やかな文明開化の一翼を担う会場として栄え、現在に至るまで多くの著名人に利用されてきました。

今回の改修ではその伝統を生かし、且つ次世代を感じさせること、公園のすばらしい環境を活かすことがデザインに望まれました。

Following the advice by Tomomi Iwakura who had returned from a tour of inspection abroad, this restaurant pioneering Western cuisine in Japan was opened in the current location in 1976. It has enjoyed the best command of view in the Ueno Park as an in-park restaurant and meeting place.

Back then, Japanese and foreign aristocrats and celebrities would visit the restaurant on carriages. It was one of the main spots to help set a direction of civilization and enlightenment in the gorgeous Rokumeikan Era and has been used by many celebrities up to present.

In this latest renovation, it was desired that the design should take advantage of the tradition, gives previews of next generation, and make the most of the wonderful environment of the Park.

「優しい炎」で迎えるエントランス。
Entrance welcoming guests with "gentle fire".

エントランスロビー、正面奥に横山大観の日本画、手前は馬越寿のガラス作品。
Entrance lobby. A Japanese painting by Taikan Yokoyama at the back and a glass artwork by Yasushi Umakoshi at the front.

改修前ロビークローク。
Cloakroom in the lobby before renovation.

改修後ロビークローク。
Cloakroom in the lobby before renovation.

ロビー検討模型
Model to review the design of the lobby.

126 第4章 商業施設

1Fレストラン。風景を映しこむ壁の鏡、反射する天井が公園の緑をインテリアに取り込みます。
Restaurant on the 1st floor. The green of the park reflected on the mirrors on the wall and reflective ceiling of the room.

1Fレストランスケッチ。
Sketch of the restaurant on the 1st floor.

改修前1Fレストラン。
Restaurant on the 1st floor before renovation.

1Fレストランスケッチ。
Sketch of the restaurant on the 1st floor.

上野精養軒 127

日本料理「JAKARTA basara」
現地の建材で造る
インドネシアの日本料理店

Japanese Restaurant JAKARTA basara
Japanese restaurant built with local construction materials in Indonesia

インドネシア、ジャカルタのオフィス街で2棟のビルの間にある和食レストランの改修工事。1階に位置した約900平方メートルのスペースをモダンで明るく清潔感のあるレストランとして日本人ばかりではなく現地のVIPなどにも利用できるプランとして計画した。

和のスピリットを、ほとんどインドネシアの素材だけを積極的に使い現地のテクニックなども取り入れて、シンプルで力強いデザインとして実現させた。またジャカルタの暑さをしのぐ涼のデザインとして客席の前面に滝を設けている。また軒を低く抑えたり、すりガラスブロックの壁、透かし彫りのスクリーン、木製ブラインドなどで涼感を演出している。家具なども色を使わず、白のレザー張りでシンプルにまとめている。

シンボルでもある中央の真っ赤な「かまど」は日本の職人が製作にあたった。またジャカルタでは少ないガラス張りのワインセラーは200本を収納できる。

客席奥には天井に昇降式のミラーを取り付けて現地の人たちと料理教室などができるようにしている。

VIP用の個室は入口を一般客席とは別途に設けて、安全性を確保している。インテリアはそれぞれ外光の取り入れ方を変えてコロニアル調、モダン調、和調とイメージを変えてデザインしている。

Client: Pt. Summitmas Property＋
Sumitomo Corporation Building Business Dept.
Construction: Pt. Jaya Obayashi
Designer: Setsuko Ando: Nikken Space Design
Location: Jakarta, Indonesia
Site area: About 900 sq m
Completion: July 2001
Material: Various materials (wood, stone, etc.) procured locally
Year of original completion: 1985

エントランス。
Entrance.

改修前エントランス。
Entrance before renovation.

This project was for renovation of a Japanese restaurant located in between two buildings in Jakarta downtown, Indonesia. It was planned that about 900-square-meter space should be renewed to be a modern, clean restaurant that serves not only the Japanese but also local VIP's.

The Japanese spirit was realized as simple and strong design by mostly using Indonesian materials and utilizing local architectural techniques. By way of airing in the heat of Jakarta, a waterfall is provided in front of the guest seats. For extra coolness, employed are such devices as low eaves, frost glass block walls, fretwork screens, and wooden blinds. No color is used for furniture, and a simple color scheme by white leather upholstery is adopted.

The red Kamado (Japanese kitchen stove) at the center serving as symbol of the restaurant was hand-made by a Japanese craftsman. The glass wine cellar not often found in Jakarta can store up to 200 bottles of wine.

The private rooms for the VIP's have an exclusive entrance for security. Their interiors have different approaches to bring in natural light, resulting in different impressions: colonial, modern and Japanese.

メイン客席。
Main guest area.

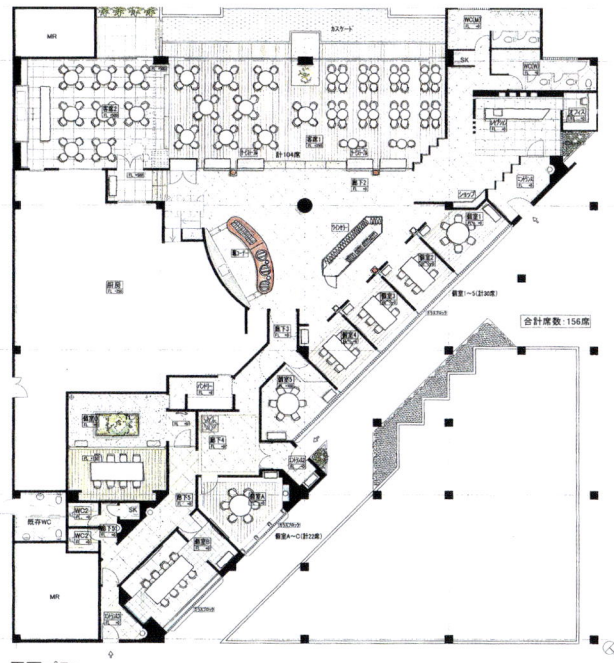

平面プラン。
Floor plan.

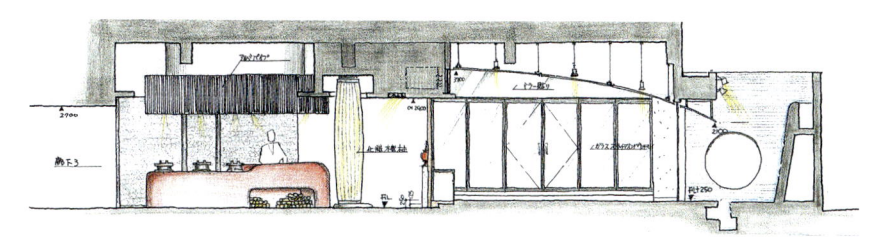

現地でよく見られる「透かし彫り」をアクセントにした個室。
Private room accentuated by locally popular fretworks.

個室。
Private Room.

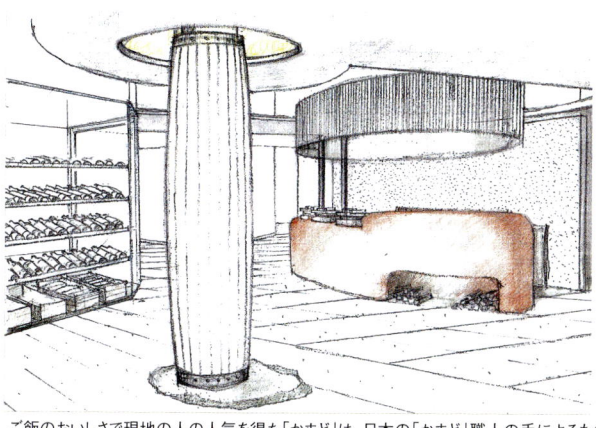

ご飯のおいしさで現地の人の人気を得た「かまど」は、日本の「かまど」職人の手によるもの。
Kamado (Japanese kitchen stove) that has become popular for tasty rice cooking was made by a Japanese kamado craftsman.

竈（かまど）コーナー。
Kamado corner.

日本料理「JAKARTA basara」

宝塚ホテルケーキショップ

新しさと伝統が
組み合わされたケーキショップ

Takarazuka Hotel Cake Shop
Cake shop combining modernity and tradition

大阪・梅田の百貨店内にある、創業1926年の老舗のケーキショップのリノベーションを計画。

ケーキショップと言えばデパ地下の代表の1つであるが、今回のショップは地階ではなく1階のメインストリートから少し外れた位置にあった。

しかし、こだわり続けた味とネームブランドが出来上がっていたので、デザイナーとしては宝塚ホテルのケーキのおいしさを多くの人に伝わるようにデザイン表現することが重要であった。

インテリアイメージとしては、新しさと宝塚ホテルの持つ伝統との融合を基本コンセプトとし空間創りを行った。

ホワイトを基調とし清潔感・明るさを表現、部分的にヴェンゲ材を使用し、空間に高級感と、老舗のイメージをもたらした。

昼間でも少し暗く感じる場所にあったため壁に光壁を設け、離れた場所からもショップが目に飛び込んでくるように工夫した。

Renovation of the long-established cake shop opened in 1926 was planned in a department store in Umeda, Osaka.
Every cake shop is one of the most popular spots in the food section in the basement of department store, but the one subject to renovation was located on the first floor, a little away from the main aisle.
As it already had an established taste and a renowned brand, it was important for the designer to express the good taste of Takarazuka Hotel bread in design to appeal to many guests.
As to its interior image, the basic concept of integrating modernity with Takarazuka Hotel's tradition was set up for spatial design.
The color of white was chosen as the predominant color to express an impression of cleanliness and brightness, and partially used wenge color brought a sense of quality and tradition to the space.
As the location gave a little dark impression even in the daytime, a wall with built in lighting was built to attract eyes to the shop even in a distance.

アートもディスプレー。（写真：庄野 新／庄野 啓[フォト・ビューロー]）
Arts are part of displays. (Photo: Arata Shono / Hiraku Shono[Photo Bureau])

Developer:	Hankyu Hotel Manegement Co., Ltd.
Cooperator maker:	Hankyu Seisakusyo Co., Ltd.
	Daiko Electric Co., Ltd.
Producer:	Seiichi Nakagawa: NEXT/m
Designer:	Toshinori Nisio: NEXT/m
	Mitsushi Emura: MHS Planners, Architects & Engineers
Location:	Kita-ku, Osaka
Renovation area:	30 sq m
Structure:	reinforced concrete
Completion:	Marchi.2004
Public wall:	Wallpaper
Public Floor:	Resilient flooring

改修前。（写真：庄野 新／庄野 啓[フォト・ビューロー]）
Before renovation. (Photo: Arata Shono / Hiraku Shono[Photo Bureau])

新しさと伝統が融合されたケーキショップ。（写真：庄野 新／庄野 啓［フォト・ビューロー］）
Cake shop with integrated modernity and tradition. (Photo: Arata Shono / Hiraku Shono [Photo Bureau])

イメージ提案。
Image proposal.

CGパース。
CG perspective.

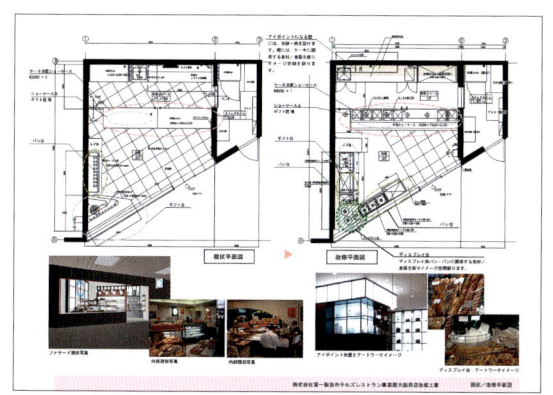

平面図。
Floor plan.

ケーキケースのCGパース。
CG perspective of the cake showcase.

宝塚ホテルケーキショップ 131

ヴァンドーム青山 銀座並木通り店

ショーケースにも
アイデンティティを求めた路面店

VENDOME AOYAMA Ginza Namiki-Dori
Street-level shop with even showcases having

有名ブランドが建ち並ぶ銀座並木通りの既成ビルの1Fにヴァンドーム青山では初めての路面店がオープンした。
ヴァンドーム青山では、2000年を期に従来の店舗デザインを一新し、プレステージの高いファッションエリアへの進出を図っている。
インテリアデザインコンセプトは「クリアー・リニアー・ストライプ」とし、ステイタスアップのキーワードとした。カラースキームはライムストーンの「アイボリーベージュ」「ダークブラウン」にシンボルカラーの「ブルー」を加え、透明感があり落ち着いた色合いの中に「ブルー」が光る上品な空間とした。
素材は、柔らかい表情を持つマイクログラスクロスを挟んだ合わせガラス、アイボリーのペイント、ライムストーン、ブナとヴェンゲの持つ木の肌などで構成しヴァンドーム青山のヴィジュアルアイデンティティを打ち出した。

The first VENDOME AOYAMA street-level shop was opened on the first floor of an existing building on the Ginza Namiki Dori Street having many brand shops.
Since 2000, VENDOME AOYAMA fully renewed the shop designs and has tried to enter the prestigious fashion market. The interior design concept was "clear, linear stripe" which also served as keyword for upgrading. The color scheme was based on ivory beige and dark brown of the limestone, accentuated with the brand symbol color of blue. The shop thus became a decent and elegant space where the color of blue is highlighted in the transparent and chic texture.
The materials used included laminated glass with micro-glass cloth, ivory paint, limestone, and Japanese beech and benge having chic wood texture to emphasize the visual identity of Vendome Aoyama.

Client: VENDOME YAMADA CORP.
Construction: Sogo Design Co., Ltd.
Designer: Risa Misawa: Nikken Space Design
Location: Chuo-ku, Tokyo
Site area: About 69 sq m
Completion: June 2000

写真：馬場祥光
Photo: Baba Yoshiteru

プランスケッチ。
Plan sketch.

改修前（別テナント）。
Before renovation (different tenant).

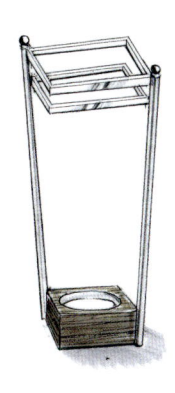

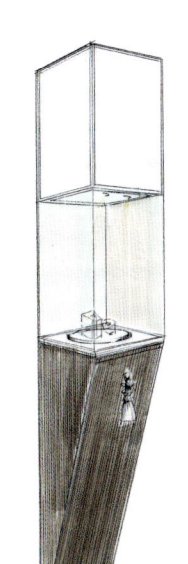

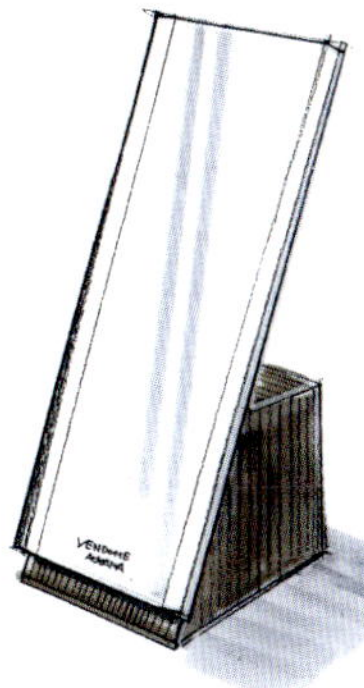

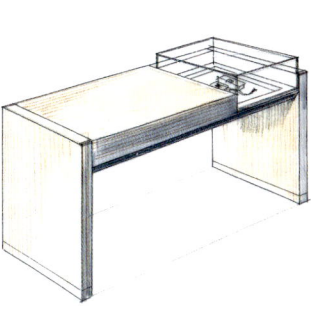

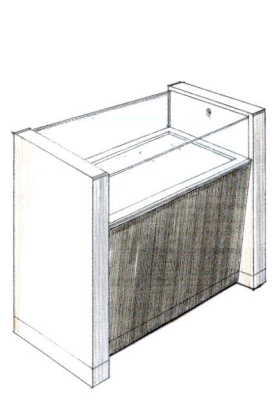

什器、小物スケッチ。
Sketches of fixtures and small articles.

店舗内。(写真：馬場祥光)
In the shop. (Photo: Baba Yoshiteru)

店舗内。(写真：馬場祥光)
In the shop. (Photo: Baba Yoshiteru)

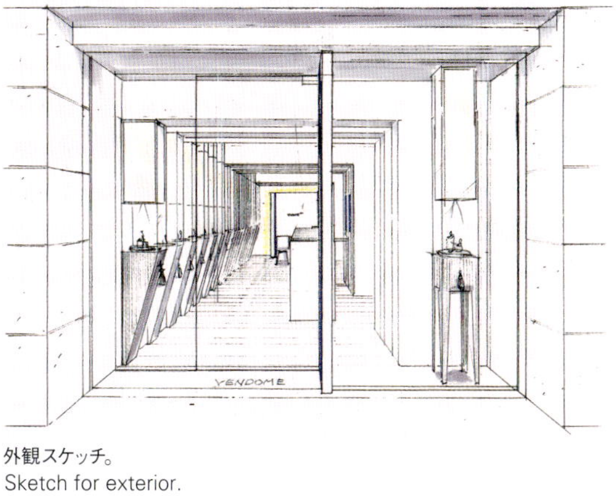

外観スケッチ。
Sketch for exterior.

メインのショーケース。(写真：馬場祥光)
Main showcase. (Photo: Baba Yoshiteru)

ヴァンドーム青山 銀座並木通り店 133

MOVIX本牧
家族で楽しめる非日常空間

MOVIX Honmoku
Non-ordinary space for families

5Fロビー。(写真:岡田和紀)
Lobby on the 5th floor. (Photo: Kazuki Okada)

MOVIX本牧は、元々は全く違う会社により運営されていたシネコンである。だが、運用会社が変わったのを機に、新たなイメージを作り、より良いサービスを提供する地元に根ざした映画館となるために、改修を行うこととなった。改修内容は、劇場内・ロビーに渡り、劇場内においては座席・スクリーン・音響を取替え、より良い状態で映画を楽しめるようにした。また、ロビーにおいては内装の仕上げを一新し、これまでとは全く違ったイメージを作り上げている。

MOVIX Honmoku was a cinema complex managed by another company. When the management company was changed, it was decided to renovate the facility in order to create a new image, provide better service and become a movie theater based on the local community.
The renovation covered inside the theater as well as its lobby. For the theater, seats, screen and sound system were renewed for better and more comfortable movie appreciation experience. The interior of the lobby was also refurbished, giving a totally refreshed image of the facility.

Developer:	Syoutiku Co., Ltd.
Architect:	MHS Planners, Architects & Engineers
Designer:	Koji Yoshihara
Location:	Honmokuhara, Naka-ku, Yokohama-shi, Kanagawa
Site area:	2,504.32 sq m
Building area:	2,095.72 sq m
Total floor area:	8,626.00 sq m
Structure:	SRC
Completion:	October 2004
Material:	Public Wall : Vinyl Wall Covering
	Public Floor : Carpet Tile

5Fロビー/グラフィック。
Lobby on the 5th floor(graphics).

5Fロビー／天井画詳細イメージ。
Lobby on the 5th floor (detailed image of the ceiling painting).

5Fロビー／天井画・グラフィック。（写真：吉原浩司）
Lobby on the 5th floor(ceiling painting/graphics). (Photo: Koji Yoshihara)

5Fロビー／天井画イメージスケッチ。
Lobby on the 5th floor(image sketch).

5Fロビー。（写真：岡田和紀）
Lobby on the 5th floor. (Photo: Kazuki Okada)

5Fロビー。（写真：吉原浩司）
Lobby on the 5th floor. (Photo: Koji Yoshihara)

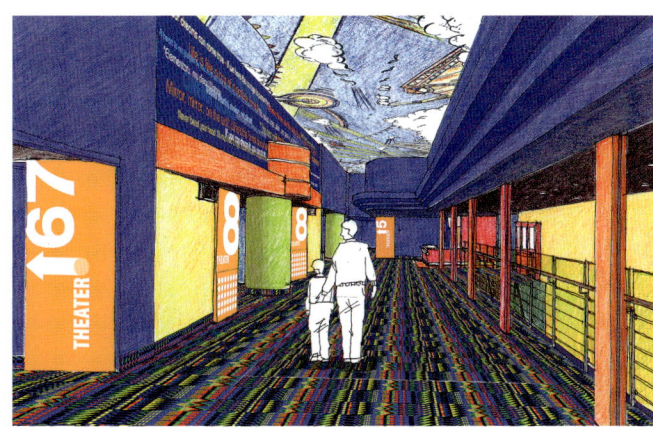

5Fロビー／イメージパース
Lobby on the 5th floor(image perspective drawing).

5階ロビーにおいては、抽象的に地元の横浜を描いた天井画と、映画のセリフをランダムに配置したグラフィックにより、現実と映画の世界を結ぶ、非現実世界を作り出している。

The lobby on the 5th floor offers a non-ordinary space to link the reality and the world of movies, taking advantage of abstract ceiling painting of the city of Yokohama and graphics randomly decorated with lines from movies.

MOVIX本牧 135

改修前（3Fロビー）。
Before renovation (lobby on the 3rd floor).

3Fロビー／イメージパース。
Lobby on the 3rd floor (image perspective drawing).

ロビーのイメージは、これまでの運用経験を踏まえた上で、地元住民の家族連れをイメージターゲットとした「家族で楽しめる非日常空間」をコンセプトとし、計画された。
コンセプトを実現化するにあたり、仕上げのみを一新する今回の計画においては、カラーリングを重要な要素として捉えて計画している。特に色彩計画においては、女性や子供に受け入れられる華やかな色使いをこころがけ、はっきりとした色相により、きらきらとしたハレの舞台を作り出している。

Based on the past management experience of the facility, the lobbies were conceived to become "non-ordinary spaces for families" mainly targeted for local family audience of the theater.
In implementing the concept, the project was to refurbish finishes only, and thus, coloring was one of the critical factors. In color planning, emphasis was on the bright and flamboyant colors appealing to females and children, and the clear color tone created beaming non-ordinary spaces.

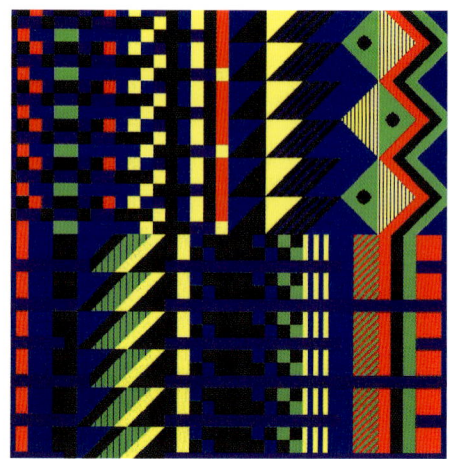

カーペットパターン。
Patterns of the carpets.

サイン計画イメージ。
Sign system (image).

3Fロビー／コンセッション。
（写真：岡田和紀）
Lobby on the 3rd floor (concession).
(Photo: Kazuki Okada)

3Fディスプレイスペース／イメージパース。
Display space on the 3rd floor (image perspective drawing).

3Fチケットセンター。（写真：岡田和紀）
Box office on the 3rd floor. (Photo: Kazuki Okada)

3Fチケットセンター。（写真：岡田和紀）
Box office on the 3rd floor. (Photo: Kazuki Okada)

2Fエントランス／イメージパース。
Image perspective drawing of the entrance on the 2nd floor.

5Fロビー／イメージパース
Lobby on the 5th floor (image perspective drawing).

MOVIX本牧 137

世界貿易センタービル スカイホール
超高層トップの
ウエディング・バンケット改修

SKY HALL, WORLD TRADE CENTER BUILDING
Renovating a wedding banquet hall at the top of the skyscraper

婚礼と会議をターゲットとした宴会施設を持つスカイホールの共用部が新しくリニューアルオープンした。浜松町の世界貿易センタービルの最上階エリアにあり、各宴会場は、それぞれ360度の東京の景色を独り占めできる施設。
施設の婚礼をターゲットとしたコンセプト「ペントハウスウエディング」に合わせ、2年間にわたって、38階の共用部通路を中心に改修が行われた。天井高が低いデメリットを、光の演出やカラースキームで効果を上げることに成功している。
エレベータホールにはポイントとなるウエルカムフラワーの台、シルバーリーフの額縁や、光を仕込んだフラワーボールをあしらい、落ち着きのある心地よさを演出した。

The public area of SKY HALL having banquet facilities targeted for bridal services and conferences are renewed and re-opened. The facilities are located at the top of WORLD TRADE CENTER BUILDING in Hamamatsucho, and each banquet room offers a panorama view of Tokyo.
Along with the new concept of "penthouse wedding" targeted for wedding ceremonies and parties to be carried out in the facilities, the renovation for a period of two years was carried out mainly focusing upon the common corridors on the 38th floor. Careful lighting arrangements and color scheme could overcome the disadvantage that overall ceiling height was low.
In order to augment a sense of comfort and serenity, a table for welcome flower, silver-leaf frame, and self-illuminating flower bowl are arranged in the elevator hall.

（写真：馬場祥光）
(Photo: Baba Yoshiteru)

改修前の38F通路。
Passageway on the 38th floor before renovation.

Client: WORLD TRADE CENTER BUILDING, INC.
Designer: Risa Misawa / Noritaka Umemura / Takayuki Nago: Nikken Space Design
Lighting design: Work Techt Corporation
Construction: Sogo Design Co., Ltd.
Location: Minato-ku, Tokyo
Site area: About 550 sq m
Construction period: August 2003 to August 2004

EVホールのウエルカムフラワー。訪れるたびに違った顔で出迎えてくれる。
Welcome flower in the elevator hall, always showing a different face to visitors.

スケッチ。
Sketch.

「PENTHOUSE WEDDING」の顔として心地よさを演出している38Fのエレベータホール。(写真:馬場祥光)
Elevator hall on the 38th floor to comfort guests as gateway to penthouse wedding ceremonies. (Photo: Baba Yoshiteru)

通路

デザインのポイントとしては、全体の色調にコントラストを効かせ、光に重点を置き、シンプルでモダンな大人っぽいペントハウスをつくり上げている。38階から39階をつなぐ階段部分は、既存の構築物をそのまま利用し、元からあったシャンデリアを取り除き、大きなアートミラーを置くことにより、階段を大きく包み込むような空間が生まれた。トイレは、小スペースをいかに効率よく、広く見せるかという点に重点を置き、開放感を大切にしている。

Passageway

As the keys of designs, the total texture is highly contrasted, and light is emphasized, resulting in a simple, modern, adult-oriented penthouse. The existing structure is used for the stairway between the 38th and 39th floors; by removing the existing chandeliers and installing a large art mirror, a space to embrace the stairs is provided with a sense of expansion. In designing bathrooms, emphasis was on how to efficiently make small spaces appear wider as well as how to give a sense of openness.

38階と39階を結ぶ階段。
Stairway to connect the 38th and 39th floors.

待合ロビーの大きなミラー額縁。(写真:馬場祥光)
Large framed mirror in the waiting lobby.
(Photo: Baba Yoshiteru)

トイレ前の通路。(写真:馬場祥光)
Corridor in front of the bathroom.
(Photo: Baba Yoshiteru)

トイレの内部 (写真:馬場祥光)
Inside the bathroom. (Photo: Baba Yoshiteru)

38F通路。(写真:馬場祥光)
Passageway on the 38th floor. (Photo: Baba Yoshiteru)

3階婚礼サロンのエントランス。(写真：馬場祥光)
Entrance to the bridal salon on the 3rd floor. (Photo: Baba Yoshiteru)

改修前（テナントエリアとして使用されていた）。
Before renovation (used as a tenant area).

婚礼サロン

38階にあった婚礼サロンと衣装室機能が3階に移転、天井照明はビル基準のものを残すことが条件の中でアクセント照明を追加し、バランスを整えた。長時間の婚礼の打合せにも充分なゆったりとしたスペースを用意した。

Bridal salon

The bridal salon and dressing room were moved from the 38th floor to 3rd floor. On the condition that the standard ceiling lighting of the building should be used, we carefully designed the lighting in a good balance. The spaces roomy enough for long bridal meetings are provided.

婚礼サロンエントランスのスケッチ。
Sketch of the entrance to the bridal salon.

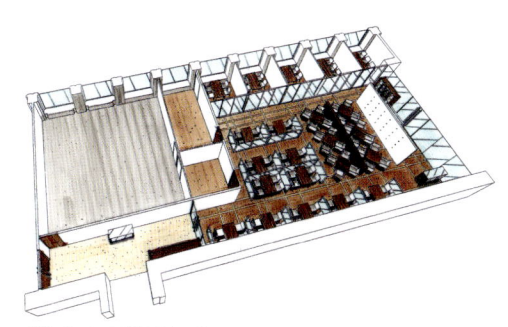

婚礼サロン内部のスケッチ。
Sketch of the interior of the bridal salon.

3階婚礼サロン。(写真：馬場祥光)
Bridal salon on the 3rd floor. (Photo: Baba Yoshiteru)

浜松町東京會舘「チェリールーム」、「天山」
夜景もリノベーションのエレメント

Hamamatsucho Tokyokaikan
Night view is another element of renovation

39階にあるチェリールーム（写真：馬場祥光）
Cherry Room on the 39th floor. (Photo: Baba Yoshiteru)

CGによる光の演出の検討。
Reviews of lighting using computer graphics.

39階改修前のチェリールーム。
Cherry Room on the 39th floor before renovation.

39階チェリールームの窓面演出。
Dressing of windows of Cherry Room on the 39th floor.

Client: Tokyo Kaikan
Designer: Risa Misawa / Noritaka Umemura / Takayuki Nago: Nikken Space Design
Lighting design: Work Techt Corporation
Construction: Sogo Design Co., Ltd.
Location: Minato-ku, Tokyo
Site area: About 410 sq m
Construction period: From August 2003 to August 2004

浜松町東京會舘の宴会場、39階「チェリールーム」、38階離宮飯店内「天山」が、リニューアルオープンした。
これはビルオーナーである世界貿易センタービルディングのスカイホールの通路改修計画の一環として行われ、会議にも婚礼にもレストランとしても対応できる演出が求められた。
コンセプトは「シック＆エンターテイメント」。最大の売りである東京のパノラマ、なかでもこの二部屋はともに東京タワーを借景とし、その景色と窓側の演出を大切にした。チェリールームでは、内照式の光の柱とカーテンに対して下から染め上げるカラーチェンジが可能なLEDを採用し、天山では、カーテンへの演出、柱にはマグネットで脱着可能なアートフレームによる演出、通常考えられる天井での照明演出を窓面や壁面へ移した。また天井は、シャンデリアを取り除き、グレアレスDLを採用、天井の圧迫感を消した。ドラマチックな演出から、フォーマルな会議まで対応できる宴会場として生まれ変わった。

写真：馬場祥光
Photo: Baba Yoshiteru

38階改修前の天山。
Tien Shan on the 38th floor before renovation.

38階にある天山。（写真：馬場祥光）
Tien Shan on the 38th floor. (Photo: Baba Yoshiteru)

柱型のアートフレームは脱着が可能。
Removable column-type artframes.

Cherry Room on the 39th floor and Tien Shan banquet room in Rikyu restaurant on the 38th floor of Hamamatsucho Tokyo Kaikan were renewed and opened.

The renovations were part of passageway renewal of the sky hall by the owner of the building, World Trade Center Building, and designs that can handle both conferences and wedding parties were required as restaurants.

The concept was "chic & entertainment". The biggest feature of these restaurants is a panorama of Tokyo. Especially, these two rooms can take advantage of Tokyo Tower as borrowed landscape, and careful attention has been paid to how to use it effectively in design.

Cherry Room now has light columns with internal lighting system and LED's that can change colors and illuminate curtains upwards; Tien Shan is dressed using curtains, removable artworks on the wall using magnets, and installation of lighting equipment on the walls or by the windows in place of normal ceiling-mount approach. By removing chandeliers and employing glareless DL's, a sense of oppression by the ceiling was removed. The renovated banquet halls can handle a variety of uses from dramatic ceremonies to formal conferences.

浜松町東京會舘「チェリールーム」、「天山」

MOKUZAI.com
インフィルは全て商品

MOKUZAI.com
All the infills are products

Producer: Seiichi Nakagawa: NEXT/m
Designer: Yoshiharu Shimura / Eriko Izitsu: FIELD FOUR DESIGN OFFICE
Marketing Planner: Toshie Suzuki
Graphic Designer: Shinichi Otake
Location: Shinjuku-ku, Tokyo
Site area: 58 square meters
Completion: Jun. 2004
Materials: floor; wood
wall; wood panel

改修前。
Before renovation.

日本人の暮らしの中から、ホンモノが少なくなって久しい。リビングデザインの為のショールームで構成された新宿のビルの一角に2004年春、MOKUZAI.comがオープンした。「無垢材」にこだわり続け創業50年の木材メーカー'マルホン'の質の高い素材を、ユーザーがいかに料理をすれば自分の生活の中に取り入れていけるのか、その接点を見出せるショールームが必要であった。
このショールームは空間そのものが「商品」である。ユーザーの潜在ニーズを引き出す為に例えば建材、家具、その間を繋ぐものなど個々の感性の中で自由に発想を膨らませていける仕掛けが施されている。木という環境の中にユーザーを置くことで無垢材であるが故の温かさ、優しさ、力強さを感じさせる。
そのためにネタである「無垢材」を、極力素朴なディテールでありながらもインパクトのあるプロポーションで見せる事を考えた。
また、ショーケースとストックヤードという必要な二つの要素を分離することなく、その間に1枚の透明ガラススクリーンを立てることにより、むこう側に存在する本社とのコミュニケーションをデザインで表現した。

サンプルウォール。持ち帰って検討できるサンプルがつまった別名おみやげウォール。（写真：川澄建築写真事務所）
Sample Wall or wall of souvenirs full of samples to take back home and review. (Photo: Kawasumi Architectural Photograph Office)

It has been long since it became difficult to find real and true things in our daily lives, but now we have MOKUZAI.com opened in the spring of 2004. This building in Shinjuku has many showrooms for living design.

Maruhon Inc., a timber manufacturer with a history of 50 years, has focused on the solid natural wood and needed a showroom to communicate with users and to indicate how they could introduce quality materials into their lives.

This showroom space itself is a product. In order to uncover potential needs of users, there are many devices enabling them to freely inflate their images based on their personalities and individual character, by taking advantage of, for example, timbers, furniture, and things to link them found in the showroom. In an environment called wood, users can experience warmth, gentleness and strength unique to solid natural wood.

For the goal, it was designed to present solid natural wood materials with very simple details and in an impact-filled proportion.

Further, instead of separating two indispensable factors of showcases and stockyard, a single transparent glass screen was erected in between to represent communications between the showroom and the headquarters beyond through design.

ベンチ側面。1つの樹種で仕上た床、壁、ベンチ、天蓋は、取替えが可能なディテールになっている。
（写真：川澄建築写真事務所）
Side view of the bench: the floor, wall, benches and the canopy are finished with a same type of wood material and can fully be replaced.
(Photo: Kawasumi Architectural Photograph Office)

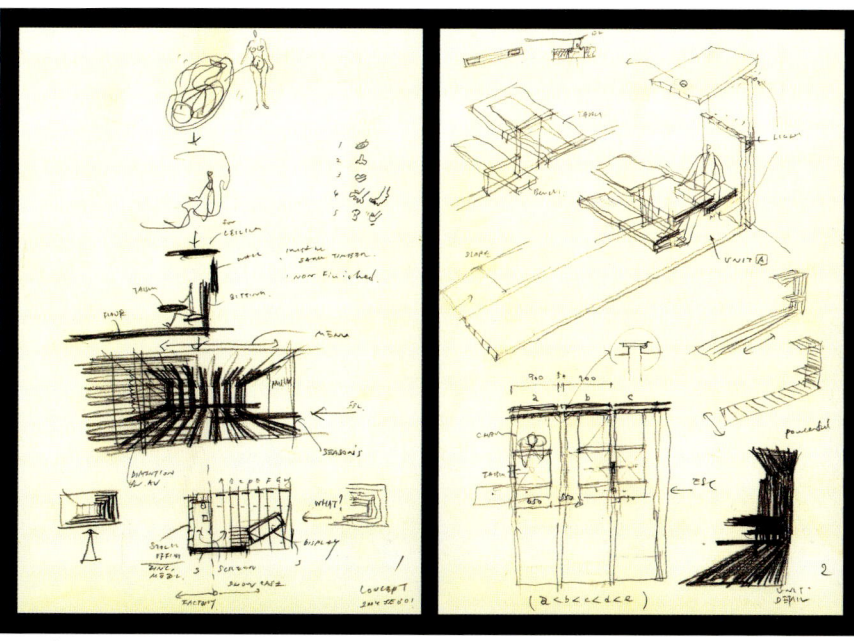

コンセプトスケッチ。ユーザーの感性に働きかける空間とは、五感に作用する空間。
それは例えば、母の胎内に包み込まれているような感覚。
Conceptual sketch: the space to appeal to sensitivity of users means that stimulating five senses. It is like being in the mother's womb.

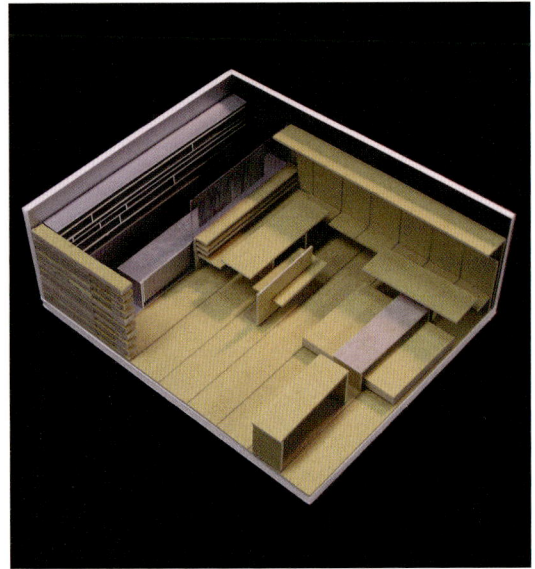

コンセプトモデル（1／100）。
Conceptual model (1／100 scale).

ブールを近景に。イベント展示のブール、
素材そのものを見せることによって
ユーザーの潜在ニーズを引き出す。
（写真：川澄建築写真事務所）
Event exhibitions 'BOULE' (Log):
hands-on experience of materials to
explore users' potential needs.
（Photo: Kawasumi Architectural Photograph Office）

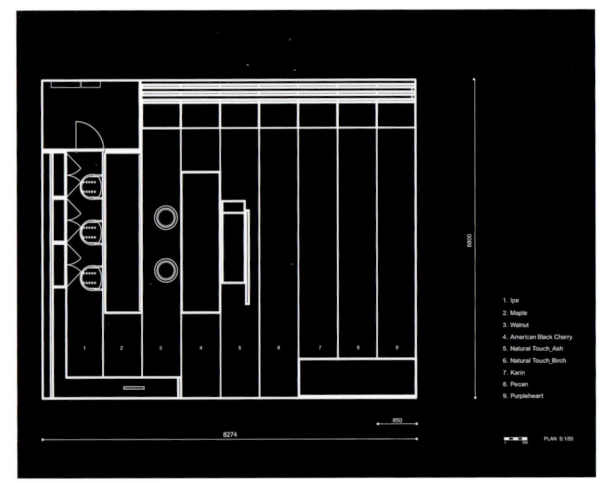

プラン、エレベーション。
Plan and elevation.

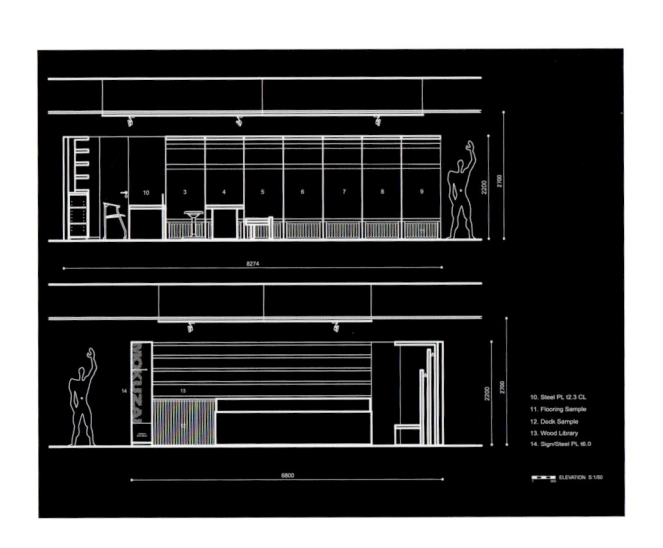

ショールーム全景。正面は木のライブラリー。（写真：川澄建築写真事務所）
View of the showroom: Wood material library at the back. (Photo: Kawasumi Architectural Photograph Office)

スクェアサンプルベンチ正面。約130種類のスクェアサンプルが用意されており、引き出してみることができる。（写真：川澄建築写真事務所）
Front of the square sample bench: available are bout 130 kinds of square samples to pull out and examine. (Photo: Kawasumi Architectural Photograph Office)

スカイビルレストエリア
リラックス&リフレッシュスペースに リニューアル

The restroom of Yokohama Sky Building
Renewal to create a relaxing and refreshing space

Owner: Yokohama Sky Building Co., Ltd.
Designer: Yuji Kobayashi / Ai Narai: Mec design International Corporation
Location: Takashima, Yokohama-shi, Kanagawa
Site Area: 7,614 sq m
Building Area: 6,321 sq m
Renovation Floor Area: 10F-54.9 sq m 11F-66.5 sq m
Structure: SRC structure / S structure
Renovation Completion: 10F: March 2005, 11F: December 2004
Materials: 10F: Ceramic tile; special paint, 11F: ceramic tile; steel metallic paint

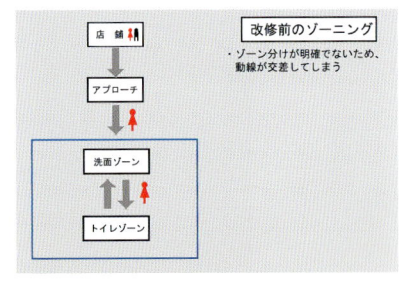

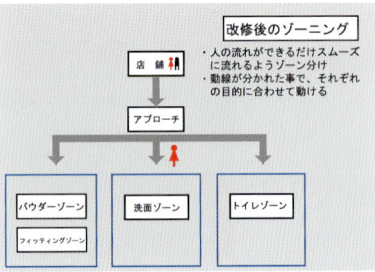

10F、11F改修前の写真。
10th and 11th floors before renovation.

街中の喧騒やビルの雑踏の中あるいは公園など、どんな場所でもトイレは必要不可欠なものである。トイレは街の中で開放されたオアシスとなる。
そのオアシスが安心して自己解放できる場所であるには、〈安全・清潔・快適〉を主に追求した。
この横浜に建つスカイビルの改修計画のトイレは飲食店フロアにあたり、利用頻度が高く老朽化が早いため、店舗改装に合わせリフレッシュする必要があると考えられた。
今回は女性客のニーズを徹底的に調査し、必要な設備・環境づくりを提案した。
人々の感性「見る・聴く・嗅ぐ・触れる・味わう」つまり五感に訴えるような楽しみの場・非日常空間の提供を追求し、人々に感動を与えるトイレづくりを目指した。
また、お客様がより安全に、より便利に、よりくつろげるレストスペースとしてフロア毎にテーマ性を持たせデザインした。

Whether we are in the hustle and bustle of the town, in crowds in the building, or alone in the park, we need restrooms; they can be oases open to public in town.
In order to let users feel safe, secure and relaxed in such oases, we mainly pursued safety, cleanliness and comfort.
The restrooms of Sky Building built in Yokohama and subject to renovations were on the restaurant floors; as they were frequently used and quickly aging, their renewal along with restaurant renovations was planned.
We made a thorough investigation on female users' needs and duly proposed necessary facilities and environments.
Our target was to create a place of enjoyment or an extraordinary space appealing to the people's five senses of seeing, hearing, smelling, touching and enjoying and establish restrooms that give strong impressions on the people.
Further, the rest room on each floor is designed with a specific theme so that it should be safer, more convenient, and more relaxing for users.

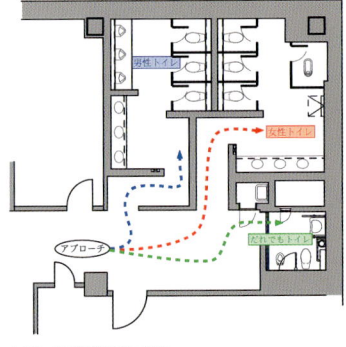

10F、11F改修前プラン。
Plans of 10th and 11th floors before renovation.

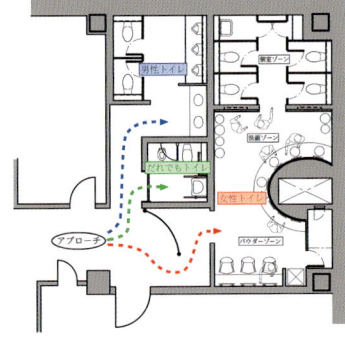

10F改修後プラン。
Plan of 10th floor after renovation.

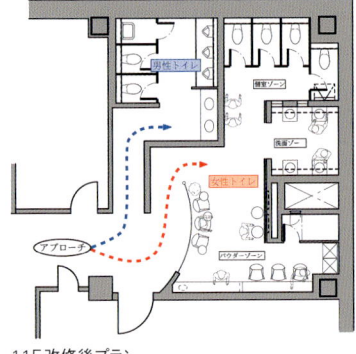

11F改修後プラン。
Plan of 11th floor after renovation.

148 第4章 商業施設

10Fコンセプトシート。
Concept sheet of the 10th floor.

内部を期待させる様なアプローチ。
Approach to raise expectations for the interior.

葉脈と風景が映し出されたモニターが埋め込まれた壁面。
Wall with an embedded monitor showing leaf veins and landscapes.

洗面台を兼ねた柱は花のグラフィックシートと生花で癒しを表現。
Lavatory-column decorated with graphic and real flowers to express its healing quality.

椅子とドライヤーを完備した落ち着ける化粧コーナー。
Comforting dressing corner equipped with a chair and drier.

自然は人々の心を癒し、花や植物などは女性の心を暖かく和ませる効果がある。デザインコンセプトとして大地の風や花の香りを感じてもらうため、草原の中の花畑をイメージし、緑を基調に、空間の中心となる楕円の柱に花を散りばめた。
カラー：グリーン……心と体の癒しの色。精神が安定。ホワイト……明るくすがすがしい気持ちになる。ピンク……優しい気分、女性らしい仕草になる。
モチーフ：花……眺めているだけで癒しの効果がある。花からもらうエネルギーで疲れた心がリフレッシュされる。
アロマ：オレンジ……甘い香りが気分を明るくし幸福感を与える。スプリングタイム……お花畑を連想させる鮮やかな香り。
ミュージック：ヒーリングミュージック……鳥のさえずり。

Nature heals the hearts of the people, and flowers and plants are capable of relaxing hearts of women. As part of the design concept to enable users to imagine breezes and scent of flowers, green is selected as the basic color, and flowers are painted on the oval columns as the focus of the space based on the image of flower garden in the field.
Color: Green: Healing the heart and body ; stable mind. White: Cheerful and refreshing Pink: Sympathetic feeling ; feminine gestures.
Motif: Flowers: Just seeing them heals; flowers give us energy to refresh our tired hearts.
Aroma: Orange: Sweet smell to cheer us up and make us happy Springtime: Fresh smell inspiring a flower garden.
Music: Healing music and songs of birds.

木目調とシンプルなタイルを組み合わせた男子トイレ。
Men's room with a combination of wood-grain and simple tiles.

内部を期待させる様なアプローチ。
Approach to raise expectations for the interior.

LED照明とモニターが埋め込まれた壁面。
Wall with embedded LED lighting and monitor.

椅子とドライヤーを完備した落ち着ける化粧コーナー。
Comforting dressing corner equipped with a chair and drier.

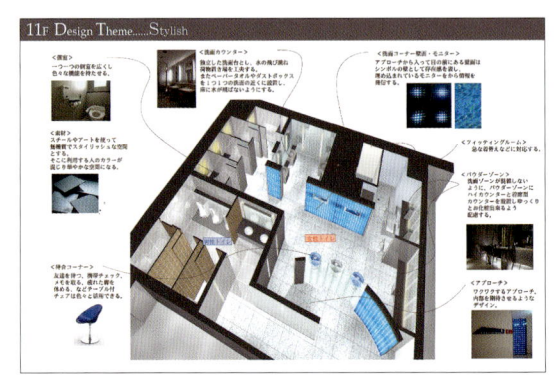

11Fコンセプトシート。
Concept sheet of the 11th floor.

モノトーンで無機質な空間は、より自分の存在を際立たせると共に、自分自身に色（化粧・衣装）をつけることで、引き立ち華やかになり、自信がつくようになる。
カラー：ブルー……物事に集中し、落ち着いて行動できる。グレー……気分が和らぐ。
モチーフ：ライト……目標。道しるべ。
アロマ：ホライゾン……都会的で清涼感に溢れた香り。ミーティング……目の覚めるようなシャープな香り。
ミュージック：シネマミュージック。

The monotonous and non-organic space highlights the presence of oneself, and by applying colors to oneself (cosmetics and costumes), one will feel confident about oneself. The message from the line illumination is the spirit to achieve the goal, and the uniform LED illumination in blue represents infinite magnificence of nightscape and stars in the sky.
Colors: Blue: Concentration and calm attitude. Gray: Relaxation.
Motif: Light: Targets; guideposts.
Aroma: Horizon: Urban and refreshing scent. Meeting: Sharp and stimulating scent.
Music: Cinema music.

第5章 クラブ施設

Chapter 5
Private Club Facilities

日本工業倶楽部会館

都心に建つ歴史的建築物の
保存再生

The Industry Club of Japan
Preservation and renovation of a historic building in the city center

Developer:	The Industry Club of Japan bldg.
Designer:	Mitsuo Iwai / Kazukiyo Sato / Ryoichi Imaeda: Mitsubishi Jisho Sekkei Inc. Masashi Teramoto / Yoko Iino: MEC Design International Corporation
Location:	1-4-6 Marunouchi, Chiyoda-ku, Tokyo
Structure:	SRC structure; RC structure
Completion:	February 2003
Materials:	Floor: parquetry; walls: plaster, gypsum, marble; ceiling: plaster, gypsum
Exterior Wall:	Exterior wall: porcelain butt end tile (western wall: stonewall tile), granite (white granite), terracotta

施工当時の外観。
Exterior after completion.

建築のあゆみ

日本工業倶楽部は、当時の実業家たちの交流施設として、1920年（大正9年）に竣工した。設計は横河工務所。古典、ゼセッションとアメリカ高層建築様式の融合とされる会館のファサードは松井貴太郎、当時の経済界の明るさを反映した華美に溢れるインテリアは鷲巣昌が担当している。

竣工後まもない1923年（大正12年）の関東大震災では甚大な被害を受けた。その後、柱の補強、耐震壁の増設などの震害補修工事を経て、80年の間建物は維持されてきたが、近年老朽化が著しく、外装タイルの剥離、建物の不等沈下、設備の陳腐化など、会館の管理には多くの労力と資金が必要となり、また、耐震性にも問題があるため、1998年、日本工業倶楽部は隣接ビルと共同での一体開発を決定した。

History of the building

The Industry Club of Japan was completed in 1920 as a meeting place for industrialists. The building was designed by Yokogawa Komuten while its facade regarded as an integration of the secessionism and American skyscraper style was by Kitaro Matsui and the grand interior reflecting the business circle in a sparkling atmosphere in the era was results of joint design efforts by Akira Washizu.

It was badly damaged by the Great Kanto Earthquake in 1923, soon after its completion. A series of repair works including reinforcement of columns and additions of antiseismic walls has been applied to the building; however, it has been deteriorated in recent years, and such troubles as external tile delamination, differential settlement of the building, and obsolescence of facilities, requiring a great amount of labor and cost of maintenance. Further, the aseismicity of the structure was insufficient. In 1998, the Industry Club of Japan decided to redevelop the area as a joint project with the neighboring building.

大ホール。躯体および壁の石の彫刻、石膏彫刻はすべて保存された。天井はスラブ補強、防災・設備機器工事を施した上で再現されている。
（写真：ナカサ＆パートナーズ）
Large hall. The skeleton, stone sculptures on the walls, and plaster figures are all preserved. The ceiling is reproduced after experiencing slab reinforcement as well as disaster prevention and equipment works.
(Photo: Nacása & Partners Inc.)

改修前の大ホール。
Large hall before renovation.

改修方針の模索

計画を進めるにあたり、各方面から寄せられた会館保存の要望に応え、日本工業倶楽部は会館の歴史的価値を明らかにすること、歴史継承について多角的視点から検討することを目的に『歴史検討委員会』（学識者・行政・事業者・設計者により構成）の設置を日本都市計画学会に依頼した。

『歴史検討委員会』では「意匠性の歴史的価値」、「構造と安全性」、「事業性と諸制度」の3つの視点から存続の可能性が議論された。建物の意匠には、内外観ともに大正期を象徴する形式が見られ、継承するだけの価値があると認められた。しかし、構造面では全面的な補強が欠かせないため、活用可能な諸制度と事業性を検討し、最も適した保存・再現の範囲を絞り込み、最終的に「建物の3分の1を保存し、残りは再現（古材利用）して躯体更新・免震は全面に施す」方法が採られるに至った。

Studies of renovation policies

Before implementing the project, people from all branches of society requested for preservation of the building. For the purpose of clarifying the historical values of the building and reviewing the possibility of maintaining its history for future in different perspectives, the Club requested the City Planning Institute of Japan to establish a Historical Review Committee (comprising of scholars, government officials, constructor, and designers).

In the committee, possibilities of the continuation of the building were discussed from three perspectives: historical values of the design; structure and safety; and business profitability and various systems that could be utilized. Both interior and exterior designs of the building were concluded that they had reasonable values for continuation; however, in terms of structure, full-scale reinforcement was indispensable. Various systems and profitability of the project were reviewed, and a range of optimized preservation and reproduction was narrowed. In the end, an approach to preserve one-third of the building and renew the rest (by using the existing building materials) with the building frame updated and antiseismic measures fully adapted.

2階来賓室。家具、シャンデリアは既存品をリフォームして利用。（写真：ナカサ&パートナーズ）
Guestroom on the 2nd floor. The existing chandeliers were reformed and used.
(Photo: Nacása & Partners Inc.)

1階広間。木製建具はすべて保存。（写真：ナカサ&パートナーズ）
Hall on the 1st floor. All the wooden fittings were preserved. (Photo: Nacása & Partners Inc.)

3階大ホール天井工事。再現の漆喰は下地共すべて新規材であるが、石膏彫刻は古い塗装を剥がした後、シリコンで型を取り、正確に再現している。
Ceiling work of the large hall on the 3rd floor. Though the plaster and its substrate were new, plaster figures are exactly reproduced by removing the old paint and molding with silicon.

1F
- 玄関
- 広間
- クローク
- 会館部受付
- 正面大階段
- エレベーターホール

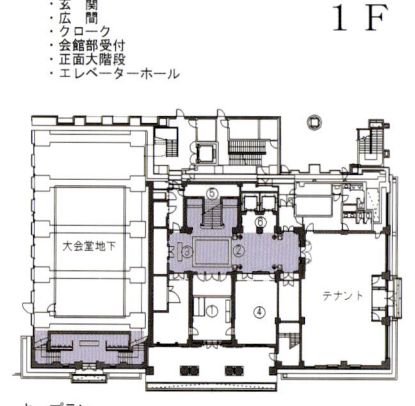

2F
- 大会堂（103坪）
- 役員会議室（15坪）
- 来賓室（15坪）
- 特別会議室（15坪）
- バー＆ラウンジ（40坪）

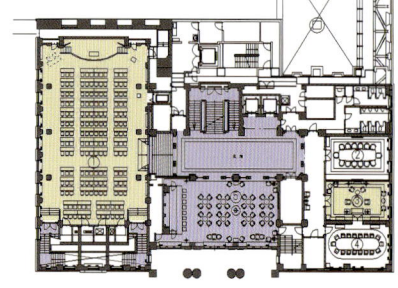

3F
- 大ホール（113坪）
- 中ホール（44坪）
- レストラン（60坪）

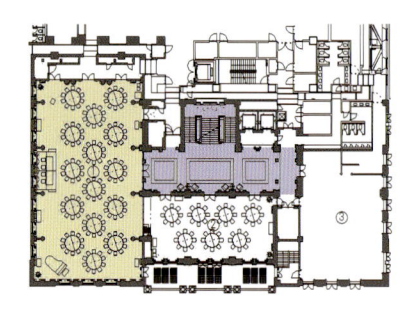

キープラン。
Key plan.

2階大会堂。大ホールと同じく躯体、壁面の仕上げ共保存された。(写真：ナカサ&パートナーズ)
Large assembly hall on the 2nd floor. As was the case with the large hall, its skeleton and wall finish were all preserved. (Photo: Nacása & Partners Inc.)

3階広間工事。
Hall renovation on the 3rd floor.

2階広間解体風景。
Disassembly of the hall on the 2nd floor.

- 第一会議室（20坪）
- 第二会議室（17坪）
- 第三会議室（17坪）
- 第四会議室（40坪・3分割可）
- 和 室（10坪）
- 和食堂（20坪）

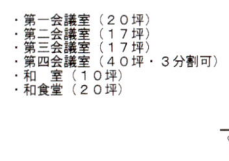

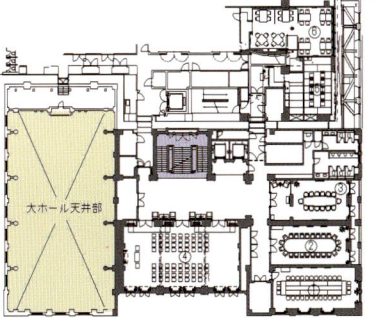

4F

- 第五会議室（19坪）
- 第六会議室（41坪・3分割可）
- 第一～五小会議室（各10坪）
- 医 局
- 理髪室
- 撞球室

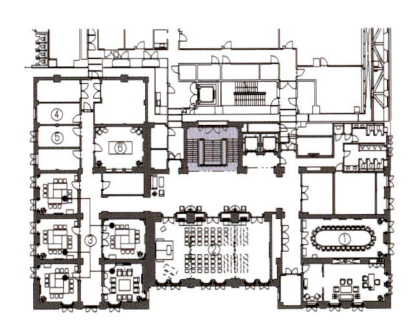

5F

キープラン。
Key plan.

日本工業倶楽部会館 155

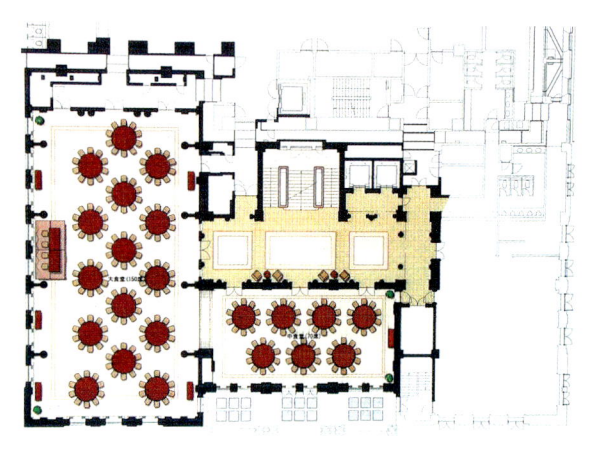

3階レイアウト。
3rd floor layout.

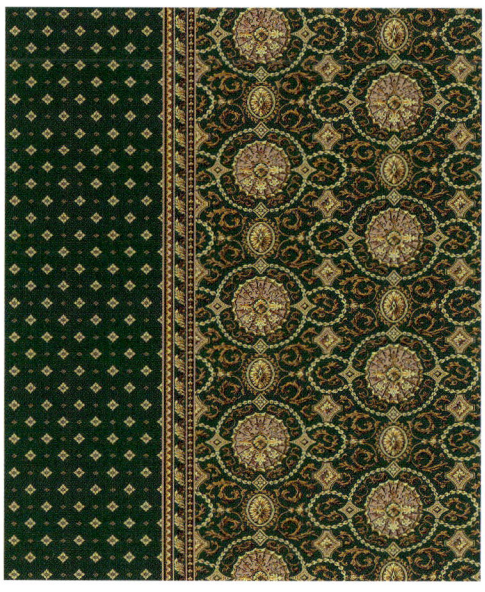

カーペットデザイン画。
Carpet design.

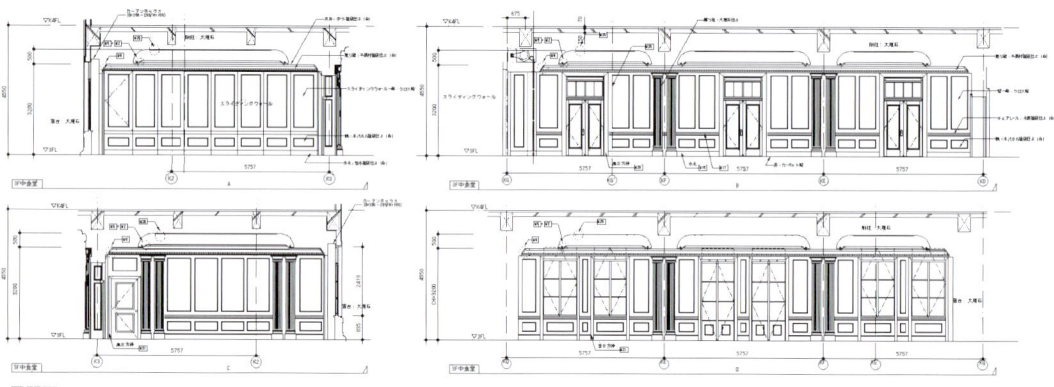

展開図。
Developed view.

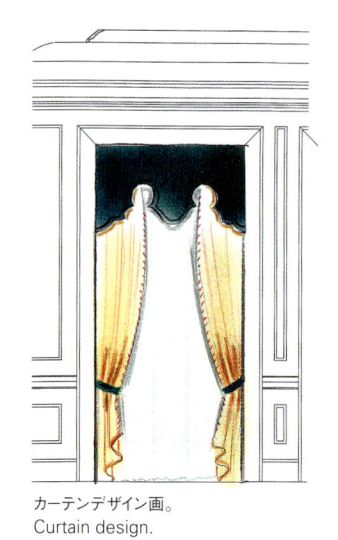

カーテンデザイン画。
Curtain design.

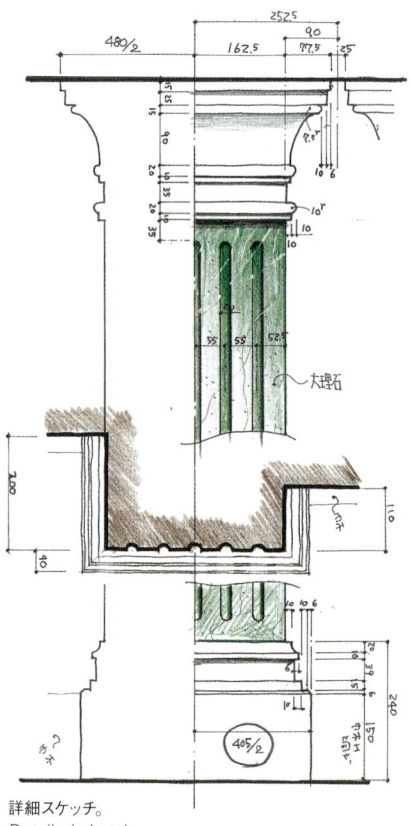

詳細スケッチ。
Detailed sketch.

カラースキームボード。
Color scheme board.

156　第5章　クラブ施設

スケッチ。
Sketch.

改修前の中ホール。
Medium-sized hall before renovation.

3階中ホール。隣接する大ホール（保存）のデザインに準じた内装。
（写真：ナカサ＆パートナーズ）
Medium-sized hall on the 3rd floor. The interior is based on that of the adjacent large hall（preserved）.
(Photo: Nacása & Partners Inc.)

5階広間。3階広間までの再現範囲のデザインと同時代の様式を採用。(写真:ナカサ&パートナーズ)
Hall on the 5th floor. Maintaining the design style reproduced for the halls on the 3rd floor or below. (Photo: Nacása & Partners Inc.)

2階広間。木製建具はすべて保存。(写真:ナカサ&パートナーズ)
Hall on the 2nd floor. All the wooden fittings were preserved. (Photo: Nacása & Partners Inc.)

倶楽部建築としての再生

歴史的街並み保存の観点から、外観については通りに面した大部分を残すことになった。

内部は歴史的なインテリアのシークエンスを重視し、1階玄関ホールから大階段を経由して3階までの各階広間、2階ラウンジは再現、2階大会堂、3階大食堂（大ホール）の空間は完全保存した。

保存・再生エリアのインテリアについてはカーペット・家具・シャンデリア等の老朽化が激しく、再利用が困難であると判断されたため、一部を除いてFF&Eの更新が必要となった。竣工当時の写真資料や原状のインテリア空間を調査し、更新の方向性を探った。

その結果、アダム様式を基軸とし、インテリア及びFF&Eの設計を進めた。4階、5階の機能を更新した宴会室及び会議室はアダムと前後するジョージアン期のスタイルを取り入れ、4階はヴィクトリアン様式、5階はリージェンシー様式でインテリア全体がまとめられた。

こうして日本工業倶楽部は単なる保存・再生ではなく、倶楽部会館としての機能を備えたままで今後も使い続けられていくことのできる建物として再生した。

Rebirth of the Club building

In view of preserving the historical townscape, most of the exterior facing the streets were to be preserved.

As to the interior, emphasis was on the sequence of the historical interior, and thus, halls between the hall on the first floor and the third floor via large stairway as well as the lounge on the second floor were reproduced while the big hall and the dining hall (large hall) on the third floor were completely maintained as-is.

It was judged that carpets, furniture and chandeliers in the preservation/rehabilitation areas were too obsolete to be reused; it became necessary to update FF&E with a few exceptions. We reviewed the photographs and documents at the time of completion and the current status of the interior spaces and examined the direction of renovation.

Based on this, it was decided that the interior and FF&E design should be based on the Adam style. The halls and the meeting rooms on the 4th and 5th floors to have new functions incorporate the Georgian style while the 4th floor interior is in the Victorian style, and the 5th floor showcases the Regency style interior.

Through this design approach, the renewed Industry Club of Japan was completed not as a simple preservation or renovation project. Instead, keeping its function as a clubhouse, it now serves as a building that can fully be utilized in future.

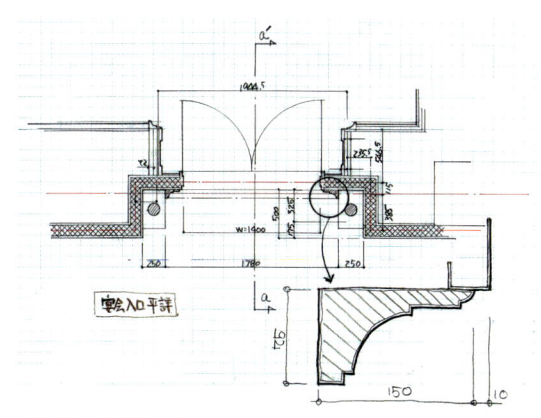

5階広間。平面詳細スケッチ。
Hall on the 5th floor. Detailed floor plan.

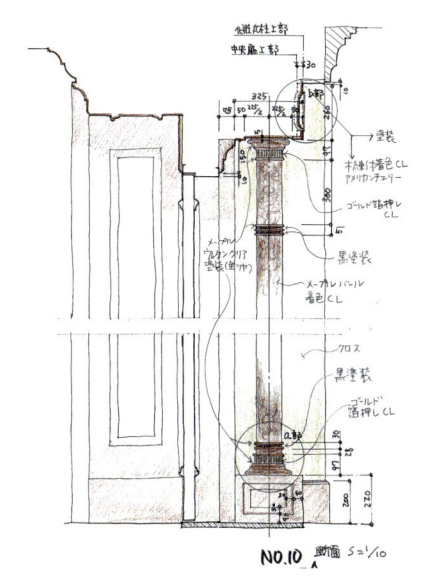

5階広間。展開詳細スケッチ。
Hall on the 5th floor. Detailed developed view.

3階広間。（写真：ナカサ&パートナーズ）
Hall on the 3rd floor. (Photo: Nacása & Partners Inc.)

4階広間。3階までの再現範囲のデザインと同時代の様式を採用。（写真：ナカサ&パートナーズ）
Hall on the 4th floor. Maintaining the design style reproduced for the halls on the 3rd floor or below. (Photo: Nacása & Partners Inc.)

交詢社倶楽部
光の密度が綾なす
知の空間デザイン

The Kojunsha Club
Space design of intelligence compiled by density of light

デザインの基本姿勢

このプロジェクトの目指したもの、それは70年前に建築された倶楽部建築の一部保存、再生、そして新築である。こうした保存建築に求められるものの最も重要なことのひとつが、空間脈絡における連続性である。原設計者の感性を尊重しつつ現代に生きる建築としなくてはならない。しかしながら全てを原設計の仕様と同一にし、復元することが真の保存ではない。その時代に即した再構成や、補強さらに新規機能が求められる。だからこそ、その建物は今までにもまして価値が高まることとなる。その意味で「保存と再生」とは「破壊を伴った創造行為」と言うことがいえなくも無い。

Principal Design Concept

The initial goal of the project was partial preservation, rebirth, and new construction based on the clubhouse architecture of 70 years ago. One of the most important aspects of the architectural preservation is the continuity of context in its space. The sense of the architect who designed the former building must be respected while the architecture must exist in the modern period.

We do not consider complete preservation and restoration as true preservation. We must consider reconstruction, restructuring, and the realization of contemporary functions to meet the needs of the times. The architecture must achieve a higher value. And by this, it can be said that "preservation and rebirth" is "creation with demolition". ―H. Ohyama

象徴的なチューダー・アーチ。（写真：清水建設）
Symbolic Tudor arch of gate. (Photo: Shimizu Corporation)

Concept CG.

新しいデザインの図書室。（写真：ナカサ＆パートナーズ）
Newly designed Library. (Photo: Nacása & Partners Inc.)

Owner:	The Kojunsha Club
Principal Architect:	Hisao Ohyama / Shimizu Corporation
Architect:	Kazuhide Sakai / Shimizu Corporation
Designer:	Atsushi Uchida / Field Four Design Office
Location:	Chuoh-ku Tokyo
Site Area:	2,054.020 sq m
Building Area:	1,878.460 sq m
Club Floor Area:	9F / 1,868.460 sq m, 10F / 1,603.752 sq m
Structure:	S, RC
Exterior Finish:	Double skin ceramic printed glass grazing
Interior Finish:	Ceiling / Wood and Painted board
	Wall / Wood and Acrylic stucco
	Floor / Wood and Carpet

交詢ビルディング（平成16年）。（写真：清水建設）
Kojun Building (2004).
(Photo: Shimizu Corporation)

旧交詢ビルヂング（昭和4年）。（写真：清水建設）
Former Kojun Building (1929).
(Photo: Shimizu Corporation)

ゲストとの歓談に使われる、新しいデザインのさろん。左側は新しい外装ダブルスキン、右側は移築した張出窓。（写真：ナカサ＆パートナーズ）
Newly designed Salon for meeting with guests. Left window is new double skin glass glazing. Right bow window is preserved parts. (Photo: Nacása & Partners Inc.)

新しいデザインの大食堂。ステンドグラスの窓とシャンデリアは移築されたもの。（写真：ナカサ＆パートナーズ）
Newly designed Main Dining Room. The stained glass window and chanderers are preserved parts. (Photo: Nacása & Partners Inc.)

新たにデザインした倶楽部空間

かつての倶楽部内装に用いられた素材や仕上とその意図を丹念に参照した上で、単なる再現ではない、現代における最適なデザインを求めた。
マコレ材の深いアメ色、マイスターの手仕事の痕跡をとどめる塗壁のテクスチャー、時間をかけて浸透するオイルフィニッシュ。チューダー様式の典型的なモチーフとしての、天井や壁、扉、面格子、カーペット柄にいたるまで倶楽部空間全体に秩序を与えるグリッドデザイン。外光、輝度の高いシャンデリア、硬い直接光、拡散反射光、透過光の使い分けが生みだす深い陰影。こうして、かつての倶楽部内装とのデザインの連続性を形づくっていった。

Newly Designed Clubhouse Space

We carefully examined the materials, finishes, and the intentions of the former club interior, not to reproduce it, but to identify the most suitable design concept for the present day. The depth of the light brown color of Makore wood, the texture of plaster walls that leaves the marks of the artisan's hand works, and the oil finish to penetrate deeper and deeper over time are key elements.
The grid pattern motif of the Tudor Style gives the clubhouse space an order of widely set-in ceilings, walls, doors, lattice, and carpeting. The proper use of various light such as outer light, the brilliancy of the chandelier, direct light, softly reflected light, and transmitted light creating deepness of shadow exist. Thus, we aimed to build a continuity of space from the interior design of the former clubhouse.—A. Uchida

新しいデザインの理事会議室。（写真：ナカサ＆パートナーズ）
Newly designed Board Meeting Room. (Photo: Nacása & Partners Inc.)

大食堂のスケッチ。
Sketch of Main Dining Room.

新しいデザインの中食堂。（写真：ナカサ＆パートナーズ）
Newly designed Smaller (sized) Dining Room. (Photo: Nacása & Partners Inc.)

新しいデザインの酒場。旧ビルヂングのチューダー・アーチの一部を飾っている。（写真：ナカサ＆パートナーズ）
Newly designed Bar. The art is a part of former building's Tudor Arch. (Photo: Nacása & Partners Inc.)

保存・復元した、談話室。（写真：ナカサ＆パートナーズ）
Preserved Member's Lobby.（Photo: Nacása & Partners Inc.）

保存・復元した、トップライトのある中庭。
Preserved Center Court with skylight.

移築された中庭のパーツ。（写真：ナカサ＆パートナーズ）
Preserved parts in Center Court.（Photo: Nacása & Partners Inc.）

移築された受付のパーツ。（写真：ナカサ＆パートナーズ）
Preserved parts in Reception.（Photo: Nacása & Partners Inc.）

（写真：ナカサ＆パートナーズ）
(Photo: Nacása & Partners Inc.)

保存・復元した、小食堂。（写真：ナカサ＆パートナーズ）
Preserved Private Dining Room. (Photo: Nacása & Partners Inc.)

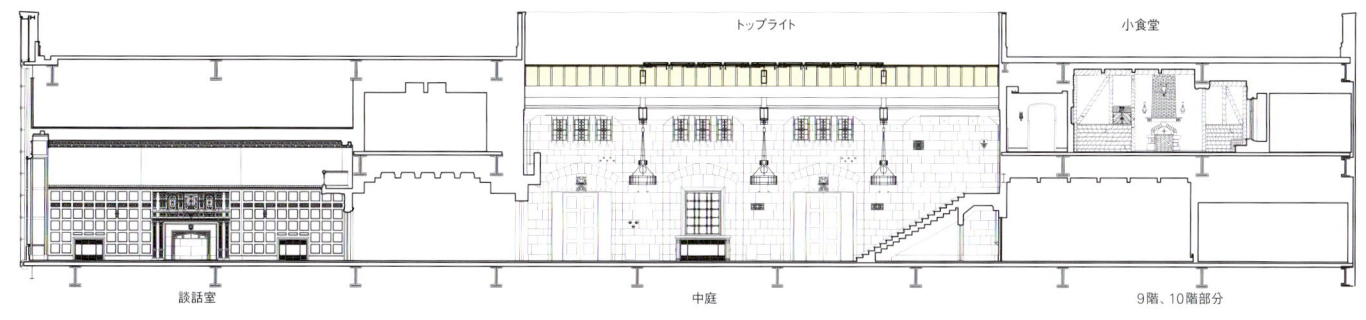

保存―トップフロアの軸
トップライトのある中庭を中心とする倶楽部空間を新しい建築の最上部フロアに移すにあたり、談話室・中庭・小食堂の木造作、彫刻の施された石などを移築した。これらは解体前の状態に戻すことを基本とし、洗浄や修復は行なっていない。採取不能だった部分は新しい材料・技術で製作した。これらにはエイジング処理は施していない。オリジナルを喪失していたシャンデリアやグリルは、竣工写真を基に復刻した。昭和期に失われた談話室出窓のステンドグラスは、保管されていたパーツを活用し、ダブルスキンのインナーサッシュとして再生した。以上の編集は、素材や技術の扱いにおいてベニス憲章（1964、ICOMOS）の考え方も踏まえている。

Preservation / Axis of the Top Floor of Clubhouse
In the transfer of club space surrounding the Center court with the skylight to the new architecture's top floors, we reconstructed portions of the wood works and sculptured stone in the Member's Lobby, Center Court and Private Dining Room. The wood and stone were preserved as such at the time of demolition and neither cleaned nor restored. The portions that could not be saved were fabricated from new materials with new technologies, and not aged. The original chandeliers and grills, lost in time, were reproduced by analyzing old photographs. Stained glass of the Member's lobby lost in the Showa Era was reproduced as an inner skin of double skin glass utilizing stored original color glass parts. This process follows the ethos of ICOMOS (1964, Venice). —K. Sakai

交詢社倶楽部

談話室。（写真：ナカサ＆パートナーズ）
Member's Lobby. (Photo: Nacása & Partners Inc.)

福沢諭吉像。（写真：清水建設）
Yukichi Fukuzawa. (Photo: Shimizu Corporation)

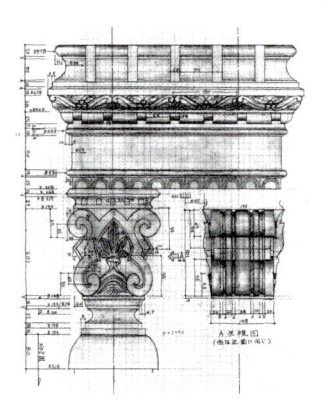

志―紳士倶楽部

いち早く欧米の文化を体感し、民間における意識の近代化を推し進めてきた福沢諭吉。彼によって1880年に創設された日本最古の紳士倶楽部、これが交詢社倶楽部である。その目的は交詢社という名前が示す通り、「知識の交換」であり、またそれらを持って「世務を諮詢」しようというものである。言い換えれば彼が目指した階級や門閥を廃した社交の場であり、知的交流の場を目的としているのである。各々が強靭な志を待ちながらも優しさをも併せ持つ真の紳士に相応しい空間とはどうあるべきか。結果として、華美とは対極的な質実さと同時に重厚さを併せ持つ、ジェントルな空間に行き着いた。

MIND / Concept of Gentlemen's Club

Yukichi Fukuza, who himself experienced Western culture, promoted the modernization of people's consciousness during the Meiji era. The Kojunsha Club, the oldest gentlemen's club in Japan, was founded by him in 1880. The name KO-JUN-SHA is derived from the original purpose of the club to provide members with the opportunity to exchange knowledge (KO) and consult with each other concerning economic matters and political affairs (JUN) at the club (SHA). In other words, it is an organization for social intercourse, eliminating status or lineage, and intellectual interchange. The design theme was the realization of space for gentlemen with strong independent minds. As a result, we realized this steady, stately and gentle space. —H. Ohyama

ロンドンのペルメル（紳士クラブ街）。（写真：清水建設）
Pall Mall (Clubland) in London. (Photo: Shimizu Corporation)

第6章 公共施設

Chapter 6
Public Facilities

秋田市立新屋図書館

新しい建物(モノ)と古き良き倉庫(モノ)の共生する地域図書館

Akita City Araya Library
Community library where a new building and a good, old warehouse coexist

上空より全体を望む。(写真:川澄建築写真事務所)
Facility as seen from above. (Photo: Kawasumi Architectural Photograph Office)

模型1。
Model #1.

模型2。
Model #2.

秋田市郊外にある「ふるさと文化創造エリア」に残る旧食糧倉庫群(1934年に建てられた木造の米倉)中の8番目の棟と、それに連結する新しい木造当による構成された文化施設が、新屋図書館である。

「古き良きモノ」である倉庫とは既存の木造架構を生かした大量の書籍を保存する静寂な空間として、「新しき良きモノ」であるRC造の本館棟は受付や新刊本を置く活動的な空間となるよう計画した。

倉庫の通り心軸上にある2本の渡り廊下は、この対比する2つの建物を結び内部循環を促し、利用者は施設を回遊しながら本と接することができる。本館棟に広がるガラスのカーテンウォールは北側からの安定した光を得ると共に、本を読む人々の姿を外部に映し出す。

倉庫棟の外観は新屋地域の人々の心象風景であったため、その歴史的景観をできるだけ変えない様に、最小限の改造程度に留めた。倉庫の構造はそのままの木造架構を利用し、その天井の高さを生かして開架書庫とした。

地域文化の継承の場としても機能する様に、新屋地区を代表する産業である酒造業に関する資料を集めた「酒の資料コーナー」を設置している。開館後には想い出深い倉庫の内部を見に来る高齢者からも好評を博した。

新屋図書館は建物の保存・再生という理念と、新しいモノとの共生という2つの理念を基に、地域社会に密着した図書館としてその機能を果たし続けている。その姿は21世紀の公共図書館の新しい姿の1つである。

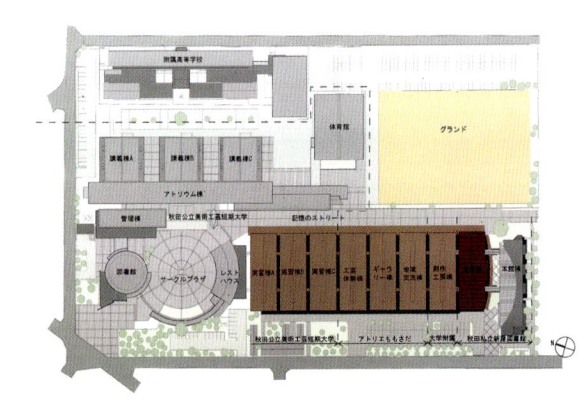

全体配置図。
General arrangement drawing.

Develop:	City of Akita
Architect & Designer:	Jiro Shimizu / Tomoko Matsuda: MHS Planners, Architects & Engineers
	Masaaki Obara: City of Akita
Location:	Akita-shi, Akita
Site area:	5,092 sq m
Building area:	1,562.71 sq m
Total floor area:	1,672.71 sq m
Structure:	RC, W
Completion:	March 1998
Public Wall:	Painting
Public Floor:	Flooring

The Araya Library is a cultural facility consisting of the 8th warehouse of the historical warehouses (rice-granaries built in 1934) and a new wooden building connected to it in the Furusato Bunka Sozo Area (Area Designated for Home Culture Creation) in the outskirts of Akita City.

It was planned that while the "good old thing" or the existing warehouse was renovated as a quiet space to archive many books by taking advantage of the existing wooden shelves, the "good new thing" or the main building with reinforced concrete construction was built as a dynamic space where the reception desk and newly published books are accommodated.

Two connecting corridors on the central axis of the warehouse promote the circulation of users who can enjoy contacts with books while going around. The glass curtain wall to the north of the main building stably takes the light in and, at the same time, reveals people reading books.

As the appearance of the old warehouse building was strongly ingrained in the mind of the locals in the Araya area, modifications were kept to minimum in order to preserve the historical scenery as much as possible. The existing wooden skeleton construction was utilized, and, by taking advantage of its height, the library adopted the open stack system.

Further, in order to add a function to preserve the local culture, the "Japanese Sake Information Corner" is established as a collection of data on the liquor industry for which the Araya area is famous. After the completion, the library has been popular among elderly citizens who pay visits to see the interior of the warehouse with full of memories of the past.

Based on the concepts of preservation & rehabilitation of the building and coexistence with new things, the Araya Library is properly functioning as a library closely tied with the local community. It presents a new shape of public libraries in the 21st century.

新旧の対峙と調和。(写真:川澄建築写真事務所)
Contrast and harmony of the new and the old. (Photo: Kawasumi Architectural Photograph Office)

地域の人々を情報発信基地へと導くエントランス。(写真:川澄建築写真事務所)
Entrance inviting people to the information base in the community. (Photo: Kawasumi Architectural Photograph Office)

円弧を描く本館棟内部。(写真:川澄建築写真事務所)
Interior of the main building forming an arc. (Photo: Kawasumi Architectural Photograph Office)

既存倉庫の木造架構をそのまま生かした『開架書庫』。（写真：川澄建築写真事務所）
Open stack system taking advantage of the wooden shelves of the existing archive. (Photo: Kawasumi Architectural Photograph Office)

倉庫と柔らかな光で演出される『軽読書コーナー』。
（写真：川澄建築写真事務所）
Softly lit light reading corner arranged in the archive.
(Photo: Kawasumi Architectural Photograph Office)

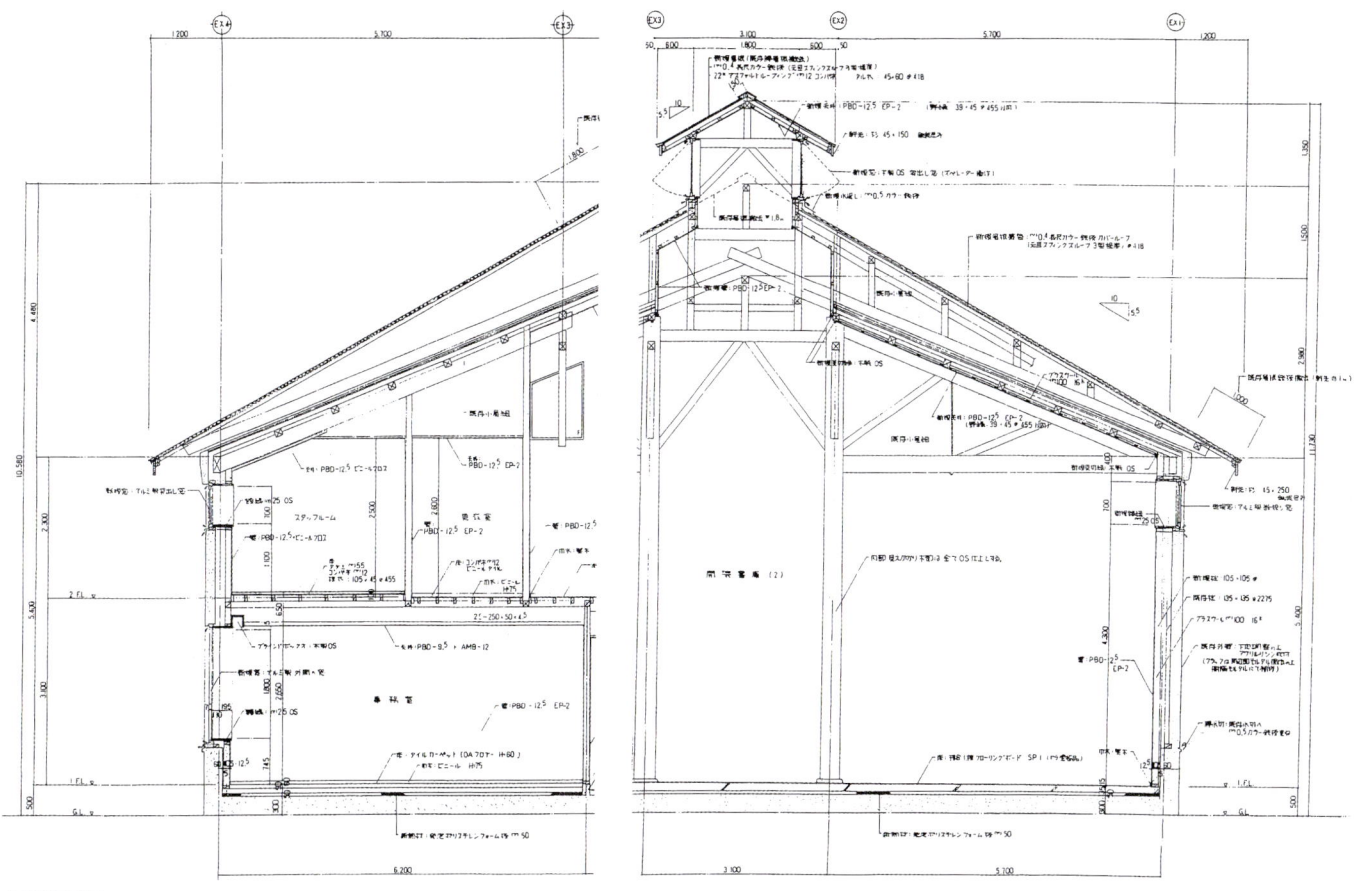

倉庫棟断面図。
Section of the archive.

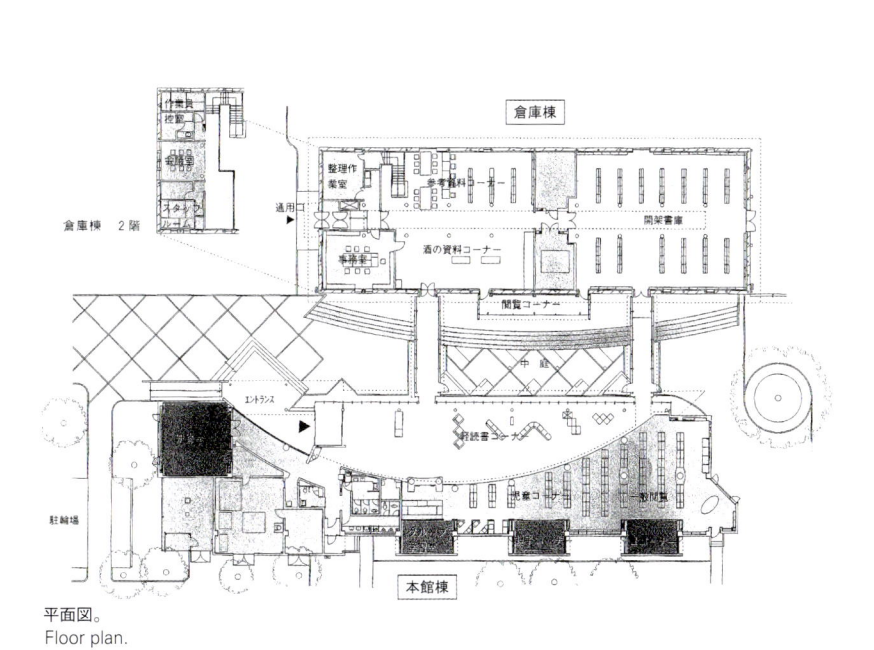

平面図。
Floor plan.

再生前の倉庫内部。
Interior of the archive before renovation.

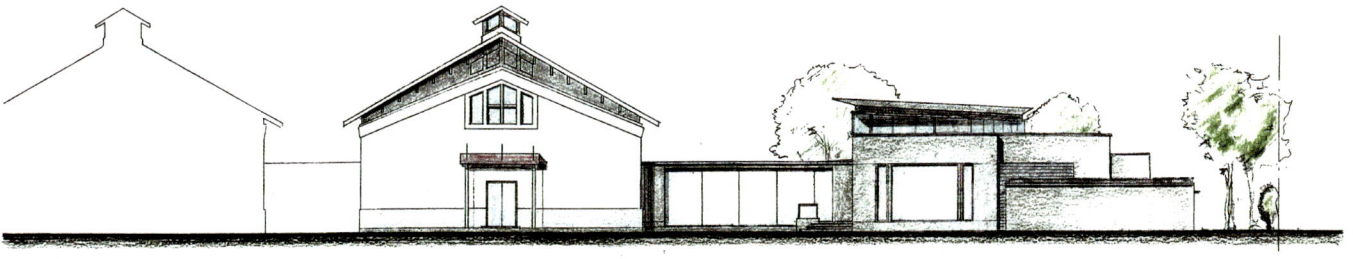

立面図。
Elevation.

秋田市立新屋図書館 171

産業技術総合研究所
自然光を生かした楽しく心和む空間にリニューアル

National Institute of Advanced Industrial Science and Technology
Renovated into an entertaining and relaxing space ulitizing natural light

Developer: National Institute of Advanced Industrial Science and Technology
Designer: Atsushi Kitamura / Tsutomu Takahashi:
NTT FACILITIES, INC.
Masashi Teramoto / Yoko Iino:
MEC Design International Corporation
Location: Hitashi 1-1-1, Tsukuba-shi, Ibaragi
Structure: RC structure(partially steel construction)
Completion: March 2004
Materials: (Main interior materials)Floor: flooring/porcelain tile;
wall: cloth; ceilihg: cloth;
EP: rock wool sound absorption board

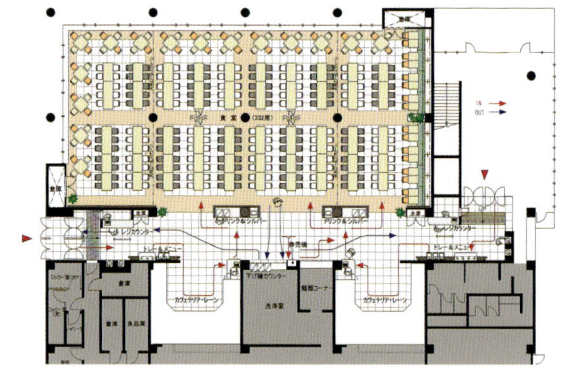

食堂プラン。
Restaurant plan.

グラフィックアートによる演出。
Decoration using graphic arts.

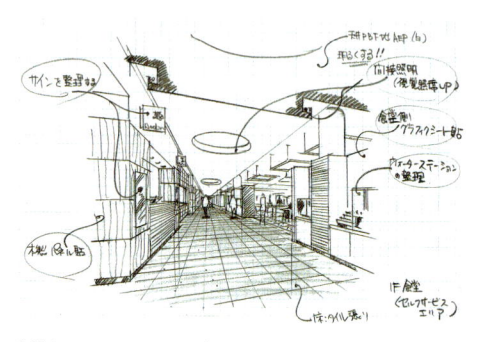

食堂カフェテリアのレーンスケッチ。
Sketch of the restaurant/cafe terrace lane.

家具レイアウトによるコーナーづくり。
Corner by the layout of the furniture.

改装前の食堂カフェテリアレーン。
Restaurant / cafe terrace lane.

明るく清潔感のある空間として再生。
Renewed as a bright space with a sense of cleanliness.

つくば産業総合研究所の広大な敷地内に点在する研究者と外来者のための食堂のリニューアルを行った。

数ヵ所ある食堂のうち、カフェテリア方式の食堂は外部環境が自然に恵まれた好立地にあるため、「明るい」「楽しい」「カジュアル」をキーワードとしてインテリアによる「食の楽しさ」の再構築を目指した。

また、動線計画の見直しを行い、カフェテリアに並ぶ長い列の煩わしさを軽減した。

家具レイアウトにも変化をもたせ、さまざまなシチュエーションに対応できるようにした。

色彩計画は白、ナチュラル色をベースに赤色のアクセントカラーを部分的に用いた。

キーワードの「明るい」「楽しい」「カジュアル」をより鮮

Renewed were restaurants for researchers and visitors that are scattered over the vast site of National Institute of Advanced Industrial Science and Technology in Tsukuba.

Among several restaurants, cafe-terrace type ones are found in favorable locations rich in nature, and the target of their renewals is set to rediscovery of "joy of eating" based on such keywords as light, enjoyment and casualness.

The circulation planning was reviewed to reduce long waiting lines in the cafe terrace.

A variety of furniture layout was provided to meet different situations.

The color scheme was based on white and natural colors, and red was used as an accent color as appropriate.

In order to emphasize the keywords of light, enjoyment and casualness more clearly in design, graphic sheets and artworks were employed for jewel the space.

The existing design details near the window were reformed, and by installing roll screens, the space was renovated as a relaxing and refreshing place taking advantage of natural light.

As the restaurant located on the second floor above the cafe terrace is also served as sort of salon used for reception, guest entertainment and parties, its design themes were set to be "repose" and "non-ordinary space" in contrast with those of the cafe terrace.

The terrace was extended to add a sense of expansion and connection with the outside, and the facility now gives an impression of a cafe terrace/restaurant in a resort where one can feel a breeze drifting through the terrace.

改装前のレストラン。
Restaurant before renovation.

イメージCG（俯瞰）。
Digital graphic image (downward view).

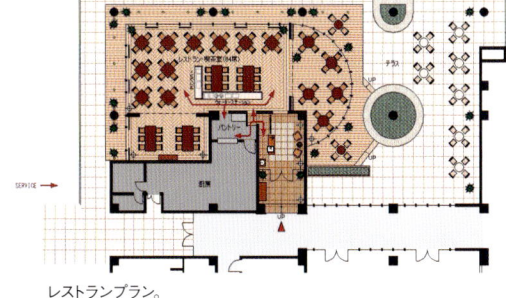

レストランプラン。
Restaurant plan.

改装後のレストラン。
Restaurant after renovation.

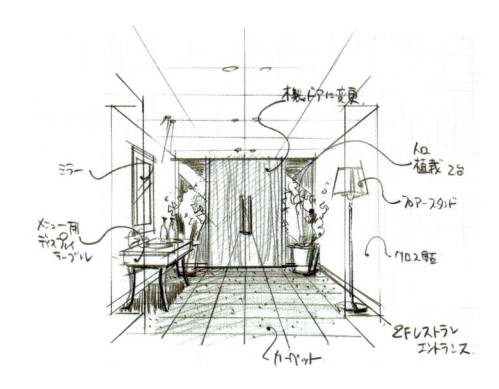

エントランススケッチ。
Entrance sketch

明に表現するためにグラフィックシートやアートワークで空間に彩りを加えた。

窓際の既存ディテールは整理し、ロールスクリーンを設置したことによって自然光を生かした心和むリフレッシュ空間として再生した。

また、この食堂の2階に位置するレストランは、応接・接待・パーティーといったサロン的な空間としても利用されるため、1階の食堂とは趣を変え、「落ち着き」と「非日常間」をデザインテーマとした。

テラス部分に増築を行い、広がりと外部空間とのつながりを持たせ、「テラスを吹き抜ける風」を感じる『リゾートカフェレストラン』のイメージを造り上げた。

テラスへの増築部分。
Extension to the terrace.

外部テラスへの増築部分イメージCG。
Digital graphic image of the extension to the outside terrace.

CLUB ANA
空港ラウンジの
部分改修

CLUB ANA
Partial renovation of an airport lounge

関西国際空港の全日空ビジネスクラス専用ラウンジ「CLUB ANA」がスペースの分煙化を機に部分改修を行ったプロジェクト。内装、家具には呼吸感のあるウッド（ビーチ）素材を使用。ラウンジの機能もバラエティーに富んだ飲食類、インターネットコーナー、プラズマディスプレイ、マッサージチェア、携帯電話ブースなどおよそビジネスとリラクゼーションに用いられるアイテムが完備された高性能なラウンジとなっている。

改修工事は設計与条件として完成度の高いデザインマニュアルが用意され、それぞれの状況に応じてそれらを適応、応用させることが改修工事の重要なファクターとなった。なかでもカウンターバックに設置の「ブルードットウォール」や100φのガラスパイプを列柱上に並べた「ガラスパイプスクリーン」はエントランスまわりを彩る必須アイテムとしてその使われ方がポイントとなった。

部分改修を前提として計画されたプロジェクトでは既存の「何を更新し」「何を残し」「何を利用するか」を見極めることが、費用対効果を考えた上での重要な初期作業となる。また同時にデザインマニュアルを読み解き、それらにプライオリティをつけ採用していくこと、さらには時代の流れにより陳腐化し始めたマニュアル上のアイテムについては積極的にリデザインしていくことがよりよいデザインにつながると判断した。

また、視覚的なデザインと同様に、改修の発端である喫煙コーナーをはじめとした空調機能の再整備、指向性スピーカーによる快適な音響環境の実現など機能面でのアプローチにも注力している。

Client: All Nippon Airways Co., Ltd.
Architect: Nikken Sekkei
Construction: Sogo Design Co., Ltd. / Obayashi Corporation / Isetan Co., Ltd.
Designer: Tomoyuki Hino: Nikken Space Design
Location: Izumisano-shi, Osaka
Site area: 240.0 sq m + 425.0 sq m
Completion: November 2004
Material: Ceiling: Painting; walls: painting; floors: tile carpet and ceramic tiles
Year of original completion: March 1998

ラウンジ全景。天井の折上間接照明はプロポーション自体を残し、繰型などの装飾を取り除くことでシンプルに生まれ変わった。奥は喫煙コーナー。（写真：柄松 稔）
View of the lounge. Adopted was indirect lighting from the coved ceiling whose original proportion was preserved while its moldings and other decorations were removed to simplify the design. The smoking corner is at the rear. (Photo: Minoru Karamatsu)

エントランスまわり。カウンターバックに見えるのが「ブルードットウォール」、左に見えるのが「ガラスパイプスクリーン」、右は手前から「飾り台」「ショーケース」「新聞、雑誌コーナー」。（写真：柄松 稔）
Entrance area. The "blue dot wall" is behind the counter. The "glass pipe screen" is to the left. A display stand, a showcase, and newspaper / magazine corner to the right (from the front first). (Photo: Minoru Karamatsu)

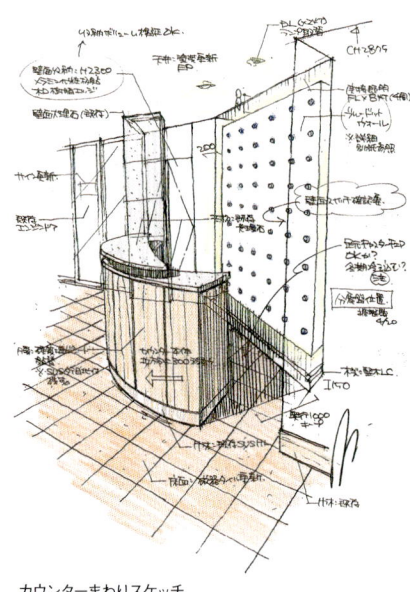

カウンターまわりスケッチ。
クライアントとの重要なコミュニケーションツール。
Sketch of the counter and its surroundings. It is a very important tool for communications with the client.

This is a project in which Kansai International airport lounge exclusive for ANA business class travelers, CLUB ANA, was partially renovated taking an opportunity of division of the lounge into smoking and non-smoking areas. Beechwood was selected to be applied to interior finishes and furniture. The lounge is now fully equipped with facilities and articles necessary for business and relaxation including a variety of food and drink offerings, the Internet corner, plasma displays, a massage chair and cell phone booths.

In this renovation work, a highly detailed design manual as design requirements was provided, and how to adapt and apply them to renewal work became an important factor. The point of argument was how to utilize the "blue dot wall" installed behind the counter and the 100mm-diameter glass pipes arranged as a glass-pipe-screen near the entrance.

On the early stage of projects where partial renovation is a premise, it is important to identify what should be updated, what should be preserved and what should be used as materials in terms of cost-effectiveness.

At the same time, we concluded that analyzing the details of the design manual, putting priorities to the requirements, and positively re-designing those items that have been rendered obsolete with the passage of time would lead to better designs.

In addition to visual designs, we also paid careful attention to the functional approaches including improvements of smoking corner and other air-conditioning facilities and realization of comfortable acoustics using directional loudspeakers.

エントランス飾り台。天井と取り合う木格子はマニュアル上パーティションとしての設定であったが、ここでは空間のアクセントとしても利用されている。
（写真：柄松 稔）
Display stand at the entrance.
The wooden grids reaching up to the ceiling was specified as partitions in the manual, but we took advantage of them as spatial accents.
(Photo: Minoru Karamatsu)

改装前のエントランス飾り台。
Display stand at the entrance before renovation.

改修前のWC。
Bathroom before renovation.

喫煙コーナー。壁面カウンターはインターネットが使用可能なLAN及び電源アウトレット付。
（写真：柄松 稔）
Smoking corner. The counter by the wall is provided with LAN ports and AC outlets.
(Photo: Minoru Karamatsu)

多目的コーナー。VIP対応など必要に応じて開閉可能な間仕切りを設けた。開放した状態（写真右）と間仕切った状態（写真左）。（写真：柄松 稔）
Multi-purpose corner. Mobile partitions are provided for handling VIP's, etc. as necessary. The partitions are open (left); the partitions are closed (right). (Photo: Minoru Karamatsu)

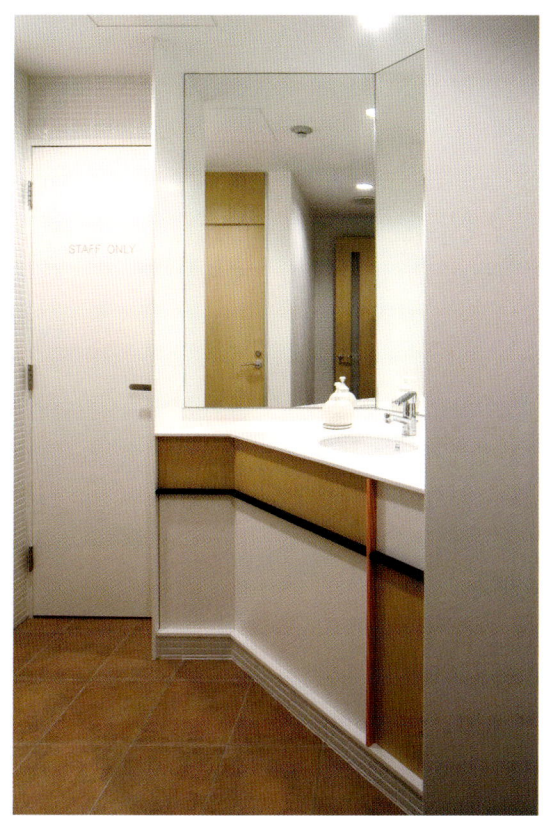

清潔感あふれるWC。スペースが狭小な場合、やはりミラーの使い方は重要。
（写真：柄松 稔）
Clean bathroom. If the space is small, how to take advantage of mirrors is important. (Photo: Minoru Karamatsu)

旧第四銀行住吉町支店
文化遺産と共存するレストラン

Former Daishi Bank Sumiyoshi-cho Branch
Restaurant in a cultural heritage

Developer:	Niigata Municipal Government
Architect:	MHS Planners, Architects and Engineers
Designer:	Inoue Keizou
Location:	Niigata-shi, Niigata
Site area:	724.71 sq m
Building area:	514.13 sq m
Total floor area:	921.91 squ m
Structure:	RC
Completion:	March 2004
Material:	Exterior Wall=granite
	Public Wall=plaster
	Public Floor=tile, linoleum and carpet

本建築は元々、1927年に第四銀行住吉支店として創建された近代銀行建築である。
道路計画のために、一旦取り壊しされることになったが、新潟市が銀行より建物部材の提供を受け、歴史的建造物として移築復原することになった。
歴史的建造物として展示設備とレストラン機能を併せ持つ施設に生まれ変わったが、特に文化財的価値をできるだけ残すこと、創建当時の佇まいを可能な限り復原することに最大限の注意が払われた。
1階銀行の営業室／執務エリア、客溜りはそれぞれレストラン客席、ショップへ、金庫室は厨房へと変貌したが、復原された照明器具やカウンタースクリーンにより創建当時の佇まいを改修前以上に取り戻すことになった。

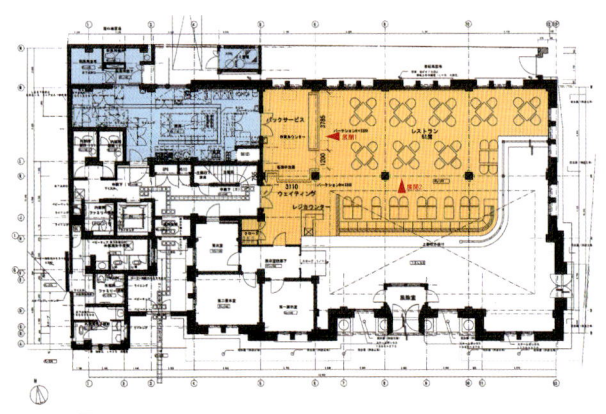

旧銀行営業室／執務エリアに配されたレストラン客席部。（写真：エスエス北陸）
Dining area built on the old banking hall/work area. (Photo: SS HOKURIKU)

1F 平面図。
Floor plan of the first floor.

改修前銀行営業室。
Banking hall before renovation.

修復後の元銀行営業室（現レストラン）。（写真：エスエス北陸）
Banking hall after restoration (current restaurant). (Photo: SS HOKURIKU)

移築前概観。
Appearance before relocation.

創業当時の銀行営業室。
Banking hall at the time of original completion.

改修前銀行営業室。
Banking hall before renovation.

This bank building was originally built as the Sumiyoshi Branch of Daishi Bank in 1927.

As part of a road plan, the building was set to be demolished; however, the bank offered the city of Niigata to provide its components, and the municipal government decided to relocate and reconstruct it as a landmark.

Though the building was reborn to have exhibition rooms as a historic structure as well as restaurant facilities, maximum attention was paid to maintain its cultural values and restore its appearance at the time of original completion as much as possible.

The banking hall/work area, the public spaces, and the vault turned into the dining room, the shop and kitchen, respectively; however, thanks to restored lighting fixtures and counter screens, the appearance of the facility became closer to its original form than that before restoration.

独立柱頭飾り、再用石膏彫刻取付様子。
Attaching a capital ornament and renewable gypsum sculpture.

古色塗り手法による大理石模様修復色合わせ様子。
Color-matching the marble patterns using a technique to give a timeworn look.

女子美術大学

自然の色彩にビビッドなカラーがマッチするファサードの再生

Joshibi University of Art and Design
Facade renewal where natural colors are in perfect harmony with vivid colors

女子美術大学は1900年に、芸術による女性の自立、地位の向上を掲げて創立された学校である。

1935年に杉並キャンパスに移転してから約65年の間に、周囲は多くの緑の大木を残しながら住宅地へと大きく変貌を遂げる。

改修や増築を経ながら、百周年の節目を迎える2000年に、歴史を踏まえながらも新しい表情を持つファサードの再生が計画された。

大通りから住宅地に入り込むアプローチの中で、木々の葉の間から垣間見えるアイキャッチャーとなるように、スクールカラーを内包する7mのシンボルタワーを設置。

敷地の角に位置するエントランスは、桜の大樹を包み込むように円弧状のウォールを設置することで、セキュリティを確保しながらも都市に開かれた女子大らしい優しいしつらえで校内へと導く。

既存の2つの建物を統括するレイヤーは緑の光や風が抜けるガラスをもちい、フェンスは都市との接点がまっすぐに引かれた境界線ではなく、より自然な形になるように木々を縫って走り抜ける。

65年を経た敷地内の自然やその形状を極力活かしたキャンパスの顔を都市の中に作ることを多様な機能・条件を持った既存建物を可能な限り残し、最低限のスクラップアンドビルドで実現させた。

カフェテリアはカラーリングによるリノベーションである。緑に囲まれた環境の中、白で統一された教室から開放された時、ビビッドカラーが気持ちをリフレッシュさせてくれる。

大学正門廻り改修前。
Main entrance before renovation.

Architect: Shimizu Corporation
Designer: Yoshiharu Shimura / Eriko Izitsu: FIELD FOUR DESIGN OFFICE
Location: Suginami-ku, Tokyo
Site area: 1,145 sq m
Completion: October 2001

大学正門。(写真:川澄建築写真事務所)
Main entrance of the university. (Photo: Kawasumi Architectural Photograph Office)

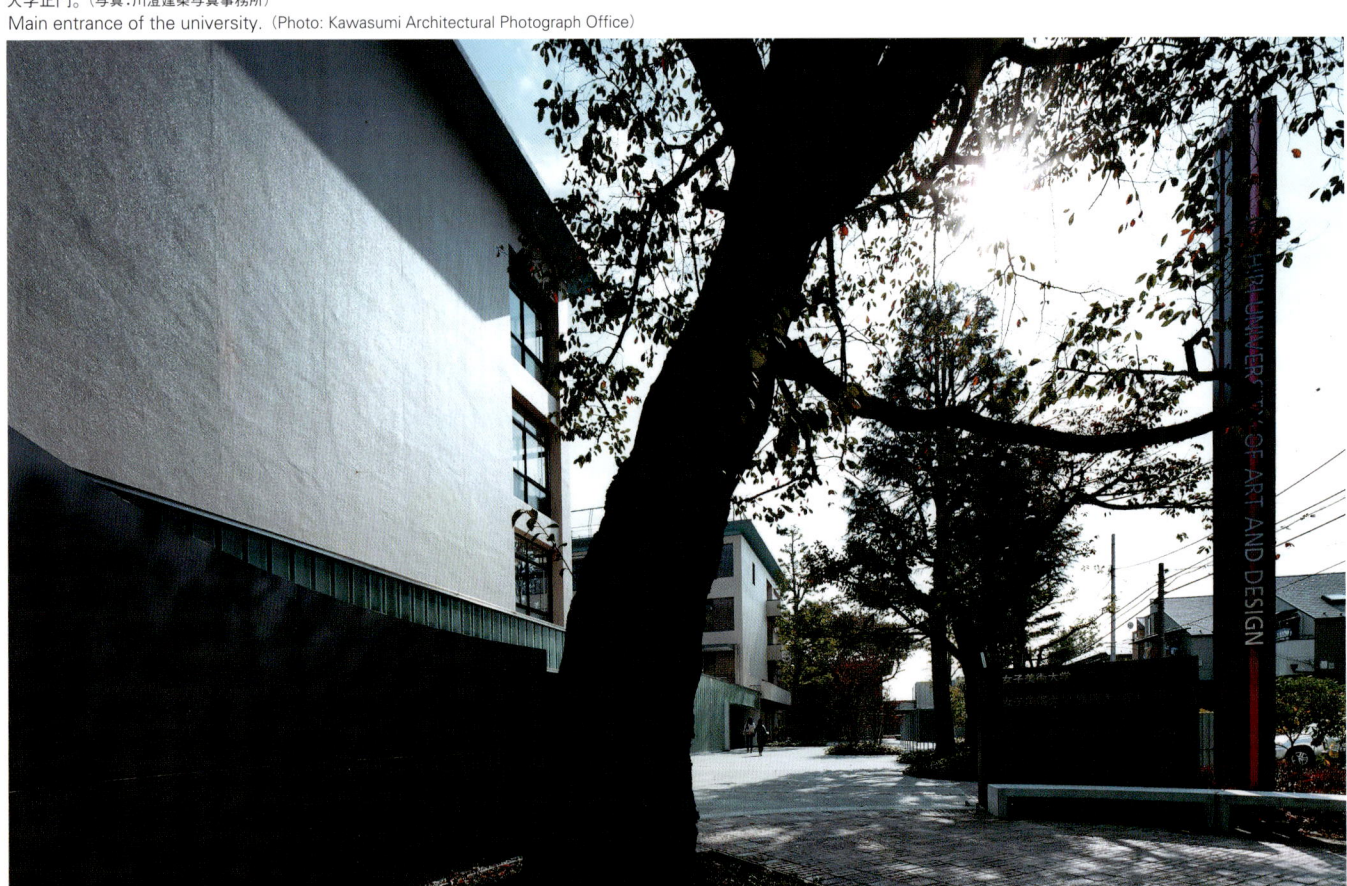

大学正門全景。（写真：川澄建築写真事務所）
General view of the main entrance of the university. (Photo: Kawasumi Architectural Photograph Office)

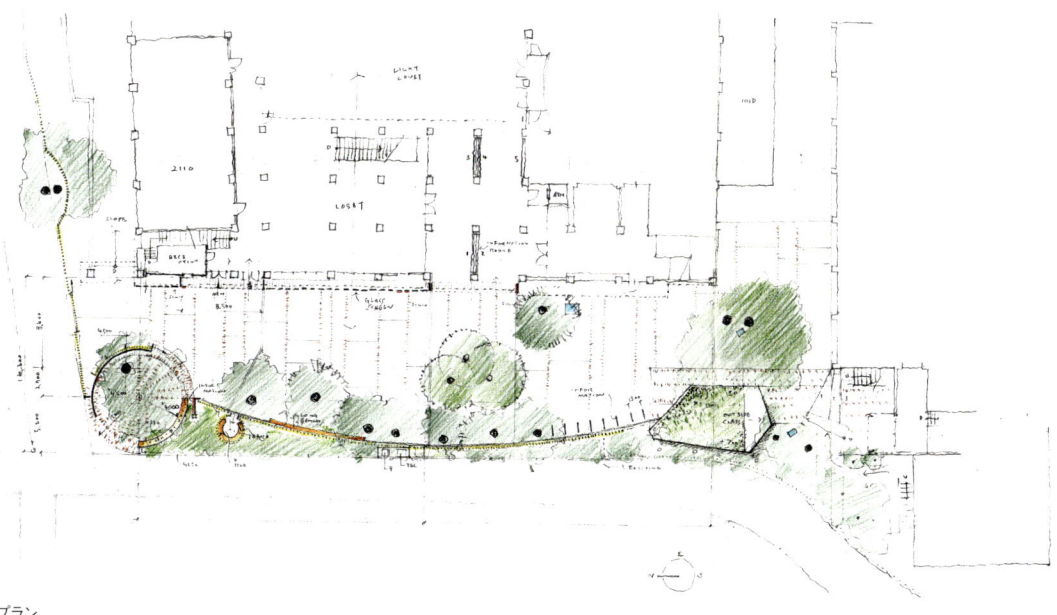

プラン。
Plan.

This women's university was founded in 1900 to empower the self-reliance and to improve the social status of women. In about 65 years after the university moved to the Suginami campus in 1935, the surrounding areas drastically changed into residential blocks while maintaining many big, green trees.

After a number of renovations and extensions, it was planned to renew the facade in the year 2000 celebrating the university's 100th anniversary. The purpose of this renovation was to give the facade a new look based on its history and tradition.

A 7-meter symbol tower with the school color was erected so that it should serve as an eyecatcher of which one can catch a glimpse while approaching to the residential area from the main street.

Leading to the campus is the entrance at the corner of the site, provided with circular walls around big cherry trees for achieving security and giving a soft and gentle image of a university open to the city.

As a layer to interface the existing two buildings, glass walls to pass light and wind are installed; the fences weave through trees so that the border with the city should not be straight lines but should have a more natural shape.

In order to realize a new face of the campus by taking maximum advantage of the 65-year-old natural environment and its shapes in site, the existing buildings having various functions and conditions were utilized as much as possible while the scrap and build approach was kept to minimum.

Coloring was used for renovation of the cafe terrace. When students get liberated from classrooms in white, the vivid colors of the cafe terrace will refresh their mind.

付属正門改修前。
Main entrance of the attached schools before renovation.

付属エントランス。（写真：川澄建築写真事務所）
Entrance of the attached schools. (Photo: Kawasumi Architectural Photograph Office)

付属正門。（写真：川澄建築写真事務所）
Main entrance of the attached schools. (Photo: Kawasumi Architectural Photograph Office)

大学食堂改修前。
Before renovation.

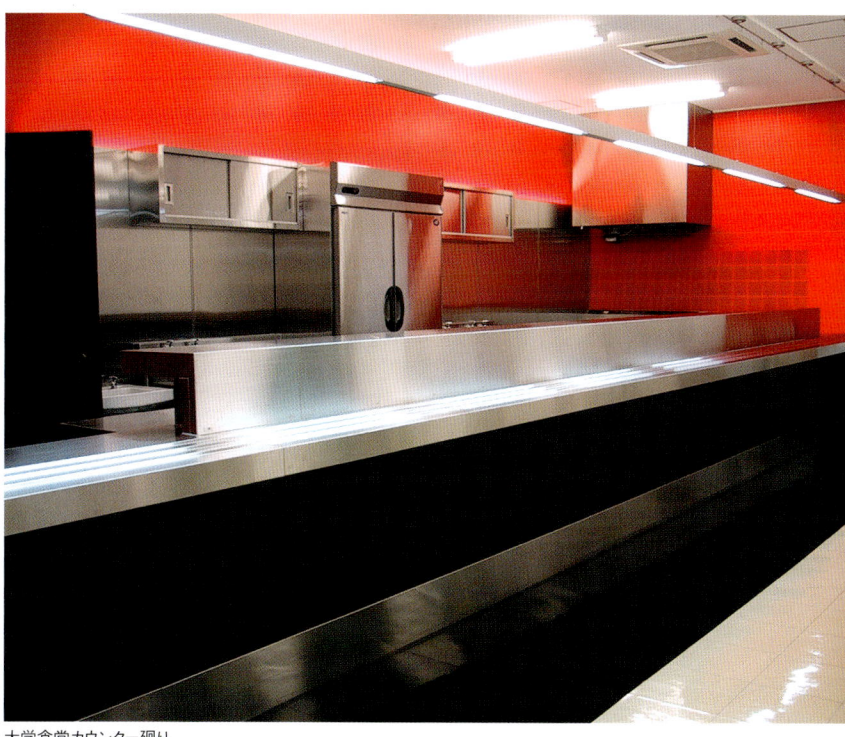

大学食堂カウンター廻り。
Counter of the student dining hall (university).

付属生徒食堂。(写真:川澄建築写真事務所)
Student dining hall (attached schools). (Photo: Kawasumi Architectural Photograph Office)

付属生徒食堂改修前。
Student dining hall (attached schools) before renovation.

女子美術大学 **181**

展示係留保存船「羊蹄丸」

海上文化交流施設として
生まれ変わった連絡船

Floating Pavilion "YOTEI MARU"

A ferryboat renovated as a floating cultural exchange facility

『船の科学館』前に係留された「羊蹄丸」。
Yoteimaru moored in front of the "MUSEUM OF MARITIME SCIENCE".

Developer:	Japanese Foundation for the Promotion of Maritime Science
Architect:	Mitsui Engineering & Shipbuilding Co., Ltd.(hull architect) / Ocean Consultant. Japan Co., Ltd(mooring facilities design)
Consultant:	MHS Planners, Architects and Engineers
Location:	Koto Ward, Japan
Building area:	2,068,62 sq m
Completion:	March 1996

レストスペース（船楼甲板階）。
Rest Space (superstructure deck).

シアター（旧第2甲板階）。
Theater (old 2nd deck).

現役連絡船だった頃。
Yoteimaru serving as a ferryboat.

内部（旧グリーン席）。
Interior (old first class cabin).

青函トンネルの開通に伴い、青函連絡船は80年余りの歴史に幕を閉じた。

そこで、永年親しまれてきた、最後の青函連絡船「羊蹄丸」を歴史的・文化的遺産の保存といった意味も含め、展示・展望施設・ホール等様々な機能を織り込み、東京湾青海地区に係留する"フローティングパビリオン"としてリノベーションすることとなった。

保存の原則は「原形保存」であったが、船舶という特殊性から、一般公開に際して充分でない部分が多く、原形を損なわない範囲で関係法令に適合すべく改造を行った。

海上文化交流施設として生まれ変わった「羊蹄丸」は、将来臨海副都心として発展していく青海地区、更には東京湾岸における文化交流の中核として、地域に潤いと憩いを与える施設となることを目指した。

The completion of the Seikan Tunnel ended the 80-odd-year-old history of the ferryboat connecting Aomori and Hakodate, Yoteimaru.

In consideration of preservation of this historic and cultural heritage popular among the general public for many years, it was decided to renovate the vessel as a floating pavilion to be moored in the Aomi area of the Tokyo Bay by incorporating various facilities including exhibition rooms, observation facilities and halls.

Though it was intended to preserve the Yoteimaru in its original form, it was found that many of the original facilities were incompliant with the relevant laws and regulations for public viewing and safety, and the vessel was thus modified without affecting the original structure.

The Yoteimaru reborn as a floating cultural exchange pavilion is expected to serve as a core facility to enrich not only the Aomi area, a coastal conurbation in development, but also the Tokyo Bay Area.

展示スペース。
Exhibition space.

アドミラルホール（旧普通席）。
Admiral Hall (old ordinary cabin).

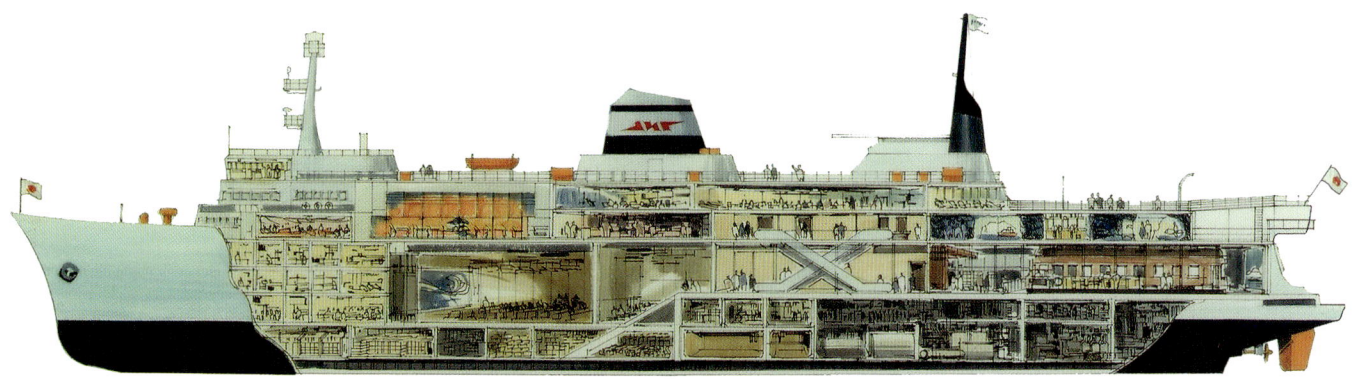

断面スケッチ。
Section sketch.

夜ライトアップされた「羊蹄丸」。
Yoteimaru lit up at night.

陸上との接合は、横方向:ドルフィン係留、縦方向:チェーン係留とし、陸との連絡は、船楼甲板レベルに設置する2基の桟橋より行う事とした。又、中甲板レベルの船首及び船中央部に1基ずつ非常連絡橋を常設し、非常時においても各方向の避難を可能にしている。

内部は連絡船であった当時の情緒と威厳を残しつつ、機能性とエンターテイメント性とが共存し、子供から大人まで幅広く楽しめる知的エンターテイメント空間となるよう心がけた。

1992年、イタリア・ジェノヴァで開催された「国際船と海の博覧会」においては、フローティングパビリオンとしてジェノヴァ港に入港。日本の歴史と文化を紹介する日本館として活躍した。

立体的に再現構成された青函ワールド。
The world of the Seikan (Aomori-Hakodate) ferry line reproduced three-dimensionally.

Mooring was by the dolphin mooring system in the horizontal direction and by the chain mooring system in the vertical direction. Two gangways on the superstructure deck level are used for loading to the vessel. In addition, emergency gangways are provided at the bow and the stern on the main deck level for emergency evacuation.

The interior of the ship maintains the atmosphere and dignity at the time of ferryboat days while offering a space for intelligent entertainment for a wide audience from children to adults, combining functionality and entertainment.

At the Genoa Expo '92 on the theme of ships and the sea, the Yoteimaru entered the Genoa port as a floating pavilion and served as the Japanese Pavilion to introduce the history and culture of Japan.

バイオグラフィ

Biographies

バイオグラフィ

株式会社伊藤喜三郎建築研究所
建築は、なかば恒久的な社会の財産として存在することを義務付けられています。であれば、その基盤となる設計という行為は、建築物の内外に想定される様々な活動の的確な予測に始まるはずです。
依頼主との信頼関係の構築も欠かすことが出来ません。伊藤喜三郎建築研究所は、永年、この着実な方法論に拠って、機能性、人間性、さらには将来への視点をも備えた建築空間の創出に取り組んできました。ここにご紹介するのは、そうしたプロセスに基づく成果の一例です。

〒141-0022　東京都品川区東五反田1丁目2-33　白雉子ビル
TEL：03-5798-8181
URL：http://www.k-ito.co.jp

株式会社日建スペースデザイン
株式会社日建設計より1994年設立。東京・大阪・名古屋に設計室。総スタッフ65名で専業のインテリアデザイン事務所としては国内最大規模。「ヒューマンスケールによる社会環境デザイン」「スペースヴァリューを高めるデザイン＆マネジメント」を標榜し、インテリアに関わる設計監理、小規模の建築設計監理、プロダクトデザインなどを主な業務としている。ホテル、商業施設、オフィス、銀行、病院、学校、図書館とシェアは全分野に及び、主な作品に住友商事本社、大阪・成田・関西空港・大分などの全日空ホテル、大阪・東京の日航ホテルリノベーション、ホテルニューオータニ、住友信託銀行、新宿・札幌のシティバンク、住友病院、早稲田・明治・立教などの大学施設、上海の中国銀行銀行家倶楽部、京都迎賓館家具設計など多数。

〒102-0083　東京都千代田区麹町5丁目4-19　セタニビル
TEL：03-3264-6609　FAX：03-3264-6697
URL：http://www.nspacedesign.co.jp

株式会社ネクスト・エム
2002年12月16日設立。都市・建築・インテリアに関わる、企画・プロデュース・コンサルティング・設計・監理・及び販売。リサーチ、コンサルティング、マネジメントを中心に業務を展開。

〒107-0051　東京都港区元赤坂1-4-21　赤坂パレスビル5階
TEL：03-3408-1771　FAX：03-3403-7384
URL：http://www.next-m.co.jp

安藤勢津子
日建スペースデザイン東京設計室　チーフデザイナー
工学院大学非常勤講師
インテリアプランナー
［主な作品］
ホテルデザインを中心に多くの施設デザインを担当。成田全日空ホテル、大分全日空ホテルオアシスタワー、長野ホテル犀北館、オークラ千葉ホテル、ホテルニューオータニ幕張、ホテルニューオータニ東京改修、ホテル日航東京改修、ヴィラフォンテーヌ六本木、IT健保保養所、ジャカルタbasara、ホテルニューオータニ東京改修、シティータワー高輪マンション、六本木泉ガーデンレジデンスなど。
1997年グッドデザイン賞（INAX）。2004年グッドデザイン賞（イヨベ工芸社家具）。

Email：ando_sd@nikken.co.jp

Email：info@next-m.co.jp

株式会社フィールドフォー・デザインオフィス
1989年（株）清水建設設計部門より独立したインテリアデザイン事務所として設立され、その後2000年に同部門からランドスケープを併合し、総勢25名で現在に至っている。
インテリアとランドスケープをメインにFFE（家具什器備品）サイン等、デザインコンサルティングから企画・監理まで幅広く業務展開し、次世代に誇れる質の高いクオリティー空間創りを目指している。

〒100-0011　東京都千代田区内幸町2-2-2　富国生命ビル27階
TEL：03-3539-2881　FAX：03-3539-2883
URL：http://www.field4.co.jp

株式会社松田平田設計
1931年（昭和6年）9月設立。松田軍平による創立以来75年に渡り、都市計画、再開発事業、先端的高機能業務ビル、大規模スポーツ施設、医療・福祉施設、公共施設インテリアデザインの設計のみならず、建物のリノベーションや改善、維持管理の協力、PFI、PM、CMなどの業務にいたるまで、巾広い業務で実績を築く。
リノベーションにおいては、2000年に「甦る建築」をめざす組織として、BEEMS室（現・BEEMS部）を設立。
都市と建築、さらにそれを取り巻く環境を再構築し、社会に貢献することを目指す。

〒107-8448　東京都港区元赤坂1-5-17
TEL：03-3403-6161
URL：http://www.mhs.co.jp

株式会社メック・デザイン・インターナショナル
1972年3月10日設立。インテリアの設計／監理／施工。FF＆Eの設計／製作／販売。マンションリフォーム設計／施工。サイン、アート、ランドスケープの設計。コンサルティング業務(PM. FM. CM. PA. M&E)。

〒105-0014　東京都港区芝1-10-11　コスモ金杉橋ビル5F
TEL：03-6400-9000
URL：http://www.mecdesign.co.jp

内田 淳
株式会社フィールドフォー・デザインオフィス　デザインディレクター
1981-90：清水建設株式会社　設計本部
1990-91：マリオ ベリーニ スタジオ（ミラノ）
1992-99：清水建設株式会社　設計本部
2000～：フィールドフォー・デザインオフィス　デザインディレクター
［主な作品］
1998：スイスホテル大連
2000：クレイトンベイホテル「クリスタルチャーチ」（JCDデザイン賞 奨励賞）（AIDIA作品展 一等）
2003：タラサ志摩ホテル＆リゾート「チャペルジュレ」
2004：ザ・ビーチタワー沖縄
2005：ホテルユニバーサルポート

〒100-0011　東京都千代田区内幸町2-2-2　富国生命ビル27F

TEL：03-3539-2881　FAX：03-3539-2883
URL：http://www.field4.co.jp
Email：uchida@field4.co.jp

大山尚男
清水建設株式会社　設計・プロポーザル統括
　首席（プリンシパルアーキテクト）兼デザインセンター所長
早稲田大学非常勤講師
［主な作品］
東芝本社ビルディング
マレーシア大使館（最優秀東京建築賞）
横浜・ホテルニューグランド（BCS賞）
兼松ビルディング（BCS賞）
信濃町煉瓦館（日本建築士事務所協会連合会全国大会優秀賞）
テレビ東京天王洲スタジオ（BCS賞）
銀座・交詢ビルディング

〒105-8007　東京都港区芝浦1-2-3　シーバンスS館
TEL：03-5441-1111
Email：ooyama@shimz.co.jp

坂井和秀
清水建設株式会社　設計・プロポーザル統括デザインセンターグループ長
［主な作品］
信濃町煉瓦館
清水建設技術研究所新本館
銀座・交詢ビルディング

〒105-8007　東京都港区芝浦1-2-3　シーバンスS館
TEL：03-5441-1111
Email：k-sakai@shimz.co.jp

志村美治
株式会社フィールドフォー・デザインオフィス　取締役デザイン部長
1979-89：清水建設株式会社　設計本部
1985-86：チャダ、シィエンビエナアソシエイツ
1989～：フィールドフォー・デザインオフィス　取締役デザイン部長
1993～：武蔵野美術大学工芸工業デザイン学科特別講師
［主な作品］
1997：資生堂パーラー銀座4丁目
1999：テレビ東京天王洲スタジオ
2000：魚半別亭「モーラー邸」（インテリアプランニング賞）
2001：女子美術大学 杉並校舎（グッドデザイン賞・SDA賞）
2002：トヨタ車体開発センター（インテリアプランニング賞・SDA賞）
2004：モクザイ・コム（SDA賞・JCD賞）

〒100-0011　東京都千代田区内幸町2-2-2　富国生命ビル27F
TEL：03-3539-2881　FAX：03-3539-2883
URL：http://www.field4.co.jp
Email：shimura@field4.co.jp

寺本昌志
株式会社メック・デザイン・インターナショナル　インテリア部　部長
［主な作品］
丸ノ内ホテル

東京臨海病院
日本工業倶楽部
ボストンコンサルティンググループ、等

〒105-0014　東京都港区芝1-10-11　コスモ金杉橋ビル5F
TEL：03-6400-9000
URL：http://www.mecdesign.co.jp

中川誠一
株式会社ネクスト・エム代表取締役
松田平田設計のインテリア設計部長から、リノベーション専門のBEEMS室を立ち上げ、現在はNEXT／mを設立し、企画・プロデュース業務を中心に活躍。
［主な作品］
総合デザインプロデュース：ホテル日航金沢、ホテル日航関西空港、第一ホテル東京シーフォート、ラグーナ蒲郡
コンサルティング：阪急第一ホテルグループ（第一ホテル東京、ホテル阪急インターナショナルなど15ホテル）、ホテルJALシティ（四谷、長野など10ホテル）

〒107-0051　東京都港区元赤坂1-4-21　赤坂パレスビル5階
TEL：03-3408-1771　FAX：03-3403-7384
URL：http://www.next-m.co.jp
Email：seiichi_nakagawa@next-m.co.jp

名取政春
株式会社伊藤喜三郎建築研究所　横浜支所　支所長
［主な作品］
市立豊中病院
宮城社会保険病院
青梅市立総合病院救命救急センター
横浜市立みなと赤十字病院

〒231-0023　神奈川県横浜市中区山下町74-1　大和地所ビル5階
TEL：045-661-3522
URL：http://www.k-ito.co.jp
Email：mnatori@k-ito.co.jp3.

渡辺真人
株式会社松田平田設計　総合設計室インテリア設計部　副部長
1988年松田平田坂本設計事務所（現・松田平田設計）入社。オフィス、ホテル、集合住宅等のインテリアデザインはもちろん、巨大スタジアムの内装から消火栓のデザインまで、インテリアに関わる幅広いデザインを守備範囲とする。
［主な作品］
日本航空　サクララウンジ・エグゼクティブラウンジ
茨城県庁舎
セコム本社
THE RIVER PLACE（下丸子プロジェクト）
三井ガーデンホテル銀座

〒107-8448　東京都港区元赤坂1-5-17
TEL：03-3403-6161
URL：http://www.mhs.co.jp

Biographies

K. Ito Architects & Engineers Inc.
Architecture is in part obligated to serve as a permanent mirror of society's values. It is therefore essential to establish a trusting relationship between client and architect.
Havingu implemented this methodology for many years, we at K.Ito Architects and Engineers are dedicated to the creation of functional,user friendly spaces with futuristic architectural value.Here within we present some examples of design based on this process.

Shirakiji Bld. 1-2-33 Higashigotanda Shinagawa-ku Tokyo 141-0022
TEL; 03-5798-8181 URL; http://www.k-ito.co.jp

NIKKEN SPACE DESIGN LTD.
Established in 1994 as a spin off from Nikken Sekkei Ltd. Ateliers in Tokyo, Osaka and Nagoya.
Sixty five personnel; one of the largest professional interior design office in Japan. Specializes in "Social Landscape Design on a human scale" and "Design & Management for raising space value". Main services include; supervising interior design and supervising small scale construction architect and product design etc.
Moreover, their service spans a variety of businesses such as; hotels, commercial facilities, offices, banks, hospitals, schools and libraries. Completed works; Sumitomo Corporation Head Office, ANA Hotels at international airports of Osaka, Narita, Kansai and Oita, Renovation works at Nikko Hotels in Osaka and Tokyo, Hotel New Otani, Sumitomo Trust & Banking Co.,Ltd., Ciibank offices in Shinjuku and Sapporo, Sumitomo Hospital, facilities for Waseda, Meiji and Rikkyo Universities, Bank of China Tower Bankers Club in Shanghai, Kyoto State Guest House and others.

Setani Bld. 5-4-19 Kojimachi Chiyoda-ku Tokyo 102-0083
TEL; 03-3264-6609 FAX; 03-3264-6697
URL; http://www.nspacedesign.co.jp

NEXT/m Produce
Founded: December 16, 2002. Summary of business: Consulting, urban planning, design, management, and sales, both overall construction and interiors. Primarily involved in research, consulting, and management.

Akasaka Palace Building 5F, 1-4-21 Moto Akasaka Minato-ku, Tokyo Japan 107-0051
TEL; 03-3408-1771 FAX; 03-3403-7384
URL; http://www.next-m.co.jp Email; info@next-m.co.jp

FIELD FOUR DESIGN OFFICE
Established in 1989 as an independent interior design office, from an offshoot of the Design Division of Shimizu Corporation. In 2000 merged with the landscape section of the same division, and now boasts a talented staff of 25. With interior design and landscaping as its main focus, Field Four covers an extensive range of activities from design consulting, such as FFE (Furniture, Fittings and Equipment) and signs, to planning and supervision, and aims for the creation of high-quality spaces that the next generation can be proud of.

Fukoku Seimei Building 27F, 2-2-2 Uchisaiwai-cho Chiyoda-ku, Tokyo Japan 100-0011
TEL; 03-3539-2881 FAX; 03-3539-2883
URL; http://www.field4.co.jp

MHS Planners, Architects and Engineers
Founded: September 1931 (Showa 6). Summary of business: urban planning, redevelopment, not only interior design for state-of-the-art highly functioned commercial buildings, large scale sports complex, medical, welfare and public facilities, but also solutions for renovation and improvement, maintenance and management for diverse projects from PFI, PM, to CM for 75 years since Showa 6 (1931) when founded by Gunpei Matsuda.
Set up "BEEMS" ("Department of BEEMS" at present) in 2000, aiming "Reviving Architecture".
Overall planning office, contributing society through restructuring city, architecture, and those surroundings.

1-5-17 Moto Akasaka, Minato-ku, Tokyo Japan 107-8448
TEL; 03-3403-6161 URL; http://www.mhs.co.jp

MEC design international corp.
Year of establishment March 10 1972. Design / supervising / constructing interiors. Design / create / sales of FF & E (Fixture, furniture and equipment). Designing and construction for condominium remodeling. Design signs, art pieces and landscape. Consulting (PM, FM, CM, PA, M&E).

5F Cosmo Kanasugibashi Bld. 1-10-11 Shiba Minato-ku Tokyo 105-0014
TEL; 03-6400-9000 URL; http://www.mecdesign.co.jp

Setsuko ANDO
Chief designer at Tokyo atelier of NIKKEN SPACE DESIGN LTD.
Instructor of Kogakuin University.
Interior planner.
[Major works]
Specializes in hotel design and other facility design. Previous projects; ANA HOTEL NARITA Corporation, ANA Hotel Oita Oasis tower, The Saihokukan Hotel, Okura Chiba Hotel, Hotel New Otani Makuhari, remodeling of Hotel New Otani Tokyo, remodeling of hotel nikko tokyo, Hotel Villa Fontaine Roppongi, Recreation House of T-Health Insurance Union, JAKARTA basara, remodeling of Hotel New Otani Tokyo, City Tower Takanawa (condominium), Roppongi Izumi Garden Residence and others.
Award: Good design award / 1997 (INAX) Good design award / 2004 (IYOBE KOGEISHA Furniture)

E-mail:ando_sd@nikken.co.jp

Atsushi UCHIDA
FIELD FOUR DESIGN OFFICE Design Director
1981-90: SHIMIZU CORPORATION DESIGN DIVISION
1990-91: STUDIO ARCH. MARIO BELLINI, MILAN
1992-99: SHIMIZU CORPORATION DESIGN DIVISION
2000〜: FIELD FOUR DESIGN OFFICE Design Director
[Major works]
1998: Swissotel Dalian

2000: Crystal Church, Clayton Bay Hotel (JCD Design Award) (first prize in AIDIA Competition)
2003: Chapel Juler, Thalassa Shima Hotel& Resort
2004: The Beach Tower Okinawa
2005: Hotel Universal Port

Fukoku Seimei Bldg. 27F, Uchisaiwai-cho 2-2-2, Chiyoda-ku, Tokyo, Japan 110-0011
TEL; 03-3539-2881 FAX; 03-3539-2883
URL; http://www.field4.co.jp Email; uchida@field4.co.jp

Hisao OHYAMA
Principal Architect, Director of DESIGN CENTER, Planning, Design & Consulting, SHIMIZU CORPORATION
WASEDA UNIVERSITY Lecturer
[Major works]
Toshiba Main Building
The Embassy of Malaysia (Tokyo Best Architecture Prize)
Yokohama, Hotel New Grand (BCS Prize)
Kanematsu Building (BCS Prize)
Shinanomachi Rengakan (Awards for National Contest of Japan Association of Architectural Firms)
TV Tokyo Tennoz Studio (BCS Prize)
Ginza, Kojun Building

SEAVANS-S 1-2-3 Shibaura, Minato-ku, Tokyo 105-8007
TEL; 03-5441-1111 Email; ooyama@shimz.co.jp

Kazuhide SAKAI
Architect, Manager of DESIGN CENTER, Planning, Design & Consulting, SHIMIZU CORPORATION
[Major works]
Shinanomachi Rengakan
Shimizu Corporation Institute of Technology Main Building
Ginza, Kojun Building

SEAVANS-S 1-2-3 Shibaura, Minato-ku, Tokyo 105-8007
TEL; 03-5441-1111 Email; k-sakai@shimz.co.jp

Yoshiharu SHIMURA
FIELD FOUR DESIGN OFFICE Director of Design Division
1979-89: SHIMIZU CORPORATION, DESIGN DIVISION
1985-86: Chhada, Siembieda & Associates
1989〜: FIELD FOUR DESIGN OFFICE Director of Design Division
1993〜: MUSASHINO ART UNIVERSITY Department of Industrial, Interior and Craft Design Special Lecturer
[Major works]
1997: SHISEIDO PARLOUR, GINZA 4-chome
1999: TV TOKYO TENNOZU STUIDIO
2000: UOHAN ANNEX-MAURA RESIDENCE (Interior Planning Award)
2001: JOSHIBI UNIVERSITY OF ART AND DESIGN (Good Design Award and SDA Award)
2002: TOYOTA AUTO BODY DEVELOPMENT CENTER (Interior Planning Award and SDA Award)
2004 : MOKUZAI.com (SDA Award, JCD Award)

FukokuSeimeiI Bldg.27F, Uchisaiwai-cho 2-2-2, Chiyoda-ku, Tokyo, JAPAN 100-0011
TEL; 03-3539-2881 FAX; 03-3539-2883
URL; http://www.field4.co.jp Email; shimura@field4.co.jp

Masashi TERAMOTO
Manager of Interior Div. MEC design international corp.
[Major works]
Marunouchi Hotel
Tokyo Rinkai Hospital
The Industry Club of Japan Bld
The Boston Consulting Group, and others

5F Cosmo Kanasugibashi Bld. 1-10-11 Shiba Minato-ku Tokyo 105-0014
TEL; 03-6400-9000 URL; http://www.mecdesign.co.jp

Seiichi NAKAGAWA
Managing Director of NEXT/m Produce
Previously the chief of interior design at MHS Planners, Architects & Engineers, then designed for BEEMS, which specialized in renovations. Now works mainly in planning and production at NEXT/m.
[Major works]
Total design planning: Hotel Nikko Kanazawa, Hotel Nikko Kansai Airport, Dai-ichi Hotel TOKYO SEAFORT, LAGUNA GAMAGORI
Consulting: Hankyu Daiichi Hotel Group (15 hotels, including the Dai-ichi Hotel Tokyo and the Hotel Hankyu International), Hotel JAL City (10 hotels, including Yotsuya and Nagano locations)

Akasaka Palace Building 5F, 1-4-21 Moto Akasaka Minato-ku, Tokyo Japan 107-0051
TEL; 03-3408-1771 FAX; 03-3403-7384
URL; http://www.next-m.co.jp
Email; seiichi_nakagawa@next-m.co.jp

Masaharu NATORI
Chief of Yokohama Branch K. Ito Architects & Engineers Inc.
[Major works]
Toyonaka city hospital
Miyagi social insurance hospital
Oume city general hospital emergency center
Yokohama city Minato Red Cross hospital

5F Daiwajisho Bld. 74-1 Yamashitacho Naka-ku Yokohama city 231-0023
TEL; 045-661-3522
URL; http://www.k-ito.co.jp Email; mnatori@k-ito.co.jp

Masato WATANABE
Sub chief of Interior Design Dept. Total Planning Division at MHS Planners, Architects and Engineers
Joined Matsuda Hirata Sakamoto Designing Office (MHS Planners, Architects and Engineers at present) in 1988, specializing in interior design, not only office, hotel, cooperative houses, but also diverse planning, relating interior design from a large scale stadium to a small article such as a fireplug.
[Major works]
Japan Air Lines, Sakura Lounge, Executive Lounge;
Governmental office building of Ibaragi Prefecture;
Headquarter of Secom Co., Ltd.;
THE RIVER PLACE (Shimomaruko Project);
Mitsui Garden Hotel Ginza.

1-5-17 Moto Akasaka, Minato-ku, Tokyo Japan 107-8448
TEL; 03-3403-6161 URL; http://www.mhs.co.jp

あとがき

この本はインテリアプランニングに日ごろ深く関わっている方々の実作例を通して、これからのリノベーションを展望するというスタンスで編集されたものである。私が代表を務める事務所からも作例を提供させていただいたが、改めてインフィルとしてのインテリア空間がその時代やニーズに合わせて適切なリノベーションをしていく重要性や、成熟した社会における空間創造のありかたを思うものとなった。掲載にご同意いただいたクライアントや建築家、写真家の方々に深く御礼申し上げたい。

……………浦 一也[日建スペースデザイン]

あるクライアントの耳の痛くなる一言『建築家は、新築設計の時は一生懸命力を注ぐがリノベーションになると親身になって取り組んでくれない』。インテリア設計の専門家は、リノベーションはごく当たり前、日常茶飯事のように取り組んでいる。しかし、リノベーションは正直言って大変手間のかかる難しい仕事。フレームが決まっている中で解く、パズルの様だ。しかし、完成すると以前よりも見違えるような空間が出来上がる。インテリアの魔術師の技である。

……………中川誠一[ネクスト・エム]

リセットしようとしているスケルトンは、とても美しい。時を経て眠っていた躯体が現れた瞬間に、デザインの段階でまだ見ぬ君に思い巡らせた気持ちを、果たしてそれで良かったのかと問われる。
その場の緊張感がたまらない。
限られた時間の中、アイデアの構築と再構築の繰り返しを経て、生まれ変わったインフィルには、次の時代のデザイナーに見つけてもらえるための骨格を、少しだけ覗かせておく事にしている。

……………志村美治[フィールドフォー・デザインオフィス]

住宅のリノベーションがTV番組になっている。
毎回使い勝手の悪くなった古い住宅を、ひとりのデザイナーが、感動的に蘇らせるという企画のものだ。入居者に涙して感謝されようとまでは意気込まないが、リノベーションの設計では古き良きものを蘇らせたいと考えている。元設計には元設計のアイデアがあり、それを解きながら進める作業は、新築の設計では味わえない面白さがある。

……………渡辺真人[松田平田設計]

以前、イタリアへ石材検査に行った際、北イタリアの山の中にある小さな村に立ち寄ったことがある。村は2000年以上前に出来た城の中にあり、今も日常生活がその中で営まれていた。二千数百年前に出来た石の空間で営業しているレストランで食べたイタリアンの味には、その美味しさとは別に何か特別な感慨があった。この空間は2000年以上という時間の中でどれ位そのインテリアが変わってきたのだろうか。当然考えも及ばない時間である。今もこの空間はインテリアのリノベーションを行うことで、生きた空間となり、社会に貢献している。建築はその空間を出来るだけ長い期間維持できるよう日々研究を重ね技術を高めている。そして、その空間の中で人が社会生活を行うために必要な道具としてインテリアがある。社会が変わり、人が変わり、目的が変われば、道具はその必然性の中で変わっていかなければならない。その積み重ねがカルチャーとなって行き、そのカルチャーが人から人へと繋がり財産となっていくのだと思う。
インテリアデザインはよい環境を作るという目的の他に、リノベーションという行為から、社会の中で一つの文化を創る大事な役目も持っているようだ。

……………寺本昌志[メック・デザイン・インターナショナル]

before→after「目を疑うばかりの変貌！」という見出しで作品紹介を華々しく発表してみたいところだが、ふれあい横浜ホスピタルの場合は、高層ホテルを病院と高齢者ホテルとして異種用途への再生（コンバージョン）事例である。そもそも異種用途への再生の場合は既存建物の要素を出来るだけそのままの形で利用し、改修にかける費用も最小限に押さえつつ、新たな用途へ如何にコンバージョン出来るか？……に設計の手腕が問われる課題である。従ってそういう意味からは究極のコンバージョンはbefore = afterとも言えるのではないだろうか。

……………名取政春[伊藤喜三郎建築研究所]

Afterword

Through the actual experiences of people who are deeply involved in interior planning on a regular basis, this book is edited from the stance of developing future renovations. Some examples were also provided by the office that I head, and it made me realize more deeply the importance of carrying out appropriate renovations of interior spaces as infill, to suit the needs of the era, as well as the philosophy behind the construction of spaces in a mature society. I would like to express my heartfelt thanks to all the clients, architects and photographers who agreed to have their work appear in this book.

Kazuya URA
[NIKKEN SPACE DESIGN LTD.]

I'm sure this sentiment of a particular client is quite familiar to you: "Architects get very involved in creating new designs, but in the case of renovations, they don't take it seriously enough." In contrast, specialists in interior design carry out renovations as a standard procedure, on a daily basis. However, to be frank, renovation is a difficult job that takes a lot of time and effort. It's like trying to work out a puzzle to fit within a set frame. However, once it's finished, a new space has been created that looks entirely different. This requires the skill of a magician.

Seiichi NAKAGAWA
[NEXT/m Produce]

A skeleton that is being reset is very beautiful. For someone who had not yet actually seen the frame at the design stage, the moment of its unveiling, after a long period of "sleeping," is fraught with concern as to whether or not it had really worked properly. The feeling of tension at that moment is incredible. The infill, which is reborn through the construction and reconstruction of ideas within a limited amount of time, allows you to see, if only briefly, the framework that designers in the next era will be able to find.

Yoshiharu SHIMURA
[FIELD FOUR DESIGN OFFICE]

There is now a television program about home renovations. In each program an old, inconvenient house is dramatically transformed by one designer. Although I don't get so involved as to return the place to the residents in the hope of thanks, I do want to revitalize the house in a positive way through the renovation design. The original design had its own solid basis, and the work of unraveling the thinking behind that is something very interesting that cannot be experienced in the design of new works.

Masato WATANABE
[MHS Planners, Architects & Engineers]

Once, when I was in Italy to study building stones, I dropped in at a small village in northern Italy. This village was inside a castle that was built 2000 years ago, and daily life carried on there as in ancient times. The Italian taste of the food in a restaurant that was operating within a space among the stones of more than 2,000 years ago had something very special about it, quite apart from its delicious taste. I wondered just how much the interior of this space had changed, throughout its history of over 2,000 years. This is a length of time that is difficult for us to comprehend. Even now, through renovation of its interior, this space has been kept alive and is contributing to society.
Architecture advances its technology by steadily refining its ongoing research, so that spaces like this one can be maintained for as long a period as possible. Moreover, the interior exists as a necessary tool for people to carry out social activities within that space. As society changes, people change, and the purpose of use changes, the tool itself must also naturally change as necessary. I believe that over time this becomes culture, and that this culture connects people with each other, and eventually becomes an asset.
Apart from its objective of creating a good environment, through the activity of renovation, interior design seems to play an important role in creating one culture within society.

Masashi TERAMOTO
[MEC Design International]

"Such a radical transformation from 'before' to 'after' that you won't be able to believe your eyes!" I would like to introduce the product colorfully with a headline like this, but Fureai Yokohama Hospital is an example where a high-rise hotel has been converted for two completely different kinds of uses, as a hospital and as a hotel catering for the elderly. In cases of conversion for a different type of use, the designer faces the challenge of working out how to convert the existing building for its new use, while maintaining the original elements in their present form as much as possible, and keeping the costs of repairs and improvements as low as possible. So, in that sense, for the ultimate conversion, we can also say that 'before = after'.

Masaharu NATORI
[K. Ito Architects & Engineers Inc.]

Afterword

Through the actual experiences of people who are deeply involved in interior planning on a regular basis, this book is edited from the stance of developing future renovations. Some examples were also provided by the office that I head, and it made me realize more deeply the importance of carrying out appropriate renovations of interior spaces as infill, to suit the needs of the era, as well as the philosophy behind the construction of spaces in a mature society. I would like to express my heartfelt thanks to all the clients, architects and photographers who agreed to have their work appear in this book.

Kazuya URA
[NIKKEN SPACE DESIGN LTD.]

I'm sure this sentiment of a particular client is quite familiar to you: "Architects get very involved in creating new designs, but in the case of renovations, they don't take it seriously enough." In contrast, specialists in interior design carry out renovations as a standard procedure, on a daily basis. However, to be frank, renovation is a difficult job that takes a lot of time and effort. It's like trying to work out a puzzle to fit within a set frame. However, once it's finished, a new space has been created that looks entirely different. This requires the skill of a magician.

Seiichi NAKAGAWA
[NEXT/m Produce]

A skeleton that is being reset is very beautiful. For someone who had not yet actually seen the frame at the design stage, the moment of its unveiling, after a long period of "sleeping," is fraught with concern as to whether or not it had really worked properly. The feeling of tension at that moment is incredible. The infill, which is reborn through the construction and reconstruction of ideas within a limited amount of time, allows you to see, if only briefly, the framework that designers in the next era will be able to find.

Yoshiharu SHIMURA
[FIELD FOUR DESIGN OFFICE]

There is now a television program about home renovations. In each program an old, inconvenient house is dramatically transformed by one designer. Although I don't get so involved as to return the place to the residents in the hope of thanks, I do want to revitalize the house in a positive way through the renovation design. The original design had its own solid basis, and the work of unraveling the thinking behind that is something very interesting that cannot be experienced in the design of new works.

Masato WATANABE
[MHS Planners, Architects & Engineers]

Once, when I was in Italy to study building stones, I dropped in at a small village in northern Italy. This village was inside a castle that was built 2000 years ago, and daily life carried on there as in ancient times. The Italian taste of the food in a restaurant that was operating within a space among the stones of more than 2,000 years ago had something very special about it, quite apart from its delicious taste. I wondered just how much the interior of this space had changed, throughout its history of over 2,000 years. This is a length of time that is difficult for us to comprehend. Even now, through renovation of its interior, this space has been kept alive and is contributing to society.

Architecture advances its technology by steadily refining its ongoing research, so that spaces like this one can be maintained for as long a period as possible. Moreover, the interior exists as a necessary tool for people to carry out social activities within that space. As society changes, people change, and the purpose of use changes, the tool itself must also naturally change as necessary. I believe that over time this becomes culture, and that this culture connects people with each other, and eventually becomes an asset.

Apart from its objective of creating a good environment, through the activity of renovation, interior design seems to play an important role in creating one culture within society.

Masashi TERAMOTO
[MEC Design International]

"Such a radical transformation from 'before' to 'after' that you won't be able to believe your eyes!" I would like to introduce the product colorfully with a headline like this, but Fureai Yokohama Hospital is an example where a high-rise hotel has been converted for two completely different kinds of uses, as a hospital and as a hotel catering for the elderly. In cases of conversion for a different type of use, the designer faces the challenge of working out how to convert the existing building for its new use, while maintaining the original elements in their present form as much as possible, and keeping the costs of repairs and improvements as low as possible. So, in that sense, for the ultimate conversion, we can also say that 'before = after'.

Masaharu NATORI
[K. Ito Architects & Engineers Inc.]

浦 一也

1947年	北海道札幌市生まれ
1972年	東京芸術大学大学院美術研究科修了
1972年	株式会社日建設計入社
1994年—	株式会社日建スペースデザイン
現在	同社代表取締役
	東京芸術大学非常勤講師
	東京インテリアプランナー協会副会長

[主な作品]
ロテル・ド・ロテル
成田全日空ホテル
日建設計飯綱山荘
ヨコハマグランドインターコンチネンタルホテル
ピンクハウス本社ビル
ホテル・モリノ新百合丘
SONYお台場メディアージュ
O HOUSE

[著書]
『建築計画チェックリスト事務所および宿泊施設』(共著・彰国社)
『現代建築集成・商業施設』(編纂・プロトギャラクシー)
『旅はゲストルーム』(東京書籍、光文社)

[受賞]
空調衛生工学会賞振興賞
福岡市都市景観賞
JCDデザイン98ホテル部門奨励賞

Kazuya URA

1947	Born: Sapporo-shi, Hokkaido
1972	MFA; Tokyo National University of Fine Arts & Music
1972	Nikken Sekkei Ltd.
1994	NIKKEN SPACE DESIGN LTD.
Present	President; NIKKEN SPACE DESIGN LTD.
	Instructor (P/T); Tokyo National University of Fine Arts & Music
	Vice Chairman; Tokyo Interior Planner's Association

[Previous Projects]
L'Hotel de L'Hotel
ANA HOTEl NARITA
Nikken Sekkei Iizuna Sanso
Intercontinental The Grand Yokohama
Pink House Head Office
Hotel Morino Shin-yuri
SONY Mediage
O HOUSE

[Publication]
Architecture Plan Check List Office and accommodations
(A joint work / Shokokusha Publishing Co., Ltd)
Modern Architecture Collection / Commercial institution
(Editing / Protgalaxy Inc.)
Guest Rooms of Travel
(Tokyo Shoseki Co., Ltd. / Kobunsha Co., Ltd.)

[Award]
The Society of Heating Air Conditioning and Sanitary Engineers Promotion Prize
Fukuoka City Urban Landscape Award
JCD Design Award 1998 Hotel Section Encouragement Prize

インテリアSuperリノベーション

発行	2005年10月25日 初版第1刷発行
編纂	浦 一也©
発行者	久世利郎
発行所	株式会社グラフィック社
	〒102-0073
	東京都千代田区九段北1-14-17 三創九段ビル4F
	Tel:03-3263-4318／Fax:03-3263-5297
	郵便振替:00130-6-114345
	http://www.graphicsha.co.jp
印刷・製本	錦明印刷株式会社

©2005 本書の内容は、著作権上の保護を受けています。
著作権者及び出版社の文書による事前の同意を得ずに、
本書の内容の一部、あるいは全部を
無断で複写複製、転載することは禁じられています。

本書の内容における電話での質問はお受けできません。

乱丁・落丁はお取り替えいたします。

ISBN4-7661-1630-5 C3052